THE UNCERTAIN TRIUMPH

FEDERAL EDUCATION POLICY IN THE
KENNEDY AND JOHNSON YEARS

FEDERAL EDUCATION POLICY IN THE KENNEDY AND JOHNSON YEARS

THE UNCERTAIN TRIUMPH

by Hugh Davis Graham

The University of North Carolina Press

Chapel Hill and London

© 1984 The University of North Carolina Press
All rights reserved
Manufactured in the United States of America

LIBRARY OF CONGRESS CATALOGING IN PUBLICATION DATA

Graham, Hugh Davis.
  The uncertain triumph.

  Includes bibliographical references.
    1. Education and state—United States—History—20th
century. 2. Federal aid to education—United States—
History—20th century. I. Title.
LC89.G73 1984   379.73   83-23424
ISBN 0-8078-1599-3

For Janet

Contents

Preface and Acknowledgments

My commitment to write this book evolved in a curiously indirect fashion. In the fall of 1979 I was invited by historian Robert A. Divine of the University of Texas at Austin to participate in a symposium designed to explore research and historiography on the Johnson administration. The symposium was sponsored by the Lyndon Baines Johnson Foundation, and my topic was collective violence.[1] But during my first week of research in the Lyndon Baines Johnson Library, I quickly became fascinated with the rich documentary evidence on the domestic policy process, and especially with that on the secret Johnson task forces. So what began as an essay on collective violence evolved into a rather schizophrenic essay on education, youth, and violence, until eventually the force of both logic and evidence forced a divorce into two separate essays, one on violence and one on education as a case study in the policy process.[2] My essay, entitled "The Transformation of Federal Education Policy," was published as chapter 5 in Robert A. Divine's anthology *Exploring the Johnson Years*.[3]

Another generous grant-in-aid of research from the LBJ Foundation in 1980 allowed me to return to Austin to continue my research, and most important of all, in 1981 I received a two-year research grant from

1. I had been co-director, with political scientist Ted Robert Gurr, of the Historical and Comparative Task Force of the National Commission on the Causes and Prevention of Violence in 1968–69. Gurr and I coedited *Violence in America* (Washington: Government Printing Office, 1969), which was also published in hardcover by Praeger and in paperback by Bantam and New American Library. In 1979 a thoroughly revised edition was published by Sage.

2. The essay on collective violence was published as "On Riots and Riot Commissions: Civil Disorders in the 1960s," *The Public Historian* (Summer 1980), 7–27.

3. (Austin: University of Texas Press), 155–84.

the National Institute of Education that enabled me to complete the research in the Johnson and Kennedy libraries, the National Archives, and the Office of Education archives in the Education Library of the NIE, to conduct nineteen interviews, read thirty oral histories, and ultimately to write the book. Hence I am indebted to a lot of helpful people. In addition to Robert Divine in Austin, I must mention the unfailingly helpful Nancy Smith and Linda Hanson, who as archivists at the LBJ Library patiently helped me to learn to ask the right questions. The staff archivists at the John F. Kennedy Library in Boston and at the National Archives were no less helpful, as were the staff librarians at the University of Maryland Baltimore County, and Joanne Cassel at the NIE Library, who was especially helpful in exploring the resources available through the Educational Resources Information Center (ERIC) and Dr. Catherine Heath's exceptional collection. My energetic research assistants, Charles Harrison and William Levine, were essential to my keeping to my timetable.

At NIE, my project officer, Grace Mastalli, together with her colleagues, Donald Burnes and Lana Muraskin, made my two years on the NIE grant a pleasurable professional circumstance. During the period from 1980 to 1982, I enjoyed two rather different institutional associations in Washington. One was a year as a research associate with the American Council on Education, which provided me with general access to that marvelous holding company of education associations at One Du-Pont Circle, and special mention must be made of Sheldon Steinbach, Charles Saunders, and Robert Atwell at ACE. Additionally, during 1980–82 I was appointed visiting associate scholar at the American Enterprise Institute for Public Policy Research, where my AEI colleagues Howard Penniman, Austin Ranney, Denis Doyle, Sid Moore, Tom Mann, and Norman Ornstein contributed to an unusually stimulating intellectual atmosphere—while Randa Murphy so competently ran the place. I also enjoyed discussions with Paul Hill at RAND, and Henry Aaron and Charles Schultze at the Brookings Institution. In all nineteen of my personal interviews (listed in my essay on method and sources), my questions were responded to with becoming candor.

The manuscript was read and criticized by six scholars whose expertise ranges across a broad spectrum that includes American political history, the history of education, political science, public administration, and public policy research. These were political scientist Thomas Cronin of Colorado College, historian (and brother) Otis Graham of the University of North Carolina at Chapel Hill, historians John Jeffries and James Mohr in my own department at the University of Maryland Baltimore County, policy scientist George LaNoue of UMBC, and historian of education Marshall Smith of the University of Wisconsin at Madison. They clearly are not responsible for any errors of fact or judgment.

HUGH DAVIS GRAHAM
University of Maryland
Baltimore County

Introduction

In the spring of 1983, the National Commission on Excellence in Education issued a devastating thirty-six-page report that indicted the nation for having "squandered the gains in student achievement made in the wake of the Sputnik challenge."[1] As indicators of this alarming decline, which was eroding the nation's educational foundations with a "rising tide of mediocrity," the report found that 23 million American adults were functionally illiterate, as were 13 percent of all seventeen-year-olds and 40 percent of minority youths. Average high school student achievement on most standardized tests was lower than when *Sputnik* was launched twenty-six years earlier. Scholastic Aptitude Test scores had demonstrated an unbroken decline from 1963 through 1982, as had both the number and proportion of students demonstrating superior SAT scores. Science achievement scores of United States seventeen-year-olds had demonstrated a parallel decline, and between 1975 and 1980 remedial mathematics courses in public four-year colleges had increased by 72 percent to constitute one-fourth of all mathematics courses. Lest the report be dismissed as merely a partisan attack by the Reagan administration against the Democratic legacy of the Great Society (which, to some extent, it was), a private task force sponsored by the Twentieth Century Fund shortly thereafter issued a reinforcing indictment of a pattern of "federal intervention that has been counterproductive, entailing heavy costs and undesirable consequences."[2] The task force was chaired by Robert Wood, director of urban studies at the University of Massachusetts and former under secretary of housing and urban development in the Johnson administration.[3] And yet a third panel in the spring of 1983, a group of forty-one governors, business leaders, scientists, and educators chaired by North Carolina's Democratic governor, James B. Hunt, severely criticized America's faltering public school system, especially in comparison with Japan's, for failing to train the technical manpower needed to sustain economic preeminence.[4]

How could such a dismal diagnosis square with the claimed and, for the most part, statistically documentable record of giant strides taken (especially at the federal level) since the Brown decision had focused the nation's attention on the schools in 1954, *Sputnik* had so alarmingly reinforced qualitative concerns in 1957, and the maturing postwar baby boom had highlighted the quantitative challenge in the 1960s? Indeed how, most poignantly, could this contemporary description of decline and disarray square with the spectacular breakthroughs of the Great Society? And as federal initiatives in such a volatile field of public policy, spectacular they were. In his sixth and final Budget Message to Congress, former schoolteacher Lyndon B. Johnson proudly catalogued the educational achievements of his presidency to 1969: Title I of the Elementary and Secondary Education Act of 1965 (ESEA) was assisting in the education of 9 million children from low-income families, while Head Start covered 716,000 preschool children, and Follow Through sought to preserve the early gains of 63,500 more. Since 1964, new federal programs had been created to aid the instruction of 182,000 handicapped children. By 1970, under the Higher Education Act of 1965 (HEA), 2 million federally funded grants, loans, and interest subsidies for guaranteed loans would reach one out of every four college students. Also by 1970, under the Kennedy legacy of college construction aid, federal funds would have assisted in the construction of $9 billion in classrooms, libraries, laboratories, and related instructional facilities.

This extraordinary transformation of federal education policy was most dramatically a function of the 1960s and Democratic administrations, but Democratic congresses had nurtured it under Republican regimes, first under Eisenhower with the post-*Sputnik* National Defense Education Act (NDEA) of 1958, then under Nixon with the important higher education amendments of 1972, which massively accelerated federal aid to college students. The result, in combination with demographic pressures, was that from 1955 through 1974 the numbers of American college students soared from 2.5 million to 8.8 million, and the proportion of eighteen- to twenty-four-year-olds attending college rose from 17.8 percent to 33.5 percent. The number of blacks attending college rose even more dramatically, from 95,000 to 814,000, and the percentage of women attending college jumped from one-third to one-half. Not surprisingly, this momentum was sustained by the administration of Jimmy Carter, who was the first presidential candidate to be officially endorsed by the National Education Association, and who repaid the debt by creating a federal Department of Education in 1979. By 1980, the percentage of American children attending nursery school or kindergarten had risen in a decade from 37 to 57 percent, and college enrollment had soared to a record 12 million.

Dramatic changes in federal policy clearly had a great deal to do with this striking change, which witnessed federal intervention on an unprecedented scale into realms of educational policy that had hitherto been almost the exclusive preserve of state and local and private jurisdictions. The results, as both the booster statistics of the 1970s and the alarums of the 1980s attest, were a decidedly mixed blessing. How the federal government became involved in all this is my story. It is a story of policy—*not* of education per se. I shall refer to the educational impacts of these policy changes only in the epilogue—and then probably too briefly (and probably too critically) for the critics.

It is, overall, a mixed story of initial failure and frustration, of political brilliance and luck, of partial success, of unintended consequences, and ultimately of being overwhelmed, even in triumph, by stronger forces. It is an intensely political story, which properly befits the policy process in a democracy. For to propose federal "intrusion" into the sanctity of the state-local-private preserve of education was to stride boldly into a uniquely dangerous political mine field that pitted Democrat against Republican, liberal against conservative, Catholic against Protestant and Jew, federal power against states rights, white against black, and rich constituency against poor in mercurial cross-cutting alliances. Liberal partisans of the New Frontier and the Great Society insisted that in an era characterized by Cold War, *Sputnik*, poverty and race riots, and exploding demographics, the national interest demanded a federal role in the country's education policy—and they were right. Conservatives, impelled by a variety of fearful impulses, ultimately repaired to the ancient wisdom of Omar Khayyám: "Whose bread I eat, whose wine I drink, his song I sing." And *they* were right.

The bitter partisan combatants of the 1960s too often tended to exaggerate the virtues of their ideological mindsets into caricatures of themselves. Congressional Republicans easily degenerated into a pattern of knee-jerk oppositionism—opposing, for instance, college scholarships for the needy because most of the recipients would likely be young Democrats (this was not, to be sure, their public rationale). Democrats generally overpromised the benefits of their largesse, and in the bargain not only invited disappointment and backlash but also, in the process of logrolling among their minority constituent blocs, created a few well-intentioned monstrosities that ranged from incompetence and waste through corruption and fraud. In the light of historical hindsight, brief as it remains, the ironies abound. Chief among them is the cruelest one: that just as the Great Society broke through to honor, in program and budget, the soaring rhetoric of its humane plea to rescue by "leveling up" the failing bottom fifth of our school population, the quality at the core of America's public schooling—that vital center of our nation's educational trust—began to collapse, spinning downward into that two-decade nosedive of painful modern memory.

There were other ironies as well, many of them centering on the Great Society's major educational triumph with the ESEA in 1965. Hailed as the long-sought breakthrough in general federal aid to education by such sober and knowledgeable voices as the *Congressional Quarterly*, ESEA created a brace of novel programs in which every penny was *categorical*, not general, and the inevitable strings attached thereto were to prove crucial to its troubled implementation (because they required too much and also too little). Properly hailed as a major victory for liberal reformers, ESEA rode through Congress as an expansion of the monumentally regressive impacted areas program. Indeed, ESEA primarily concerned elementary education and had very little to do with secondary education. Finally, the political circumstances that conditioned ESEA's birth necessarily complicated its implementation by a bureaucracy that had not designed it and was not organized or staffed or spiritually inclined to carry it out. The results were a large measure of chaos and a consequent collapse of morale by the end of the decade. This was a major and heavy price, although not a fatal one, of sudden and stunning victory against a historical backdrop that had nourished federal aid to education with a deeply troubled ambivalence, especially when it threatened heresy against the "religion of localism."

THE FEDERAL ROLE IN EDUCATION

Prior to the 1960s, one of the most distinctive attributes of America's political culture had been the tenacity with which the United States, unlike most nations, had resisted a national education policy. The United States was born in revolt against a British colonial regime that was reasserting central authority, and at the heart of classical Jeffersonian liberalism was a fear of central power. The founders assumed that the education of American children would remain a chief concern of parent and church, with its public ambit reserved for the states exclusively. Article X capped the Bill of Rights by inferentially insisting upon the nonfederal character of American education, which was conspicuously omitted in the Constitution as a legitimate concern of the national government. From the turmoil of Reconstruction emerged what might have been a turning point: the United States Office of Education. But it existed for a century as a kind of bastard child, an object of bureaucratic ridicule in Washington, skeleton staffed by third-rate "educationists" who compiled obscure statistical reports that gathered dust.[5]

Even as they resisted centralization, however, Americans continued to regard education as the keystone of the American democratic experiment, to the Americanization of a nation of immigrants. Indeed, federal aid to education predates the Constitution.[6] It was explicitly encouraged by the Congress of the Confederation in the Survey Ordinance of 1785 and the Northwest Ordinance of 1787 as a way of encouraging education and as a means of accelerating the sale of public lands. Although land was far too plentiful for such an approach to be very effective, the continuity of this policy extended for a century and a half, through the statehood acts for Hawaii and Alaska. Land being the chief historic form of federal wealth, the federal government granted a total of 98.5 million acres to the states for supporting the public schools. Federal assistance was extended to higher education by the Morrill Act of 1862 and was further reinforced in 1890 (the second Morrill Act), 1914 (the Smith-Lever Act), and 1917 (the Smith-Hughes Act). These laws funded the new land-grant colleges for the expansion of agricultural extension and provided for mechanical-vocational training and home economics programs in high schools. The World War II period brought the "impacted" aid of the Lanham Act in 1940 for school districts overburdened by non-taxed military installations, and the GI Bill was passed in 1944. Finally, the Cold War brought the National Science Foundation Act of 1950 and, in response to *Sputnik*, the path-breaking National Defense Education Act of 1958 (NDEA) to stimulate education in science, engineering, foreign languages, and mathematics.[7] In short, the federal government was clearly willing to provide categorical aid, especially in times of national crisis. But attempts to enact more general-aid programs foundered on constitutional objections, the church-state issue, fear of loss of local control, partisan wrangling, and, beginning in the 1950s, the controversy over school desegregation.[8] Throughout the long history of federal categorical aid, each successive categorical act tended to create and nurture its own constituency—farmers, mechanics, home economists, veterans, scientists, and engineers—rather than create a breakthrough toward more generalized federal assistance for schoolchildren and college students.

The debate over general federal aid had been accelerated by the discovery during the two world wars of widespread illiteracy among the conscripts, by the postwar baby boom flooding the classrooms in the 1950s and reaching college age in the 1960s, and by the alleged increasing inability of local tax resources to meet these challenges. Between 1945 and 1965, 80 million new Americans were born, and the demographic consequences for the overburdened schools became increasingly clear. By the end of the 1950s, both the Roper and Gallup polls showed an increase from two-thirds to three-quarters of Americans favoring outright federal assistance,[9] and the public record showed that most members of Congress, both Republican and Democratic administrations, and the major educational organizations endorsed more general federal aid in some form.[10] Yet by 1960, no general bill had become law.[11]

The Kennedy administration pressed vigorously for federal aid during 1961–63, but the political sources of objection to the various forms such aid might take became so locked into intransigent patterns of resistance and mutual veto that the Kennedy program was widely branded by contemporaries as a "fiasco." By 1962, a sympathetic study of the long quest for general federal aid still concluded with deep pessimism that the prospects for general elementary and secondary aid, which had seemed so bright in 1960, were now exceedingly dim.[12] Then came Kennedy's assassination, the successful Johnson drive to enact the major Kennedy reform proposals in 1964, the Democratic landslide against Goldwater, and consequently the dramatic breakthrough for federal school aid in 1965. This breakthrough was exploited by the Johnson administration skillfully and relentlessly, even when the momentum of the Great Society was sapped by the congressional elections of 1966, the escalation of the Vietnam War, the continued spiral of inflation, and ghetto and campus rioting. By the end of 1968, the major new federal commitments were in place—the landmark Elementary and Secondary Education Act and the Higher Education Act of 1965, the National Endowments for the Arts and the Humanities, Teacher Corps, Head Start, Follow Through, guaranteed student loans, college work-study, scholarships for the needy, school breakfasts, public television, aid for school construction, developing institutions, the handicapped, community colleges, bilingual education—it was a bumper harvest, and one that has generally been well documented, at least externally.

During the 1960s, federal aid to schools and colleges surged from $1.8 billion to more than $12 billion annually, with the most novel and striking increases flowing to elementary and secondary education (in 1960 such federal aid amounted to about half a billion dollars; by 1970 this had risen to about $3.5 billion).[13] Federal educational programs proliferated like Topsy, from approximately 20 to 130, scattered throughout more than a dozen departments and agencies and more often than not only minimally coordinated with one another. From the perspective of the 1980s, with the Reagan administration seeking to reduce severely or dismantle much of this liberal program legacy of the 1960s, and in the wake of critical analyses of such change-oriented programs as ESEA Title I, it is difficult to recapture the excitement of the partisans and social scientists who drove the New Frontier and Great Society programs through.

This book of course builds upon the substantial body of literature on federal education policy that has accumulated since the embittered battles of the Kennedy years and the breakthrough under Lyndon Johnson. I have critically surveyed that literature elsewhere,[14] and here I acknowledge its obvious strengths. Helpful books by such respected analysts as Stephen Bailey, Edith Mosher, Eugene Eidenberg, Roy Morey, and Norman Thomas were prompt and contemporary assessments,[15] researched and written by scholar-practitioners who enjoyed privileged access to policy actors whose memories were fresh. These remain important studies of congressional, agency, and constituent group behavior, and their case-study methods combined legislative hearings of agency and interest group testimony with customarily anonymous interviews, which sought to maximize candor by masking sources. But they inescapably lacked the perspective that only time could bring. Their anonymous interviews blocked the evidential specificity that historians demand, and the somewhat episodic quality of their case studies encouraged both a discontinuity of process and a short-ranged view of policy evolution. Neither their approach nor mine is inherently superior to the other; the genres are inherently different, and both are needed. I hope to demonstrate that historians who wait for the archives to open, and who hence enjoy both access to a great mass of new evidence and the advantage of (in my case) at least a decade of historical perspective, have an important and clarifying contribution to offer.

PRESIDENTIAL LEADERSHIP AND THE TASK FORCE DEVICE

Now that the Kennedy and Johnson archives are open,[16] this book will center on an internal analysis of the primary archival evidence that reveals the evolution of educational policy formulation from the perspective of the executive branch, that is, the cockpit of the presidency; the White House nerve center; the Bureau of the Budget (BOB); the Department of Health, Education, and Welfare (DHEW); the United States Office of Education (USOE); their constituencies in the world of American education; and their links to Congress. My central thread of continuity will be executive planning through presidential task forces.

The task force device was by no means novel to the 1960s, and in 1960–61 President Kennedy employed a rather traditional version of it when, immediately after his election, he and his closest aides, especially Theodore Sorensen and Myer Feldman, summoned scores of volunteer outside experts to form twenty-nine task forces in a crash program to sharpen policy priorities for the transition.[17] But the recommendations of the education task force, chaired by Frederick L. Hovde, president of Purdue University, were widely reported in the media in January 1961, and their huge price tag caused a damaging political backlash—a fact whose meaning was not lost on Vice-President Lyndon Johnson. Thereafter Kennedy confined his policy planning more closely to the traditional "central clearance" process of legislative agenda formulation, whereby the agencies routinely generated their recommendations through the cabinet officers for central clearance by way of the Bureau of the Budget to the White House.[18] And again traditionally, the price of the coordinating advantage of central clearance tended to be the rather routine percolating of legislative proposals up from the agencies, through tiers of bureaucratic filters that produced incremental legislative recommendations rather than bold policy innovations—a phenomenon whose significance also was not lost on Vice-President Johnson, nor on the senior staff of BOB.

In the spring of 1966 the historian William Leuchtenburg published a tantalizing article in *The Reporter* entitled "The Genesis of the Great Society."[19] In it he described how in the spring of 1964 President Johnson, anticipating both a landslide victory over Goldwater and overwhelming Democratic dominance in the Eighty-ninth Congress a year hence, decisively moved to forge a reform program of his own that could be presented as legislative proposals to the new Congress in January. From this commitment sprang the Johnson task forces—roughly 135 of them, by recent count.[20] Students of public administration have been fascinated by their strategic design, which represented an attempt by the president to short-circuit the normal central-clearance process.[21] Thus the task force device was designed to interrupt the normal bureaucratic flow, provide for innovation, combat the inherent inertia and boundary maintenance of the agencies, and maximize the leverage of the president (with his battalion of a thousand short-term political appointees) over the entrenched, permanent subgovernment (with its army of 2.5 million civil servants) backed by its powerful allies in the congressional subcommittees and clientele groups.[22] Unlike the visible Kennedy task forces, however, the Johnson task forces would be secret. They would also be small and modestly staffed, oriented to policy rather than politics, and would link the administration to the world of the university and the practitioner through an executive secretary from the government (mainly from the Bureau of the Budget) and a liaison man from the White House staff. By the summer of 1964, while Lyndon Johnson's election campaign was crushing the hapless Goldwater, the president's secret task force engine for designing the Great Society was in place. His electoral triumph was quickly followed by the Great Society's major legislative breakthrough of 1965. Then came the Republican counterattack in the off-year congressional elections of 1966, and with it a quiet sea change. Against the swell of ghetto riots and wartime inflation, the Johnson administration largely and successfully fought a holding action in 1967. But because Johnson's formidable task force operation had generated its own momentum, the culminating and ostensibly lame-duck year of the Johnson administration, 1968, witnessed a curious paradox that centered on what appeared to be a vast contradiction, as new Great Society programs poured through Congress when the president's power was at its nadir.

THE PARADOX OF THE GREAT SOCIETY

In one sense the autumn of 1968 clearly represents an ebb tide in the Johnson administration's policy planning process and suggests a kind of pathological cycle that reflects what we have come to expect as the natural flow and ebb of presidential power. The glow of early success generates expectations that performance cannot match and enthusiasm cannot sustain. As Johnson's honeymoon patina wore off under the pressures of domestic violence, the Vietnam War, and inflation, the early euphoria of the Great Society faded, congressional resistance stiffened, and Johnson's popularity plummeted. Innovative outside task forces increasingly gave way to interagency groups in which agency resentments festered and competition for scarce resources increased. Seasoned cabinet officers resented the directives of Joseph Califano and his burgeoning young staff, and Califano's remarkably sustained generation of new task force projects met stiffened agency resistance. By 1968 the extraordinary Johnson task forces, like the beleaguered Johnson administration, seemed to have pretty well run their courses.

Yet in an important sense, the autumn of 1968 was not anticlimactic. Johnson's chief education aide, Douglass Cater, who was in a position to know, has testified to Johnson's shrewd conviction that once programs to aid clientele groups get on the statute books, they survive despite underfunding and delays in implementing them.[23] As a matter of the politics of the Hill, Johnson sensed intuitively that new clientele groups would form protective alliances with sympathetic congressional subcommittees and agency administrators—those symbiotic "iron triangles" of political science lore whose entitlement programs were so deeply woven into the fabric of the modern state. So Johnson and his aides drove unrelentingly even to the end, as Califano formed nineteen new task forces in 1968, and Congress responded in the field of education alone by passing the Indian bill of rights, school breakfasts, guaranteed student loans, aid to handicapped children, and vocational education. From the perspective of the late 1960s, such a phenomenon was viewed by many officials in DHEW and USOE with considerable ambivalence, including frustration and dismay at the prospect of further underfunding and hamstringing of the programs generated by their earlier triumphs. From the perspective of the early 1980s, when the federal budget had ruptured dangerously under the burden of proliferating entitlement programs and double-digit inflation, Johnson's political and legislative instinct seems abundantly vindicated—for better and worse.

One final observation is in order before turning to the narrative in chapter 1, and that concerns a disclaimer about my research design and the assumptions behind it. By concentrating on the evolution of education policy, I necessarily risk a kind of tunnel vision; obviously, the development of education policy was not the dominant event in Washington during the 1960s, nor were ad hoc education task forces the primary concern of the federal executive. Moreover, readers deserve to be alerted to one structural or organizational problem that focusing attention on task force planning inherently invites. Because at any given moment in the policy process, the White House staff would simultaneously be dealing with immediate legislative goals as well as task force planning for legislative implementation a year or more hence, writing about such activities required a certain contrapuntal style, back and forth from task force notion, to legislative enactment or rejection, then back to the planning groups again in a continuous cyclical process, at least during the Johnson administration.

The first two chapters of the book speak mostly of failure. They describe the tortured efforts of the Kennedy administration, on behalf of general aid for teachers' salaries and school construction, where repeated fiascoes over religion and desegregation and federal control were partially redeemed late in 1963 by a major legislative accomplishment in construction aid to higher education. Assassination prevented President Kennedy from signing the Higher Education Facilities Act of 1963, an achievement for which he deserved the full credit that Lyndon Johnson properly accorded him when as the new president, he signed the bill into law. Chapter 3 analyzes the classic Johnson effort of 1964–65, with Bill Moyers coordinating the task forces that led to the construction of the Great Society's programmatic base. John Gardner's celebrated task force on education has dominated the literature ever since. Chapter 4 interrupts the narrative flow to concentrate on the question of how best to reorganize the federal government's executive branch to serve traditional goals of efficiency and economy, and especially to pursue the new program goals of the Great Society. Chapters 5 through 7 trace the transition from the initial Moyers-led effort to the evolution of the highly elaborate system constructed by Califano and his new domestic policy aides. Chapter 8 assesses the paradoxical dimensions of the culminating year of LBJ's administration, 1968, which closed with Johnson retiring to the ranch in late January of 1969. The final chapter is an epilogue that brings us from January 1969 to the present, with special attention to the implementation and evaluation of the major education programs that lay at the heart of the Great Society.

In all this, what the task forces do provide is a fascinating and revealing window on the policy process, but not the only window. They are a point of entry into a much larger world, which in this case picks up with the presidential campaign of 1960 between Kennedy and Nixon. There we begin with the striking anomaly that education came to figure significantly in a presidential contest at all, much less prominently. As Chester Finn has observed, "Presidents seldom think about education. . . . As seen from the White House, education is a low-level issue that commands no precedence on the ever-lengthening list of presidential concerns. It probably ranks with housing and nutrition, which is to say it gets more heed than Indian affairs and mental health, but less than welfare, energy, or pollution."[24] At least, presidents and presidential candidates had historically thought and talked very little about education. But beginning with the presidential campaign of 1960, education as an issue of presidential debate and national significance, and of presidential task forces and national commissions, was destined to enjoy far more than its one brief, shining moment in Camelot.

THE UNCERTAIN TRIUMPH

FEDERAL EDUCATION POLICY IN THE

KENNEDY AND JOHNSON YEARS

1 / JOHN F. KENNEDY AND EDUCATION
From Congress to the White House

KENNEDY AND FEDERAL AID

In his memoir, *Kennedy*, Theodore Sorensen claims that "the one domestic subject that mattered most to John Kennedy [was] education. Throughout his campaign and throughout his Presidency, he devoted more time and talks to this single topic than to any other domestic issue."[1] But Myer [Mike] Feldman, Sorensen's chief lieutenant, concluded more recently that Kennedy had no deep personal concern for public education—save for the training of the mentally retarded, which was related to the circumstance that had touched his family with tragedy—and that Kennedy's accelerating commitment to federal aid as a presidential candidate and as president owed far more to practical politics than to the kind of bedrock emotional commitment that drove the former schoolteacher Lyndon Johnson.[2]

The preponderance of evidence supports Feldman's private assessment. Kennedy attended four elite private schools, graduated from Choate and, after brief studies at the London School of Economics and Princeton University, attended and graduated from Harvard University. Then came one semester at the Stanford Business School, followed by naval service during World War II, and his election to Congress in 1946. Such a career of wealth and private schooling would not be likely to generate devotion to the public schools. When young Congressman Kennedy was appointed to the House Education and Labor Committee, he served quietly in the Eighty-first Congress; then early in the Eighty-second Congress, in 1949, he introduced a bill providing for federal funds for buses, health services, and textbooks for private and parochial schools.[3]

This gesture was popular in his heavily Catholic Eleventh Congressional District in Boston, but it was clearly doomed in a chamber and also a committee that had been historically hostile to federal aid to education, and not surprisingly Kennedy's bill died quietly in committee. Far more visible in the Eighty-first Congress had been S. 246, a Senate-passed bill providing for federal aid to elementary and secondary schools, and one that enjoyed the cosponsorship of "Mr. Republican," the conservative Senator Robert A. Taft of Ohio. Public debate over the bill was dominated by a bitter dispute between Francis Cardinal Spellman of New York, who wanted "auxiliary services" for parochial schools included in any federal aid bill, and Congressman Graham Barden of North Carolina, who chaired the special subcommittee on education and flatly opposed taxpayer aid to parochial schools. Spellman called Barden a "new apostle of bigotry," and when Eleanor Roosevelt joined the fray by opposing federal aid to church schools in her syndicated newspaper columns, Spellman accused her of launching an "anti-Catholic campaign" and of writing columns that were "documents of discrimination unworthy of an American mother."[4] When S. 246 came before the House Education and Labor Committee in 1949, Kennedy supported it generally but pressed an amendment calling for federal payment of half the cost of bus service for private and parochial school students.[5] When the committee defeated his amendment by a vote of sixteen to nine, Kennedy cast the deciding negative vote in a thirteen to twelve refusal to report the Senate-passed bill for floor action.

Kennedy was elected to the Senate in 1952, and although he was appointed to the Senate Labor and Public Welfare Committee, which handled education legislation, he generally steered clear of the volatile federal aid debate throughout the 1950s, as the church-state issue yielded primacy to the growing school desegregation issue, and a Republican president sparred inconclusively with a Democratic Congress. In *Politics and Policy*, James Sundquist ably surveys the political snarls of the "Years of Frustration" between Eisenhower's election in 1952 and the orbiting of *Sputnik* in 1957.[6] During these years, President Eisenhower persuaded Congress to create the new Department of Health, Education, and Welfare. He first appointed Oveta Culp Hobby, and then Marion P. Folsom, to preside over DHEW in the cabinet and witnessed half a decade of raucous partisan squabbling over the controversial issues that the federal aid question posed: school desegregation and the Powell amendment,[7] the National Education Association and aid for teachers' salaries, the baby boom and school construction and federal control, and the always smoldering church-state controversy. Only the Soviet launching of *Sputnik* on 4 October 1957 jarred the combatants out of their rancor and forced a consensus that superior Soviet performance in science and engineering demanded prompt federal funding of higher education in the interest of national defense.

The result was the $1 billion National Defense Education Act of 1958 (NDEA), which the Senate majority leader Lyndon Johnson reasonably and proudly referred to as "an historic landmark . . . one of the most important measures of this or any other session."[8] Sundquist called it "the most important piece of national education legislation in a century,"[9] and in hindsight it is clear that the NDEA ran formidable interference for Johnson's subsequent ESEA of 1965, especially in regard to what Sundquist recognized as "the psychological breakthroughs it embodied." This was less because of its specific categorical provisions than because NDEA explicitly asserted a legitimate *national* interest in the quality of American education. But a more central question for the future of federal aid was whether NDEA's short-term assistance to higher education in Cold War crisis might generate momentum toward a *permanent* and more generalized federal role that was regarded as legitimate and necessary. And a corollary question was whether and how such a role might include elementary and secondary schools. When the congressional by-elections of 1958 brought sweeping Democratic victories that produced gains of 48 seats in the House and 15 in the Senate,[10] the Democrats looked confidently toward the Eighty-sixth Congress with margins of 282 to 154 in the House and 64 to 34 in the Senate.[11] Because Eisenhower was constitutionally barred from a third term, the Eighty-sixth Congress presented Democrats with unusual opportunities to embarrass the Eisenhower-Nixon administration and recapture the White House in 1960. In that sense, the presidential campaign of 1960 began when the Eighty-sixth Congress convened on 7 January 1959, and an aid-to-education bill was to figure prominently in Democratic strategy.

THE CAMPAIGN OF 1960

Accounts of the partisan jockeying over education in 1959 by Sundquist, Munger and Fenno, and Bendiner ably document the frenetic but inconclusive maneuvering of the preelection period. It culminated with tortured parliamentary logic on 2 February 1960 in a tied Senate vote on a motion to table a move to reconsider a vote on an amendment to a school-aid bill that subsequently passed the Senate. But the bill never made it to conference with a companion House-passed bill because a conservative coalition of southern Democrats and Republicans on the House Rules Committee blocked a conference committee vote on a bill that President Eisenhower probably would have vetoed anyway.[12] The result of this intensely partisan maneuvering was that the successful goal of the Democrats was to trap Vice-President and certain GOP presidential nominee Richard Nixon into breaking the Senate tie by voting against federal aid for teachers' salaries and for school construction. He would thereby earn the enmity and the Democrats would earn the appreciation of the NEA's three-quarters-of-a-million voting teachers and their families.

On election eve in 1960, then, both houses of Congress had passed a general aid-to-education bill for the first time in the twentieth century, primarily because of the new Democrats elected in 1958 and the new post-*Sputnik* mood. Because both bills would fund school construction, the major differences, which promised to cancel each other out in conference compromise, were that the House bill this time around contained the Powell amendment, and the Senate bill included aid for teachers' salaries. But the customary Senate-House reconciliation was blocked on 22 June by a seven-to-five vote in the House Rules Committee when all four Republicans were joined by three southern Democrats (committee chairman Howard Smith of Virginia, William Colmer of Mississippi, and James Trimble of Arkansas) in refusing to authorize a conference. Although Eisenhower was thereby spared having to sign a bill he disapproved of or to veto an aid-to-education bill on election eve,[13] the issue was primed for the fall campaign between Kennedy and Nixon. Furthermore, as Sundquist observed, not only had the Democrats cemented their alliance with the NEA, they had implicitly escalated their vision of the federal commitment from a temporary response to baby boom and Cold War crisis to a permanent role in boosting educational quality. However, the precise rationale and mechanism for such a permanent role, especially at the elementary and secondary level, remained unclear.

When Kennedy announced his candidacy at a kick-off press conference on 2 January 1960, he listed six main issues, the third of which was rebuilding the stature of American science and education (the arms race and freedom and order in the emerging nations were first and second; the farm economy and urban decay were fourth; economic growth was fifth; and America's moral purpose completed the list).[14] Kennedy and Nixon were nominated by their respective party conventions in July, and their campaigns were dominated by Cold War posturing, especially over Quemoy and Matsu and Cuba. When they occasionally clashed on domestic issues, it usually took the form of Kennedy's attacking the flat Republican economy, and Nixon's defending seven years of peace and prosperity and attacking Democratic fiscal irresponsibility. During the campaign, Kennedy raised the education issue early and often, hammering at Nixon for casting a "tie-breaking vote killing a Democratic bill giving the states money to increase teachers' salaries."[15] On 25 September, the eve of the first radio-television "debate," Nixon released his study paper on education, and it revealed a comprehensive program of federal aid, although one that was devoid of dollar figures.[16] For elementary and secondary education, he proposed a program of debt-servicing and matching grants that would relieve state and local governments of heavy construction costs and thereby, "first in importance," release their funds for "urgent increases in teachers' pay. . . . And we will do it without menacing the invaluable freedom of our schools by inhibitive Federal control."[17] For higher education, Nixon called for "greatly expanded" programs of subsidized loans for dormitories and matching grants for the construction of classrooms, laboratories, and libraries; expanded NDEA loans; a new national scholarship program based on need and competitive examinations to be administered by and its costs shared by the states; tuition tax credits for higher education; matching grants to build new medical schools; and more federal investment for vocational education, the handicapped, and adult education. Nixon even suggested as a harbinger of the National Institute of Education that he was to establish a dozen years later, the creation of a "national clearinghouse" for research, demonstration, and gathering and disseminating information about local experience and experimentation. And he concluded with a call for the creation of a permanent top-level commission on education, a sort of CEA for education to provide advice and continuing evaluation.

It was a bold counterstroke, and it was far more specific than any previous campaign statement of Kennedy's. That same day, the *New York Herald-Tribune* published the candidates' responses to seven questions on education. But the candidates answered selectively and thereby blunted perception of their differences.[18] Nixon ducked the *Herald-Tribune*'s question on aid to private and parochial schools but encouraged consideration of tuition tax credits. Kennedy ducked the tax credits but called for aid to public schools only. Nixon was for state matching grants without any equalization formula; Kennedy was for supplemental federal funds to assist the poorer states. Nixon proclaimed that "the problem of teachers' pay is the greatest single challenge confronting our American educational system today," but he insisted that federal control must be avoided by assisting local construction and debt service only, thereby releasing local funds for increased teacher salaries. Kennedy's first statement was, "Federal aid to education via the States is a must." But in that same first response he said that federal aid should "encompass" teachers' salaries as well as school construction, and he again attacked Nixon for his tie-breaking vote against "giving the States freedom of choice to use Federal aid to improve teachers' salaries." As for loans and scholarships and all the rest, both men were for more. Both also carefully avoided cost estimates. In such a format, their differences were blurred.

The next day, however, their differences were sharpened in the first radio-television debate in Chicago, when Charles Warren of MBS asked Nixon to explain the discrepancy between his remark in 1957 that teachers' salaries were "nothing short of a national disgrace" and his tie-breaking Senate vote against federal aid for teachers' salaries in 1960. Nixon's response, in part, was as follows:

> I think that the reasons that I voted against having the federal government uh . . . pay teachers' salaries was probably the very reason that concerned Senator Kennedy when in January of this year, in his kick-off press conference, he said that he favored aid for school construction, but at that time did not feel that there should be aid for teachers' salaries—at least that's the way I read his remarks. Now, why should there be any question about the federal government aiding . . . teachers' salaries? Why did Senator Kennedy take that position then? Why do I take it now? We both took it then, and I take it now, for this reason: we want higher teachers' salaries. We need higher teachers' salaries. But we also want our education to be free of federal control. When

the federal government gets the power to pay teachers, inevitably in my opinion, it will acquire the power to set standards and to tell the teachers what to teach.[19]

In reply, Kennedy ducked the allusion to his January kick-off press conference and quickly turned to the February tiebreaker:

When uh . . . the Vice President quotes me in January, sixty, I do not believe the federal government should pay directly teachers' salaries, but that was not the issue before the Senate in February. The issue before the Senate was that the money would be spent for school construction or teacher salaries. On that question the Vice President and I disagreed. I voted in favor of that proposal and supported it strongly, because I think that provided assistance to our teachers for their salaries without any chance of federal control and it is on that vote that the . . . Mr. Nixon and I disagreed, and his tie vote uh . . . defeated . . . his breaking the tie defeated the proposal. I don't want the federal government paying teachers' salaries directly. But if the money will go to the states and the states can then determine whether it shall go for school construction or for teachers's salaries, in my opinion you protect the local authority over the school board and the school committee.[20]

Education figured only marginally in the second and third debates, and the fourth was devoted entirely to foreign policy. Most of the debates and most of the campaign, in fact, featured jousting over international issues. Domestic issues centered on the performance of the economy, and to a lesser degree on civil rights, on which both candidates rather carefully hedged. Nixon's substantial education program appeared to have blunted somewhat the edge of Kennedy's attack, but Kennedy kept pressing his appeal for federal aid for construction and teachers' salaries, securing an informal but de facto endorsement from the NEA,[21] and toward the campaign's close, on 2 November 1960, he pledged in a speech in Los Angeles that "in 1961, a Democratic Congress—under the leadership of a Democratic President—will enact a bill to raise teachers' salaries as well as fund school construction."[22] Given his winning plurality of only 112,803 popular votes out of 68,329,895 votes cast, those three-quarters-of-a-million NEA teachers seemed well worth wooing. But with victory on 8 November came the responsibility of translating promises into programs, and the ambiguity of Kennedy's mandate was exemplified by his negative coattail effect, as the Democrats lost twenty seats in the House and two in the Senate.

THE KENNEDY TASK FORCES

The previous summer, immediately following his nomination, Kennedy had appointed, with maximum publicity, a series of advisory committees whose reports were to be delivered during the transition period.[23] These high-profile exercises involved such prominent chairmen as Adlai Stevenson on foreign policy, Stuart Symington on defense, Paul Nitze on national security, W. Averell Harriman on Africa, Senator Joseph Clark and Congressman Emanuel Cellar on civil rights, and Congressman Frank Smith on natural resources. But after 8 November, president-elect Kennedy appointed Sorensen special counsel to the president and promptly charged him, together with Mike Feldman, to recruit a series of unannounced task forces from the ranks of the professions, foundations, and university faculties.[24] First on the list was an antirecession task force, and Harvard's Paul A. Samuelson was recruited to head it. Then came task forces on depressed areas, housing, health and welfare, education, space, taxation, and Latin America.[25] Sorensen's list grew to include thirteen task forces involving "close to one hundred men" who received neither compensation nor expense money nor staff support, although public release of the reports in January 1961 brought considerable public attention to at least the task force chairmen, and the task force operation proved to be an excellent recruiting device.[26] Sorensen also reports that no one refused to serve on the task forces.

The task forces were not to report until January, so Sorensen and Feldman joined with senior Bureau of the Budget staff to begin a parallel and centralized process of transition in November and December by preparing a master checklist of legislative, budgetary, and administrative issues that might constitute Kennedy's new program agenda.[27] This massive tome, or "Kennedypedia," was compiled from unenacted legislation left over from the Eighty-sixth Congress, the Democratic platform of 1960, Kennedy and Johnson's campaign pledges, and expiring laws in need of renewal and revision. It contained, according to Feldman, approximately

1,500 pages of analysis and 500 pages of commitments. When Feldman, Kennedy's transition liaison with the Bureau of the Budget, delivered it to the president-elect, he exclaimed, "My God, Mike, what'd you get me into?"[28] On 21 December, in an all-day and late-night session in Palm Beach, Kennedy reviewed the list with his top advisors, commenting, "Now I know why Ike had Sherman Adams."[29] Thus the initial process of building a legislative agenda was begun well in advance of the task force submissions. They would have to be "fitted in" later. In the meantime, the Bureau of the Budget held the high ground, linking the executive agencies to the incoming administration and defining, through transition team memorandums and dialogues, the questions that would in turn shape the direction of the new legislative agenda.[30]

THE HOVDE TASK FORCE ON EDUCATION

Chairman of the president's six-man task force on education was Frederick L. Hovde, president of Purdue University.[31] The other five members of this blue-ribbon group were Alvin Eurich, a vice-president of the Ford Foundation; Francis Keppel, dean of the Harvard School of Education; John Gardner, president of the Carnegie Corporation; Russell Thackery, executive secretary of the American Land-Grant Colleges Association; and Benjamin Willis, superintendent of public schools in Chicago (and soon to be president of the American Association of School Administrators).[32] It was, as Hugh Douglas Price observed, a "distinguished body," one that could speak with authority on matters of higher education especially. But it was also one that contained "no representatives of the conservative, southern Democratic, Catholic Church, or NAACP positions" on the volatile question of federal aid to schools.[33]

When Kennedy first launched the task force operation, he cautioned Sorensen and Feldman on the potential danger of its backfiring: "Let's keep it pretty confidential. Let's not let the press have access to it until we know what the results are going to be."[34] Kennedy, according to Feldman, "felt that this could be very embarrassing to a new administration if people that he didn't know, people over whom he had no control made statements that were released to the press. And his fears were actually realized in a couple of the releases that we had."[35] Through the fall and early winter, the Hovde task force labored in silence, but on Friday, 7 January, Hovde and several of his colleagues journeyed to Kennedy's penthouse atop New York's Carlyle Hotel to present their report to the president-elect. Kennedy's press secretary, Pierre Salinger, quickly handed out copies of the seven-page report as a press release.

The most eye-opening aspect of the Hovde recommendations was its price tag: it called for more than $9,390,000,000 in grants and loans over the next four-and-one-half years, with $5,840,000,000 of this to go to the *public schools only* in the form of grants to the states (for construction, salaries, or other appropriate educational purposes, but not for reducing local levels of expenditure). This amounted to an annual expenditure of $2,310,000,000, which was far in excess of even the most generous Senate bill that had failed the year before, when the Democrats enjoyed a more robust margin in Congress. Of the report's three main parts, the first, calling for $1.46 billion in aid for public schools, would provide a politically attractive base for *all* public schools of $30 per annum per pupil, based on average daily attendance in public schools, but it would also add an equalization bonus of $20 per child for poor states (defined as having personal income below 70 percent of the national average, with most of these being in the South) and for cities with populations exceeding 300,000. Part 3 would increase the loan program for college dormitories (where room rents help repay the loans) and add a grants-and-loans program for academic buildings, private as well as public. Part 2 called for a five-year extension and expansion of the NDEA, extending the forgiveness features on loans to *all* teachers rather than just public school teachers. Clearly, the Hovde report envisioned a massive and *permanent* federal role in education, including some aid to private and parochial schools in the higher education programs, but with elementary and secondary aid reserved for the public schools only.

As Keppel later recalled, "We came up with a report that if Mr. Kennedy had adopted, would probably have broken the federal government's bank in no time at all."[36] Hovde told the press that "anything less than this would not be significant for a program of uplifting education," and Kennedy hedged only slightly in public, saying that there was "great value" in the report but adding, "I don't know whether we have the resources immediately to take on the whole program, but we'll have to decide the degree of need and set up a list of priorities."[37] Privately, however, Feldman recalls that Kennedy was "quite annoyed, quite upset because it contained what he thought was a very unrealistic program.

And he correctly felt the press would feel that this was the program he was going to put into effect."[38] "You couldn't control these people," Feldman complained. "They put in their report whatever they wanted to. They were completely independent. So we accepted it. We had a one or two day headline, and we were attacked by the conservative press."[39]

But the most damaging reaction came two weeks later, and just three days before the inauguration, when Cardinal Spellman savaged the Hovde task force recommendations at a rally at Cardinal Hayes High School in the Bronx. "It is unthinkable," he declared, "that any American child be denied the Federal funds allotted to other children which are necessary for his mental development because his parents chose for him a God-centered education."[40] The cardinal repeatedly announced his disbelief that Congress would accept the task force proposals, which would deprive parochial school children of "freedom of mind and freedom of religion" and would thereby "use economic compulsion to force parents to relinquish their rights to have religion taught to their children." If the task force report was designed in part as a trial balloon, it had predictably rallied the NEA, but the Catholic thunder was ominous.

FORGING KENNEDY'S EDUCATION PROGRAM: THE ROLE OF THE BUREAU OF THE BUDGET

During the two months following Kennedy's electoral victory, while the Hovde task force was deliberating, the staff of the Bureau of the Budget had been planning the transition to an activist Democratic administration that was clearly committed to a breakthrough in general federal aid. Enjoying and exploiting their considerable advantages of a strategic location in the executive branch, an elite civil service reputation, and organizational initiative vis-à-vis an adjourned Congress and an as yet unorganized new administration, the BOB staff in the Office of Legislative Reference and the Division of Labor and Welfare (which subsumed education programs) began circulating transition memorandums designed to shape the context of the transition, and hence to maximize BOB's leverage in guiding the legislative policy formulation of the Kennedy regime. In his political history of the Office of Management and Budget, Larry Berman argued that the senior staff members of the Bureau of the Budget had been extremely frustrated by their "green eyeshade" role during the Eisenhower years, wherein the BOB felt largely reduced to an enclave of accountant-administrators; hence the bureau longed to return to the "golden years" of directors Harold Smith under Roosevelt and James Webb under Truman.[41] On the eve of Kennedy's victory, his advisor Richard Neustadt, a former BOB staffer under Webb, recommended re-activating the bureau as the primary policy and program-planning unit in the executive office of the president.[42] Kennedy appointed David Bell, another Webb staffer, as budget director, and the smooth transition to the Kennedy administration, which centered on close working relationships between White House aides Sorensen, Feldman, and Lee White and the bureau's Bell, Elmer Staats, and Phillip Hughes, was reflected in the BOB's newfound élan.[43]

In a transition memorandum to the director dated 13 December 1960, the Division of Labor and Welfare staff viewed the imminence of general aid to education as a "unique opportunity" to restructure both the form of the aid and, through it, the federal role in education. The memorandum observed that "the financing of education in the United States is at present a State, local, and private rather than a Federal responsibility," with local government providing 50 percent of the funds, the states providing 41 percent (half of this consisting of state grants to local governments), and the federal share being only 9 percent. Moreover, that federal share, which amounted to about $1 billion in fiscal year 1961 (or about 1 percent of all federal expenditures), consisted primarily of aid to impacted areas, which was by far the largest program, and special categorical programs designed to aid land-grant colleges, vocational and technical education, veterans, science education, libraries, college housing, and the like. If total national expenditures on education would have to double in the next decade simply to meet enrollment demand, then four conclusions followed: First, federal aid should maximize its leverage or multiplier effect so as to stimulate the much larger state-local and private financial requirements rather than substitute for them. Second, the newly expanded federal role should be clearly defined in relation to state and local responsibilities, "otherwise, there is a risk that education will gradually become an activity largely or mostly federally financed," which in turn "would raise questions as to the desirability, necessity, or nature of Federal controls that might follow." Third, and dear to the hearts of the planners and policy rationalizers at BOB, the new federal role should be planned within the context of "broader problems of intergovernmental fiscal relations." The transition memorandum concluded:

Many and varied kinds of aid to education are now being provided and specialized training and activities are now being carried on by a number of Federal agencies, with the resultant multiple and inconsistent relationships with States and colleges and with a considerable risk that the launching of new general aid programs should be considered as an opportunity at least for examination and possibly for consolidation or elimination of special programs—also for the simplification of Federal relationships with the recipients of its educational grants, which would be achieved, for example, by consolidating numerous grants into a single one.

Finally, because properly planning such complex new relationships would require extensive review "during the next 6 or 12 months," perhaps interim measures might be recommended to Congress in the meantime.[44]

But the bureau was to have only two hectic months to review the Hovde and DHEW recommendations before the president sent his Special Message on Education to Congress on 20 February 1961 and followed it with his elementary and secondary school-aid bill on 27 February, and his higher education bill on 7 March. In his contemporary case study of Kennedy's initial drive for federal aid, Hugh Douglas Price concluded that the Hovde report "received relatively little attention in the nation at large and played no direct role in shaping the Administration's proposals."[45] Whether the producers and readers of such newspapers as the *New York Times* and the *Wall Street Journal* represent the nation at large is debatable, but Price was wrong about the minimal role of the Hovde task force. Both BOB and DHEW reacted quite directly and repeatedly to the Hovde recommendations, and necessarily so. The BOB staff perforce reacted to both Hovde and DHEW, because the bureau disagreed sharply with certain portions of the Hovde report, and because, as was repeatedly observed in the prefaces of BOB staff memorandums, "The proposals for aid to education developed by the Department of Health, Education, and Welfare generally follow the Hovde Task Force recommendations with certain modifications."[46]

BOB's major differences with Hovde centered on one of its major recommendations, a special aid formula designed for urban schools, and on three BOB convictions that Hovde basically did not address (nor, for the most part, did DHEW). As far as aid to urban schools was concerned, Hovde had recommended a special grant of $20 per child in average daily attendance in the public schools for cities exceeding 300,000 in population. The bureau complained that this was both arbitrary and demographically unsound, because the nation's metropolitan growth was occurring most dramatically in the suburbs, whereas the central cities were generally losing population. Furthermore, the Hovde urban recommendations "confuse[d] general support and special purpose grants"; inner city areas with severe problems are best aided by comprehensive project grants that involve "housing and urban renewal, welfare, public transportation, as well as educational services," which would only overlap existing federal programs.[47]

The bureau's next two objections were, first, that the Hovde-DHEW plan inverted the proper priority on higher education, where enrollment and construction demands would greatly exceed elementary and secondary needs in the coming decade, and Hovde had barely addressed the pressing need for greater college scholarship aid. Even using DHEW's five-year budget estimates, which were based on $15 per child (only half of the Hovde task force's per-pupil assistance formula), the federal payment for elementary and secondary education would exceed 70 percent of the total, but by that fifth year (fiscal year 1966) their enrollments would have increased by only 12 percent, whereas college enrollments would have increased by 32 percent. Second, although both Hovde and DHEW sought to avoid having federal funds substitute for state and local funds (which had been Nixon's proposal, thereby freeing up local funds for teachers' salaries), BOB called for a stimulating or multiplier effect rather than simply a maintenance of effort requirement. Having flayed the Hovde-DHEW three-part proposal for its recommendations for general aid for all public schools, equalization aid for poor states, and special aid for urban schools, because they appeared "too complex" and "fall short of meeting important national objectives," the bureau staff then boldly counterproposed "a single program of Federal grants utilizing an equalizing formula based on relative state income per child in average daily attendance. The program would also be gradually introduced, involve partial State matching based on the state's fiscal ability, and be conditional upon maintenance of past effort as well as continued improvement in all States."[48] There followed a seven-point explication of the bureau's alternative design, plus a proposed alternative budget through fiscal year 1966.

The BOB counterproposal, however rational and scientific in its design, was doomed. It was politically naïve and never had a chance, as we shall shortly see. But the bureau's fourth major recommendation was to become what Price called the administration's "1961 secret weapon."[49] This was the bureau's perception that the new general-aid bill represented an unprecedented opportunity to revise the impacted areas and vocational aid programs. Both came up for renewal on 30 June 1961, both were politically popular, hence both were customarily unassailable in Congress. But BOB quite reasonably regarded them as rigid and outdated relics of two world wars and the Korean War. The brief Hovde report had understandably ignored both. The DHEW proposals had omitted vocational education but had urged that the necessary reductions in aid to education in impacted areas that a general-aid law ought to require should be attempted later. DHEW argued this on the dual and plausible grounds that the rationales for aid to impacted areas and general aid were incompatible, and that the president might have to approve a good general-aid bill that included objectional provisions for aid to impacted areas that he could otherwise veto separately. But the bureau was unpersuaded: "By including both within the general aid proposal, consideration of interrelationships by the Congress is assured; separation would permit special focus on narrow areas of interest, encourage a disregard for overlap and duplication, and practically assure no modification by the Congress of these existing special-purpose programs."[50]

The Bureau of the Budget's fundamental challenges to the Hovde-DHEW approach were faithfully reflected in several drafts of the president's Special Message on Education, which were being shuffled between Sorensen, Feldman, and White in late January and early February. But on 13 February, Feldman met with Wilbur Cohen and Jack Forsythe, who was general counsel for the Senate Committee on Labor and Public Welfare. Forsythe reported bluntly that the further the education message strayed from S. 8 (Senator McNamara's aid-to-education bill, which had passed the Senate in 1960 by a roll-call vote of fifty-one to thirty-four), the more difficulty it would face. A bill similar to S. 8 "would probably be reported out of committee in a few days and would be passed over-whelmingly, without extensive debate on the Senate floor—marking a significant administration achievement." During the meeting the three men surmised:

> If the bill followed the lines of the Hovde report, it was doubtful that Senator Hill would sponsor the measure. Senator McNamara would have difficulty voting for the measure. Senator Morse would probably sponsor the measure reluctantly. Senator Clark would probably sponsor it, but without much enthusiasm.
>
> As a political matter, the big city congressmen already favor S. 8 and would probably vote for both measures. The rural con-gressmen have been conditioned to S. 8 and some of them, under the Hill-Elliot leadership, would vote for S. 8 but would be re-pelled by the Hovde formula.[51]

FEDERAL AID TO EDUCATION AND THE CONGRESS: THE DEBACLE OF 1961

Former Senator Kennedy therefore went with a proven Senate winner, and in his Special Message on Education of 20 February, he recom-mended a "three-year program of general federal assistance for public elementary and secondary classroom construction and teachers' sala-ries." His bill was essentially a replica of the Senate's successful bill of the previous year, S. 8, "although beginning at a more modest level of expenditures," and distributed according to S. 8's equalization formula, which was "already familiar to the Congress by virtue of its similarity to the formulas contained in the Hill-Burton hospital construction and other acts." Kennedy's message, which was read in both houses by clerks, added, "In accordance with the clear prohibition of the Constitution, no elementary or secondary school funds are allocated for constructing church schools or paying church school teachers' salaries; and thus non-public school children are rightfully not counted in determining the funds each state will receive for its public schools."[52] The president's pri-ority list of legislative proposals of 21 February ranked aid to education as seventh and aid to colleges as ninth—behind antirecession aid and wel-fare reform, area redevelopment, minimum-wage increase, and changes in the feed-grain program.

But when the administration's elementary- and secondary-school-aid bill was sent to the Hill one week later, it contained a surprise that had not been mentioned in the special message. The content of Title I was largely as advertised: federal grants totaling $3.3 billion over three years for construction or teachers' salaries in public schools only. This was based on BOB's $15-per-pupil flat rate, with the 10 percent set-aside as a rather vague gesture toward the urban school problem. The Bureau of the Budget had also prevailed upon DHEW to include a formula penalty for states that failed to maintain or increase their effort. The surprise was contained in Titles II and III. These would make permanent the aid to impacted areas (P.L. 815 for construction and P.L. 874 for operation) but would reduce the amount of each by half.[53]

On 7 March, the president followed with his higher education bill, which provided for two major programs. It would provide $2.8 billion in loans over five years for academic facilities and earmark $892 million for 212,000 four-year-college scholarships based on merit and need. Private colleges, including religious schools, stood to benefit from both programs. Thus the Hovde task force stood to get its breakthrough in college classroom construction, not to mention an extension and expansion of the dormitory loan program of 1950; and BOB stood to get its scholarship proposal. It seemed like a well-crafted package, especially in light of the previous year's passage of an aid-to-education bill by both houses of Congress for the first time in history, and now without the threat of an Eisenhower-GOP veto.

Kennedy was asked about his school-aid bills at his press conference on 1 March:

> Q: Sir, in view of the criticism that has occurred, could you elaborate on why you have not recommended Federal aid to public and to private and parochial elementary and secondary schools?
>
> *The President*: Well, the Constitution clearly prohibits aid to the school, to parochial schools. I don't think there is any doubt of that. The Everson case, which is probably the most celebrated case, provided only by a 5 to 4 decision [that] it [was] possible for a local community to provide bus rides to nonpublic school children. But all through the majority and minority statements on that particular question there was a very clear prohibition against

aid to the school direct. The Supreme Court made its decision in the Everson case by determining that the aid was to the child, not to the school. . . . [T]here isn't any room for debate on that subject. It is prohibited by the Constitution, and the Supreme Court has made that very clear. And therefore there would be no possibility of our recommending it.

Q: But you are free to make the recommendations you have made which will affect private and parochial colleges and universities?

The President: Well, the aid that we have recommended to colleges is in a different form. We are aiding the student in the same way the GI bill of rights aided the student. The scholarships are given to the students who have particular talents and they can go to the college they want. In that case it is aid to the student, not to the school or college, and, therefore, not to a particular religious group. That is the distinction between them.[54]

The school-aid question dominated discussion of domestic issues at Kennedy's 8 March press conference, where he opposed a Roman Catholic proposal for "across-the-board loans" for nonpublic schools—one that was being pushed in the House by majority leader John McCormick, who shared the president's geographic, religious, and ethnic background. Kennedy and Secretary Ribicoff also publicly opposed attaching desegregation riders such as the Powell Amendment, and Congressman Powell, who was formerly a loose cannon on the deck, but who was now attempting to appear as a responsible committee chairman, was persuaded to withhold it.

But the religious issue could not be contained. When the National Catholic Welfare Conference declared on behalf of the Catholic hierarchy that the federal aid bill was unacceptable without a loan program for parochial schools, the eighty-eight Catholics in the House became potential allies with obstructionistic Republicans and balking southern Democrats. This was especially true on the crucial Rules Committee, where the eight-man "Rayburn majority" of the newly packed committee included three Catholic Democrats: Ray Madden (Ind.), James Delaney (N.Y.), and Thomas P. O'Neill (Mass.).

KENNEDY'S BACKDOOR STRATEGY:
THE COVERT CATHOLIC "SWEETENER"

In response to this dilemma, Kennedy's strategy was to insist publicly on a public-school-aid bill that excluded private and parochial schools but to have Ribicoff and Sorensen secretly negotiate for a compromise with Bishop Hannan and Monsignors Tanner and Hurley of the NCWC. According to this plan, the administration would send to Congress a series of noncontroversial revisions to the NDEA; then, in the markup sessions, Senators Clark and Morse would add an amendment to Title IV, Section 305, which would expand private-school loans beyond defense-related equipment to include the construction of classrooms that are used for science, mathematics, foreign languages, plus English, physical fitness, and the school lunch program. This in effect would enable church schools to obtain low-interest, government-guaranteed loans to construct virtually any structure short of the chapel. For a Catholic president to appear to be a party to such an agreement would be politically suicidal. So Sorensen closed his "administratively confidential" memo with the stipulation that "there was to be no mention or indication that the Administration had played any role or taken any position on this amendment or course of strategy."[55] It would appear to be merely a matter of congressional discretion, and the president at his press conferences consistently denied being a party to such maneuvers.

Accordingly, on 20 April Ribicoff sent Kennedy his proposed noncontroversial amendments to the NDEA. Meanwhile, Senator Morse's committee duly held hearings and after markup reported out S. 1021, which authorized $2.5 billion in public-school grants for operation, maintenance, construction, and also for teachers' salaries. On 25 May the Senate passed S. 1021 by a vote of forty-nine to thirty-four (Democrats, forty-one to twenty-one; Republicans, eight to twenty-two). On 1 June the House Education and Labor Committee reported a clean bill (H.R. 7300) similar to the Senate-passed bill and sought a rule for floor hearing. But the Rules Committee, under heavy Catholic pressure, especially from Delaney and O'Neill, held up considering H.R. 7300 until it received the NDEA amendments with the new provision for parochial-school loans.

Despite Kennedy's denials of complicity, the strategy of using NDEA revision to smuggle in aid to parochial schools was transparent. In an editorial on 20 June the *New York Times* charged that NDEA revision in Congress had been "dominated by efforts to write into this legislation provisions for aid to private and parochial schools," which was "now being used as a cover under which there is an attempt to slip through large-scale Federal aid to non-public schools."[56] The *Times* supported the original Kennedy bill being sponsored by Congressman Frank Thompson (D., N.J.) in the House, opposed the NDEA gambit for sweetening the Catholic lobby, and urged New York City's Congressman Delaney to support fellow Catholic Thompson's bill in the Rules Committee. But Delaney and O'Neill held the Thompson bill hostage in Rules until the NDEA bill arrived, so Powell's committee shortly complied by reporting out the NDEA bill, H.R. 7902. Even so, the tense jockeying in Rules still held up all the bills. On 3 July the *Times* editorially complained that the NDEA ransom had been paid, but still the school-aid hostage remained imprisoned in Rules: "Even in the unsavory business of holding hostages, it is customary to set the victim free once the ransom has been paid. The amended NDEA was the ransom; and so the public-school bill ought to be by any rules of this nasty game, liberated from the Rules Committee, where it has unconscionably been held by a strange coalition."[57]

Then, on 18 July, Virginia's Judge Smith teamed up with Mississippi's Colmer and the Catholic Delaney in a strange coalition to join the five Rules Committee Republicans in killing the public-school bill, the NDEA bill, *and* the college-aid bill in an afternoon of acrimony and slaughter. The Republicans wanted no bill at all, nor did the southern Democrats Smith and Colmer. The Catholics wanted the NDEA "sweeteners" for parochial schools, but three southern Democrats—Carl Elliott of Alabama, Homer Thornberry of Texas, and James Trimble of Arkansas—objected to such thinly disguised church aid in the unlikely name of defense. The key was Delaney, who reflected understandable Catholic fears that federal aid for public school teachers' salaries posed potentially ruinous competition for poorly paid Catholic lay teachers. The paralysis was complete.

"FIASCO"

When news of the butchery in Rules reached the White House, Kennedy called Wilbur Cohen into the Oval Office and inquired, "Wilbur, why couldn't you get one more Republican on the Rules Committee to vote with us?" Cohen recalls his response: "Impetuously and somewhat annoyed, I retorted: 'Mr. President, why can't you get one more Catholic?' The President shrugged his shoulders, half-smiled and dropped further discussion."[58]

At Kennedy's press conference on 19 July, he was asked, "Mr. President, the whole bundle of your school legislation was torpedoed in the House Rules Committee yesterday, and it's clear that one of the things that largely helped to sink it was the religious issue. Will you discuss that problem, including the report that you have just about given up on passing school legislation in this first session of this Congress?" President Kennedy replied:

> Well, I know that we were defeated in the Rules Committee by a vote of 8 to 7. I will say that 7 of those 8 votes came from members of Congress who were in the last election. They have, of course, their responsibility to meet. But the fact of the matter is that there are procedures available to the House of Representatives to adopt this bill, in spite of the action yesterday, before the session ends.
>
> Now, the Senate passed it by a generous majority and it came out of the House Committee with support. I consider it to be probably the most important piece of domestic legislation. I'm hopeful that the members of Congress who support this will use those procedures which are available to them under the rules of the House to bring this to a vote, and that a majority of the members of Congress will support it.[59]

The procedure Kennedy was referring to was the seldom-used and rarely effective device of Calendar Wednesday, which was designed to short-circuit the House committee structure in an emergency. But Ribicoff and Cohen preferred to attempt through normal channels (which necessarily included the Rules log jam, and especially Delaney), a compromise that would drop the two most controversial items in the original package: aid for teachers' salaries and the NDEA sweetener for Catholics.[60] Instead it would extend school construction in impacted areas only in overcrowded districts (by the same amount the House had passed in 1960). A separate title would provide $300 million for constructing college facilities. Supporting the last-ditch compromise, Sorensen emphasized that $180 million of the college aid would be in grants rather than loans—"and to accept grants as well as loans is a major change from the original admin-istration position."[61] On 14 August Sorensen advised Kennedy that "there is no real possibility of the bill receiving approval without clearing the House Rules Committee. This means that it must receive the support of either Congressman Delaney or a Republican member." He further added that "the compromise measure advanced by Secretary Ribicoff last week failed to win a commitment from key House leaders, apparently because it went too far—and from key Senate leaders, apparently because it did not go far enough."[62] Sorensen even argued that the compromise was not the "anemic" bill that Senator Hubert Humphrey had denounced, but rather "in some ways a better bill than before." He added the Nixonian rationale that "it is the old bill without teachers' salaries, which is what both Houses have passed before. Teachers will be glad to get any Federal aid to education after 40 years—and local funds will thus be freed for salaries."[63]

Kennedy accepted the compromise proposal, and Congressman Thompson introduced it as H.R. 8890. The drastically watered-down, one-year "emergency" school construction bill was denounced by Catho-lics as discriminatory, by the NEA as woefully inadequate, and by House Republicans as a railroad job. When Congressman Powell sought its consideration on 30 August on the House floor through the Calendar Wednesday procedure, he was trounced in a roll-call vote of 170 to 242 (Democrats, 164 to 82; Republicans, 6 to 160). Price observed of this stunning defeat for the administration that "the massive opposition con-sisted of 160 Republicans, 70 southern Democrats, and 12 non-southern Democrats."[64] The higher education companion bill, H.R. 8900, was then sent to the Rules Committee, where it remained buried.

The *New York Times* editorialized on 6 September that the "failure of leadership, in the White House, in the Department of HEW, and in the House of Representatives gives little cause for hope. Compromise has been the order of the day, and the result has been a fiasco for Federal aid to education and a disaster for the nation's public schools."[65] On 6 Sep-tember the House extended the NDEA and the aid to impacted areas bill for two years, the Senate agreed (despite Kennedy's plea for a one-year extension), and on 3 October Kennedy signed the "unsound and un-economical" bills with "extreme reluctance."[66]

At his press conference following Powell's Calendar Wednesday fail-ure, Kennedy had observed that "everyone is for education but they're all for a different education bill. . . . So we will be back next year."[67] But beyond his occasional public rhetoric, he hadn't worked very hard to push through his education program in 1961. He had ducked civil rights, provided lip service to education, and instead had placed his priorities on aid to depressed areas, expanded trade, a broadened minimum wage, and housing and foreign aid, where his congressional victories had been impressive. As the first Catholic president, he was politically condemned to oppose parochial school aid in his elementary and secondary school program. But his covert encouragement of the NDEA sweetener for Catholics was a sham that backfired on him, and his repeated denials were disingenuous. The second session of the Eighty-seventh Congress would occur in an election year, 1962, and if Kennedy seriously intended another attempt to pass legislation on federal aid to education, he would need a new formula with the same old Congress, especially in the volatile House.

2 / KENNEDY AND THE LEGACY OF ASSASSINATION

THE POLITICAL CONTEXT OF 1962

Because 1962 was an election year, the widespread sentiment in Congress favored avoidance of the controversial issues surrounding the federal aid-to-education question until 1963. Secretary of Health, Education, and Welfare Ribicoff had sent President Kennedy a five-page postmortem memo on 6 October 1961 that analyzed the failure of 1961 and flatly asserted that "a broad program of grants to states for public school construction and teachers' salaries is virtually impossible to pass."[1] Ribicoff urged Kennedy to abandon such a state grant program, or at least postpone it until 1963, and press instead in 1962 for the higher education bill and the medical professions bill,

> then, face squarely the fact that a general aid bill for construction and teachers' salaries has been killed by the House Rules Committee and cannot be enacted by this Congress, make this an issue for the '62 elections with a commitment to press for it in '63, but insist that the needs are so great that some steps must be taken now. Therefore, transmit a new bill, the Emergency Educational Opportunities Act of 1962, which would include a series of special purpose programs to aid teachers, improve course content, step up the level of needed research, etc. The bill could, if desired, be in the form of amendments to NDEA. The bill could also include, as one of its features, a one-year construction program for school districts urgently in need, or this program could be introduced in separate legislation.[2]

In retrospect, this was shrewd political advice.

But President Kennedy was determined to ask Congress for an even more elaborate education package than he had in 1961. In his annual State of the Union Message on 11 January 1962, Kennedy announced that he would continue to push for enactment of his failed 1961 programs for construction and teacher salary aid (for public schools only), and, at the college level, for federal scholarships as well as construction loans for academic facilities. He also hinted that he would ask for several new education programs in addition to those that had been rejected by the first session of the Eighty-seventh Congress.[3]

When Congress received Kennedy's Special Message on Education on 6 February, it contained a ten-point program, headed by his plea for the enactment of the previous year's general aid bills, S. 1021 and H.R. 7300—long moribund in Judge Smith's Rules Committee graveyard.[4] But appended to Kennedy's lead section on general public-school aid for construction and teachers' salaries was a novel proposal for federal scholarships and grants designed to upgrade the quality of teaching. This was included in Wilbur Cohen's original submission to the White House of 6 December, and it had elicited the enthusiastic endorsement of the Bureau of the Budget, whose staff foresaw little useful educational (as distinguished from political) impact in spreading $300 million federal dollars over a national teachers payroll of $8 or $9 billion, and who wanted instead to use federal funds to reward merit.[5] Ribicoff had made the same argument in his memo to Kennedy dated 6 October 1961.

In addition to the president's new quality-improvement proposal, there were two other new proposals: one to combat adult illiteracy and one to aid handicapped children. Other special proposals were renewed from 1961 and included aid for medical and dental education, aid to educate the children of migrant workers, and a federal advisory council to aid the arts. Kennedy also backed a pending bill, S. 205, that proposed a noncontroversial program of construction aid for educational television, and he called for increased National Science Foundation appropriations to improve high school science education. Only the last two items, which passed Congress without difficulty, ever got past the Rules Committee. The college-aid bill, H.R. 8900, which was a leftover from 1961, and which Kennedy reendorsed for 1962, fared better. H.R. 8900 had passed the House on 29 January 1962, and it passed the Senate on 6 February, with large majorities in both houses. Each version of the college-aid bill contained differing amendments, but this typical circumstance was what conference committees were designed to iron out through trade-offs. Higher education had seemed largely immune from the whiplash over race, religion, and federal control that tortured the debate over general aid to the lower schools. Catholic and Baptist and Lutheran colleges had long received federal funds to support dormitory construction and science laboratories and language instruction and the like, and the G.I. Bill had for even longer provided federal scholarships to veterans at sectarian institutions. And quite demonstrably, the postwar baby boom to which the returning G.I.'s had so heartily contributed was beginning to flood the underbuilt and understaffed college and university campuses, and the 4 million college students of 1960 were expected to double by 1970. Even the Christmas break between the first and second sessions of the Eighty-seventh Congress, ironically enough, had seemed to calm the nasty religious wars of 1961, and on the very day that Kennedy sent his Special Message on Education to the Hill, the Senate passed H.R. 8900 by a roll-call vote of 69 to 17. The House had passed its version on 30 January by a thumping roll-call vote of 319 to 80. Its prospects seemed bright.

THE COLLEGE-AID DEBATE OF 1962

But there were political land mines scattered about. One involved the distinction between federal loans and grants for the construction of academic facilities. In 1961, the Kennedy administration had requested generously subsidized federal loans. But committee testimony had revealed that many colleges either could not afford to participate without raising tuitions or eliminating teachers' salary increases, or were restricted by state constitutions from borrowing. So H.R. 8900 called for both loans and grants. While taxpayer-subsidized loans to private sectarian colleges had established precedents, however, outright federal grants had none. This provision considerably increased the vulnerability of federal college aid to the religious-war crossfire, which had previously been largely avoided. In his Special Message to Congress of 6 February 1962, Kennedy attempted to finesse this problem by urging Congress "this month [to] complete its action on legislation *to assist in the building*" of academic facilities—with no reference to loans versus grants.[6]

President Kennedy strode more boldly into the other major region of dangerous terrain. This concerned the issue of federal scholarships. It involved, at the student rather than the institutional level, essentially the same loans-versus-grants dichotomy, but it triggered a partisan rather than a religious dispute. This tendency had been demonstrated in 1961, when the first college-aid bill reported by the House Education and Labor committee, H.R. 7215, which had provided for 200,000 scholarships, was killed in Rules on 18 July, mainly because the Republicans objected to federal scholarships for the bright but needy. Students should not be "induced" to go to college, the Republicans argued. So the dead H.R. 7215 was transformed into the live H.R. 8900 simply by omitting the scholarship provisions. But in February 1962, Kennedy was committing himself to a huge Democratic constituency: families earning less than $5,600 a year—one half of all American families in 1960—who could not afford to send their children to college even *with* student loans. His language was direct (although to a generation once removed by exponential inflation, his dollar amounts will appear archaic):

> The average cost of higher education today—up nearly 90 percent since 1950 and still rising—is in excess of $1,750 per year per student, or $7,000 for a four year course. Industrious students can earn a part of this—they or their families can borrow a part of it—but one-half of all American families had incomes below $5,600 in 1960—and they cannot be expected to borrow, for example, $4,000 for each talented son or daughter that deserves to go to college. Federal scholarships providing up to $1,000 a year can fill part of this gap.[7]

On aid to higher education, Kennedy could appeal with honor both to the lower-income families with college aspirations and to the restive Catholics, most of whom were Democrats. And congressional Republicans, who had largely reverted on domestic issues to their pre-Eisenhower knee-jerk posture of minority oppositionism, could be expected to play the politics of election year 1962 with faithful consistency.

By pressing for the aid to both lower and higher education bills in 1962, Kennedy was risking mutual contamination by the religious and partisan controversies. Fred M. Hechinger, who covered education for the *New York Times*, reported on 11 February that Kennedy's message had "clearly upset some of the estimates of his own supporters," who had hoped that he would not renew the drive for elementary and secondary school aid until 1963. But Hechinger also observed, "At the same time, some educators are dismayed that persons close to the White House continue to indicate that the President is reconciled to settling for the other parts of the package, without action on aid to the public elementary and secondary schools."[8] Whatever the sincerity of Kennedy's intentions, Congress basically ignored his general-aid bill, but the Roman Catholic lobby did not. The day after Kennedy delivered this education message, Cardinal Spellman told a meeting of the New York Archdiocesan Teachers Institute that the president's school-aid proposals would mean "the end of our parochial schools," and that excluding parochial schools from the program would be a "terrible crime."[9] When Kennedy was asked about his dilemma at his press conference on 7 February, he responded that "because I think it is such an urgent matter, I will do everything I can to have the Congress take favorable action on this subject this year."[10] His actions never matched his rhetoric, and his general-aid bill went nowhere. But the religious controversy was powerfully refueled, and the political atmosphere that had earlier appeared cordial to the college-aid bill was thereby severely contaminated.

The president's flawed strategy was further worsened by partisan maneuvering, bad luck, and political accident. H.R. 8900 could have avoided the House bottleneck in Rules and gone straight to conference in February, when bipartisan support was strong, but for the single objection on 8 February of Congressman Albert H. Quie, a Republican from Minnesota, which automatically sent H.R. 8900 to the Rules Committee. A respected member of the House Education and Labor Committee, Quie explained that he "just wanted to buy enough time . . . so that the House will not have to accept the Senate's scholarship provisions."[11] And buy time he did—three months of deadlock in Rules, which allowed the religious and partisan and ultimately racial controversies to reappear and fester. On 18 February, six national college associations issued a joint statement calling for both loans and grants for classroom construction, but *not* mentioning scholarships; hence they preferred the House bill to the Senate bill.[12] The higher education community was united against federal aid limited to loans because approximately forty states variously prohibited indebtedness by the public colleges, and thus federal aid limited to loans would discriminate against the public sector. But a potential compromise program of loans for only private colleges (including sectarian schools) but both grants *and* loans for public colleges produced private college resentment at unequal treatment. Finally, any compromise that would attempt to bar grants from sectarian but not from non-sectarian private colleges would run afoul of the virtual impossibility of defining the line separating the two. Add to all this the dispute over scholarships, and it is easy to see how ground for possible compromise was so difficult to find. Given such controversial jockeying, a rule was not granted for conference until 2 May, and then by only a narrow vote of eight to six, with all five committee Republicans being joined in dissent by the conservative Democrat William Colmer of Mississippi. To get a conference rule, Powell had to promise Judge Smith and his House colleagues that he would refuse to accept the Senate's scholarship provision.

But there were problems in the Senate also. Chairman Lister Hill of the Labor and Public Welfare Committee, who was a veteran New Dealer, was up for reelection against a staunch Alabama conservative, and as a result his usual strong support for education legislation, which was often crucial in wooing his fellow southerners, was greatly curtailed. Hill was adamantly opposed to the House bill's grants to private colleges, and his Senate colleague, Wayne Morse, who chaired the education subcommittee, also opposed grants to church-related colleges as unconstitutional. (Morse was also distracted during the early weeks of the conference impasse by an intense Senate floor fight over the communications satellite bill.) Opposition to grants for sectarian colleges was reinforced on 16 June when five powerful education groups, all of them involved primarily in lower education, sent telegrams to all the House-Senate conferees opposing federal grants for construction of academic facilities at sectarian colleges as a violation of the principle of separation of church and state.[13]

Then, on 25 June, the Supreme Court ruled six to one in the case of Engle v. Vitale that the reading of an official nondenominational prayer in New York State public schools was unconstitutional. The negative political reaction was sharp, especially among southern Democrats. Congressman George Andrews of Alabama expressed his double-edged moral outrage against the Warren court succinctly: "They put the Negroes in the schools and now they've driven God out."[14] Although the Kennedy administration had been unexpectedly cautious in its civil rights policies, white southern fears began to grow as the administration proposed a law to ban literacy tests in federal elections by making a sixth-grade education a presumption of literacy (this was filibustered to death in the Senate). In the executive agencies, the Office of Education in December of 1961 required a racial nondiscrimination clause in contracts with colleges and universities selected for NDEA language institutes (six southern institutions then withdrew from the program, but twenty-two remained). In March of 1962, Ribicoff announced that effective September 1963 DHEW would withhold funds from segregated schools receiving aid-to-impacted-areas funds (military bases were disproportionately located in the South). And in September, the Justice Department filed its first aid-to-impacted-areas suit to bar federal aid from racially segregated public schools in Prince George County, Virginia.[15] By September, while the conference committee remained deadlocked, the growing controversy over the admission of James Meredith to Ole Miss would further stiffen southern resistance to administration proposals (including Kennedy's announcement that he would appoint Robert Weaver as secretary of a department of urban affairs if Congress would authorize its establishment—which it did not do while Kennedy was president).

THE DISORGANIZATION OF THE EXECUTIVE BRANCH

Organizational disarray in the executive branch compounded all of these growing difficulties. It started at the top, with Kennedy's highly personal, loosely structured, and ad hoc style of organizing the presidency. The consensus of the comparative literature on organizing the executive branch is that Kennedy rejected the highly structured Eisenhower pyramid with its military style of hierarchical staff system and functioned instead as his own chief of staff, presiding with informal openness over a group of generalist aides.[16] The oral histories in Boston and in Austin depict a charming, intellectually curious young president given to a fluid style of relationships. One surprising strength of Kennedy's presidential style is that his relationship with his senior competitor, Lyndon Johnson, became one of reasonably cordial and mutual respect. All evidence testifies to Kennedy's concern that Vice-President Johnson be assigned duties of considerable magnitude, so that his vice-presidency might not be measured by the bitterness of fellow Texan John Nance Garner. The same evidence testifies to Johnson's probably surprised but gratified response to Kennedy's solicitude. This complicated relationship of competing egos produced many strengths and weaknesses that the literature thoroughly explores. But in federal education policy, where Vice-President Johnson played no discernible role, it produced primarily weaknesses. The president himself, like most modern presidents, became primarily interested in the "point" decisions of foreign policy rather than the "line" decisions of DHEW or USOE. Sorensen and Feldman in substantive policy and O'Brien in congressional liaison were exceptionally able aides, but they were spread too thin, and they were working with a Congress in which the president had no functional majority. This weakness of style and commitment at the top was transmitted to DHEW and USOE. Secretary Ribicoff grew to loathe his job at DHEW, where the paucity of "Schedule C" political appointments yielded unusual power to entrenched civil servants. "I used to be Number One in Connecticut," Ribicoff complained to Wilbur Cohen, "now I'm Number 64 here."[17] Ribicoff was uninterested and untalented in administration, regarded DHEW as "ungovernable," and was frustrated by his legislative failures on the Hill. He enjoyed a close relationship with Kennedy, but he could not seem to persuade such key congressional powers as Senator Lister Hill or Congressman John Fogarty, so he longed to join them. When Kennedy disregarded Ribicoff's advice on education policy for 1962, Ribicoff cast his eyes on a Senate seat from Connecticut, and in July of 1962 he resigned as secretary to run for (and win) that seat. Cohen's recollections of Secretary Ribicoff are not flattering: "Ribicoff left because, first he is a political animal; he is not an administrator . . . he was in fact an extremely poor administrator, one of the poorest we had as Secretary of HEW. . . . He was interested particularly in his own political future. He was very self-centered and egotistical."[18]

Ribicoff was replaced by Mayor Anthony Celebrezze of Cleveland, whom Cohen regarded as reflective of White House cynicism toward DHEW because the appointment was predicated less on merit than on the potential of Celebrezze's credentials as an Italian-American to boost Ted Kennedy's senate race in Massachusetts. In time, Cohen came to have a decent respect for Celebrezze. Although he believed that the "Kennedy people didn't have any respect for Celebrezze—they didn't think Celebrezze had the mental abilities," Cohen concluded that "now, it turned out that Celebrezze was a very good secretary, but mainly because he let the White House determine all the significant things, and the reason for that is he wanted a judgeship. So his attitude was to play it cool, do what they want, and I'll get my judgeship." [19] And indeed he did.

At the Office of Education, the Kennedy administration's appointed commissioner was Sterling McMurrin, a man Kennedy did not even know—which testifies at least indirectly to Kennedy's basic gut disinterest in education policy, at least through 1962. Actually, McMurrin was a potentially able commissioner, the first to be chosen from the ranks of higher education (he was a professor of philosophy from the University of Utah); previous commissioners had been drawn from the ranks of the public school bureaucracy and generally lacked serious claim to national distinction. But Professor McMurrin was the administration's fourth choice, after James Allen of New York and two others had declined the appointment. Francis Keppel recalls that "Ribicoff decided that he would handle all the politics on Capitol Hill and McMurrin would sit back and think high thoughts in the Office of Education. Well the politics fell apart something terrible, and . . . a bill which had been put together with baling wire for higher education got on the floor of the House." [20]

"NONREIMBURSABLE LOANS"

The conference committee deadlock over federal aid to higher education during the summer of 1962 is reflected in the frustrated reports of Larry O'Brien's pulse-takers from both houses on the Hill, which mirror the dismal prospect of a repetition of the paralysis of 1961. Charles Daly, O'Brien's House nose-counter, reported to O'Brien on the House conferees: "[Edith] Green sees the education conference as 'almost hopeless' and says there is some feeling talks should cease for a while. Most of the Senators are firmly against grants to private colleges; their idea of extending loans to private colleges and grants to public institutions would get little backing in the House. On the question of scholarships, she is working to develop some sort of acceptable compromise but here, too she is not optimistic." [21] As for Congresswoman Green's view of her Senate counterparts:

> In her view, the only place we might possibly be helpful now is in modifying the Senators' attitudes toward grants. She says Clark is okay on grants, Javits has at least swung over to the point where he acknowledges there is a difference between loans and grants. Yarborough would okay grants to non-church-related private col-

leges (presenting a problem of definition), Morse might possible [*sic*] support grants, Randolph is opposed to grants and Mc-Namara is against everything. She suggests we hit Randolph and McNamara.[22]

O'Brien's Senate nose-counter, Mike Manatos, reported on Senator McNamara's opinion of this "worthless piece of legislation," and this assessment reflected the same mood of gloom: "My meeting this morning with Senator McNamara developed the same feeling of hopelessness with regard to the Conference on Higher Education as expressed by Congresswoman Green. He is resentful of the attempt, as he construes it, of the House Rules Committee to dictate terms of the Conference to the Senate. . . . He thinks grants should go only to non-church schools and that Church supported colleges should have loans only."[23]

The dual essence of the problem was that, first, the House conferees continued to insist on grants for both public and private academic facilities, whereas the Senators insisted on loans but not grants to private colleges. Second, the House would not accept the Senate's scholarship provision. So President Kennedy "hit" Senator McNamara in late July with a proposal that, if the House conferees flatly refused to consider college student scholarships, as directed by the Rules Committee, then the Senate conferees ought to consider an inventive "student loan expansion with forgiveness of repayment for those entering occupations required by the national interest and in short supply."[24] The logic of this legislative ingenuity, which would so dilate the repayment requirements of a loan that it would approximate a de facto federal grant in the guise of a loan, or a grant under the loan rubric, was suggested by the NDEA of 1958, which "forgave" repayment requirements for students who entered the teaching profession in areas given priority by NDEA.

Wilbur Cohen, the self-proclaimed "salami-slicer" whose relentless incrementalism in social legislation was appropriately reflected in that metaphor, pounced on this elastic possibility in his tireless and effective liaison between the White House and the Hill—in this case between Edith Green and Theodore Sorensen. Cohen's confidential memo to Sorensen of 3 August 1962 summarized Mrs. Green's creative formula for transforming a student loan, upon which the House conferees insisted, into a student grant, which the Senate conferees demanded. This included requiring *no* institutional contribution (NDEA required a 10 percent institutional contribution); *no* ceiling of federal payments to an institution (the NDEA ceiling was $250,000 per year); *no* interest charge on the loans (NDEA charged 3 percent starting the second year after leaving college); and, most stunningly, a novel federal *refusal* to express *any* academic or vocational preference, especially insofar as superior student performance and therefore promise was concerned: "No preference would be given for students with superior academic backgrounds who express a desire to teach or to students whose academic backgrounds indicate superior preparation or capacity in science, mathematics, engineering, or modern foreign languages."[25] Better yet, annual repayments of principal would be limited to 5 percent of the borrower's taxable income—which would approximate $150 on a gross annual income of $4,000 for a new teacher in the early 1960s—and the "Commissioner of Education could, by regulation further reduce repayments for good cause shown."[26] But the maximum flexibility lay in the elasticity of the NDEA's precedent for "forgiveness," which under the NDEA applied only to teachers in public elementary or secondary schools: "Up to 50 per cent of loan would be forgiven, at a rate of 10 per cent of unpaid balance per year, for each year's service (subsequent to the making of the loan) in an 'area of critical manpower need in the national interest' or in the Armed Forces. . . . Such 'areas' would be determined annually by the Secretaries of Defense, Labor, and Health, Education, and Welfare."[27] To empower so many cabinet secretaries to annually determine areas of "critical manpower need" for federal loan forgiveness was indeed a flexible instrument, and it appealed to the compromising sentiments of conferees Edith Green and Joseph Clark, who convinced their conference colleagues to report out a version of H.R. 8900 on 19 September that would authorize $1.5 billion in grants and loans over five years to public and private colleges for construction of classrooms and libraries; $250 million in grants to public community colleges; and $600 in student "loans," which included a set-aside of 20 percent of the loan funds for "nonreimbursable loans" to exceptionally needy and promising students.[28]

This was Dean Keppel's higher education bill "put together with baling wire"—"what struck me as the most unlikely language I've ever heard—a provision for '*non*-reimbursable loans.' Well, for heaven's sake what's a loan!"[29] Republican Congressman John M. Ashbrook of Ohio called the "nonreimbursable loan" set-aside "semantic doubletalk," which of course it was, and there was widespread sentiment in the House that the conference committee had violated its instructions by including the Senate's thinly disguised scholarship provision. Besides, "truly needy" scholarship students were unlikely to be Republicans. Clearly, H.R. 8900's original bipartisan support was crumbling. Worse, southern Democrats began talking about defection over the religious issue. Worst of all, from the Kennedy administration's viewpoint, the resurgent church-state controversy was splintering the fragile alliance supporting federal aid even at the college level. The conference report on H.R. 8900 was filed on 19 September, and before the vote was taken the following day, Dr. William G. Carr of the NEA sent telegrams to all House members warning that the provision for federal funds for construction grants to sectarian colleges "imperils America's traditional concept of separation of church and state."[30] The NEA wanted federal aid to bolster its constituents' salaries, and Senator John F. Kennedy had embraced this proposition as a presidential candidate. To the NEA, the big battle was for teachers' salary relief in an elementary-secondary-school-aid bill for the public sector only, a goal to which college aid must be held hostage. And the NEA was not alone in the September telegram and lobbying blitz: add the American Association of School Administrators, the National Conference of Parents and Teachers, the Southern Baptist Convention, and others.

The result is best exemplified by the response of the House delegation from Alabama. Despite the conventional racist-reactionary stereotypes, Alabama's Democrats had historically inherited a powerful populist legacy, and the deans of both delegations on the Hill—Carl Elliott in the House and Lister Hill in the Senate—were deeply rooted in the progressive rural liberalism of the New Deal. But on this occasion Senator Hill lobbied the House side to oppose taxpayer aid to religious colleges, and the entire Alabama delegation voted to recommit and thereby kill the conference report. So the House, which had supported H.R. 8900 on 30 January by a roll-call vote of 319 to 80, voted on 20 September to recommit the conference report by a vote of 214 to 186. The Republican margin of opposition, 130 to 30, was not surprising. But the Democratic margin was regionally crucial. House Democrats supported H.R. 8900 by a vote of 156 to 84, but seventy-six of the ninety-nine southern Democrats voted for recommittal, which meant that thirty-three southern Democrats who voted for the bill in January had switched to oppose it in September. So in the second session of the Eighty-seventh Congress, as in the first, federal aid to education, even at the college level, where its prospects had earlier appeared so bright, was dead. The *New York Times* once again reproved the administration's faltering leadership in its postmortem editorial: "The President, who less than a year ago said federal aid to the public schools might well be the most important piece of domestic legislation, has lapsed into a strange silence. And his lieutenants in Congress and in the Executive appear just as remote from the issue as former Secretary Ribicoff, who has dropped out of the Cabinet to return to Connecticut politics."[31] The *Times* editorial deplored the "Falstaffian concept of courage" of the administration's supporters of federal aid to education, who were "in retreat or in hiding." It recalled with approval the president's original insistence that education was a vast, interconnected enterprise with public elementary and secondary schools at its foundation, and hence that federal aid to higher education, or to combat adult illiteracy, or to assist manpower retraining, were important but ancillary goals. "There was nothing wrong with the President's original diagnosis," the *Times* concluded, including his reminder that "the issue has been debated for forty years and ought to be ready for action. But now even the debate appears to be fading out."[32]

THE CONGRESSIONAL ELECTIONS OF 1962

In late July, when the education conference appeared hopelessly deadlocked, and with similar blockages facing major administrative programs in medicare, mass transit, and public works, President Kennedy set the partisan tone for the 1962 midterm elections by attacking the consistent negativism of the Republicans in his 23 July press conference. He said the November elections would give the American people a "clear" choice —whether to "anchor down" by voting Republican or to "sail" by voting Democratic.[33] The president thereafter campaigned vigorously for Democratic candidates until he was halted by October's Cuban missile crisis.

Kennedy's announcement of a naval quarantine of Cuba on 22 October and his subsequent ultimatum to Khrushchev blunted Republican hopes that Cuba might become an administration embarrassment, as it had in 1961. The result of the election was essentially a standoff. The Democrats could claim a net gain of four Senate seats against a nominal loss of four House seats. Not since 1934 had a presidential party fared so well in a midterm election. On the other hand, as the Republicans were quick to point out, the Democrats had scarcely recouped their large losses sustained through Kennedy's negative coattail effect in 1960, which had left far fewer vulnerable seats for Republicans to recapture in 1962. And the Republicans had increased their southern House seats from nine to fourteen. So when the first session of the Eighty-eighth Congress convened in January, Kennedy was still going to lack a working majority, especially in the House.

A FRESH STRATEGY FOR 1963: THE BUREAU OF THE BUDGET'S OMNIBUS SOCIAL WELFARE APPROACH

Late in October of 1962, the Bureau of the Budget's staff began constructing a "fresh approach" to a new federal education program that rejected the strategy of separate bills in the last Congress for "elementary and secondary education, quality, higher education, and for a variety of special aids (for adult illiterates, migrants, handicapped children) [which] simply resulted (1) in dredging up in bold form the issues of public school versus private and segregation versus desegregation, and (2) in arousing more support for specialized groups and needs—without any gain in support for broader programs in education."[34]

The bureau called instead for an *omnibus* bill that would embrace a broad "social welfare" approach to education, that would concentrate on "aiding people—from childhood to old age—rather than aiding institutions or another level of government." The BOB memorandum observed that the president's Special Message on Education of the previous 6 February had accepted the social welfare view conceptually, but that "curiously enough, the social welfare view of education was not pursued by the Administration politically or in fact in the structure of the legislation."[35]

The bureau's recommended social welfare approach was rooted in an "underlying rationale" about what "education is or should be in our society"—that it is "integrally connected with a person throughout his life, to his freedom, his individual social and economic welfare and in turn to the freedom, social, and economic wellbeing of the Nation." As such, education was the key to "the anticipated next stage in the development of our society, thrust upon us by changing technology, automation, leisure, urban, rural change, unemployment and population increase." Such a rationale would seek to maximize economic growth rather than blanket aid to institutions, so its programs would reach out to *people*— slum and rural children, the elderly, women whose intellectual resources were poorly tapped, people working in "ordinary jobs" who could benefit from retraining and sabbatical benefits as much as scholars and corporate executives.

Implicit in the bureau's proposal was a critique of the political tendency of line agencies in general, and DHEW and USOE in particular, to construct legislative proposals based upon the competing demands of powerful constituent groups and their institutions rather than upon the needs of people; to base programs on coalitions rather than on a unified *theory* of education. This critique from the "institutional memory" of the executive branch was to sharpen and become more explicit in the years ahead, but in the fall of 1962 the bureau's call for an omnibus bill and social welfare strategy for 1963 was based in large part on the embarrassing two years of failure of all attempts to create federal aid programs to aid "institutions or another level of Government." The bureau had also consistently warned that even a large federal-aid program was going to be tiny in relation to the more than $20 billion sum that was annually spent on public and private education in America, and therefore that federal programs should concentrate on incentives, on leverage, on stimulating breakthroughs rather than supplementing what was already being done through the vastly more massive state and local and private educational expenditures.

THE STATES' RIGHTS COUNTERATTACK

But also in the fall of 1962, a demand for a "fresh start and a creative new approach" to federal aid to education was coming from another source, and its proposed new approach differed radically from the preferences of the Bureau of the Budget. This was the Bipartisan Citizens Committee for Federal Aid for Public Elementary and Secondary Education, and its masthead reflected a truly bipartisan elite: William Benton, Barry Bingham, James Conant, Lawrence Derthick, Walt Disney, Arthur Flemming, Marion Folsom, Edgar Fuller, Earl McGrath, William Menninger, Walter Reuther, Howard K. Smith, Lewis Strauss. The blue-ribbon committee contained two former secretaries of health, education, and welfare and two former commissioners of USOE. On 9 November, committee chairman George J. Hecht, publisher of *Parents Magazine*, wrote President Kennedy urging the administration to ask Congress to construct a bipartisan bill, rather than submit an inherently partisan "Administration" bill; and to extricate itself from the church-state controversy by embracing a principle that would *"MAKE FEDERAL CONTROL ILLEGAL AND IMPOSSIBLE."* How? By transferring federal funds to "ongoing State aid education systems," which would then "be deemed State funds upon receipt by the State," and would be "distributed to local school authorities for public education purposes as defined by State law, using the same processes through which State funds are now distributed."[36]

The Bipartisan Citizens Committee proposal did call for some sort of equalization formula to benefit the poorer states, for matching requirements and penalties to prevent mere substitution of federal for state funds, and for encouraging state planning. But its essence was vintage states' rights. On 22 November, in Miami, Hecht explained the committee's proposal before the annual meeting of the Council of Chief State School Officers, whose executive secretary, Edgar Fuller, sat on the committee.[37]

In response to all these pressures, Sorensen's first draft of the proposed omnibus education bill for 1963 generally reflected the Bureau of the Budget's memo of 7 November that proposed the omnibus rationale and also its summary and budget projection of 24 November, which included the various agency submissions and called for maximizing the programmatic flexibility of existing legislation through "a more liberal interpretation of the law than has heretofore prevailed," and hence minimizing the need for new and novel (and therefore vulnerable) legislation. Sorensen's draft also included aid for teachers' salaries in public schools only. But his final point had a newly familiar ring: "Upon receipt by the states, Federal funds under the statute will become state funds, included in the existing state aid programs and administered by the state educational agency, in accordance with its own laws on equalization, organization and public purpose."[38]

The Bureau of the Budget was appalled at this. Its responsive memo of 5 December concentrated on the positive principles it was seeking to develop, that is, making maximum use of existing legislative authority (NDEA, NSF, HHFA); presenting an omnibus bill "as the No. 1 Presidential domestic objective in the first session of the 88th Congress," possibly to be considered by a joint select committee or select committees in both Houses; providing a program continuum from preschool through old age; and targeting at specific problems rather than educational levels.[39] But its strong preference was clearly for *project* grants with specific targets, where the federal granting authority determined priorities, over general grants wherein federal funds might simply disappear in the nation's vastly larger education budget.

> General grants to States for elementary and secondary schools under present budgetary limitations—even if they could be enacted—would be too small to make a dent—perhaps $500 million out of $20 billion. The State's rights, no-control-over-education drive would have the Federal Government turn the money over to the States under general "State Plans." This would be the same as "to put the money on the stump and run." Federal money would merely replace local funds and it would take large sums just to overcome this substitution and to make a real impact and achievement of national objectives would be difficult.[40]

The BOB even suggested that the omnibus bill "might best leave out controversial proposals which renew the church-state issue—such as grants for forgiveness of loans to colleges and general aid." But the crucial decisions were up to the president, to be summarized in his annual State of the Union Message in mid-January and in his Special Message on Education in late January.

COMMISSIONER FRANCIS KEPPEL

In the early autumn of 1962, when the administration's education program was foundering for the second year in a row, Commissioner McMurrin of the USOE followed Secretary Ribicoff in resigning. Francis Keppel, who had been dean of Harvard's School of Education since 1948, recalls the circumstances, as told to him by former fellow Harvard dean, McGeorge Bundy.

> Mr. McMurrin could hardly bear the thought—poor fellow— and resigned. He resigned, incidentally, through his congressman, as I recall, from Utah, so that Mr. Kennedy read it in the morning paper. The story I now have to tell you comes from Mac Bundy, who was one of the White House aides. The following morning they had some kind of a meeting. And Mr. Kennedy

said, "What's all this about this fellow resigning as Commissioner of Education, apparently by way of Capitol Hill? What's going on! I never heard of the fellow!"

And Mac Bundy's response was: "Mr. President, that's exactly the trouble. You never heard of the fellow!"[41]

So Kennedy turned to an educator he knew, Harvard's Dean Keppel, and had him sworn in as commissioner (a job that Keppel conceded "had a very bad smell to it") in a highly visible White House ceremony (Justice Frankfurter was scheduled to give Keppel the oath, but he was too ill). A Yankee Episcopalian, the Harvard-educated Harvard dean was well suited by background and temperament to mediate between the Kennedy administration and the contending interest groups, especially the Catholics and the NEA, and the lower-versus-higher-education lobbies.

The new commissioner accompanied Secretary Celebrezze, Wilbur Cohen, and Mike Feldman to the annual pre-Christmas legislative strategy session in Palm Beach in December of 1963. The veteran Cohen was the chief legislative strategist, together with Sorensen. Their 1963 omnibus strategy, which drew heavily from the BOB's policy recommendations, sought to unite the bickering education lobbies behind one bill that offered something for everybody and that emphasized the necessary interrelatedness of the broad educational enterprise, from preschool to adult learning, from vocational to doctoral levels. But it was politically centered on a proposed package of aid for higher education facilities based on the accepted Hill-Burton model, which had been providing federal funds for constructing hospitals affiliated with religious denominations since 1946.[42] Keppel recalls his diplomatic assignment.

It was obvious that the best hope that one could have would be to keep a program before the Congress . . . and try to keep the lobbyists from killing each other, oh, because the higher education fellows were so mad at the NEA fellows they wouldn't speak to them. In fact, I can recall negotiation at a private meeting between Mr. Logan Wilson (a Texan, by the way, a former president [of the University of Texas] representing the higher education interests) and William Carr, who represented the National Education Association. These two men [who] had worked with each other for probably five or ten years were so cross at each other in early 1963 that I personally had to invite them to dinner, and they didn't dare turn me down. This was literally the case.[43]

Keppel saw his "delicate" first task as getting the lobbyists—"Catholic, NEA, American Council on Education, land grant colleges, and all the others . . . to shut up about things they didn't like and only talk about things they did like."[44]

THE AMBIVALENT OMNIBUS BILL OF 1963

Kennedy's State of the Union Message of 14 January began with emphasis on his proposed tax cut, but he also emphasized the need for qualitative improvements in four main areas of national concern, the first being investing in America's youth through expanded education, manpower training, and a domestic version of the Peace Corps (the other areas were health, civil rights, and such national resources as transportation and parks). Like most such annual messages, the rhetoric was general and uplifting, and more than half of this one was devoted to foreign affairs. But his 17 January Budget Message contained three specific hints about his new strategy for aid to education. As the BOB had urged, it would broadly interpret the existing legislative authority of USOE and NSF and focus selectively on critical problems rather than spread federal monies thinly across the board. Also, while its programmatic scale would be considerably broadened, its budgetary scale would be slightly reduced and phased in over five years. (The *New York Times* estimated a total of $5.3 billion over 1964–69, with only $1.2 billion requested for fiscal 1964, for the twenty-five-item package.)

Kennedy's Special Message on Education of 29 January and its accompanying bill revealed the details of the new strategy. First, the single omnibus bill, the proposed National Education Improvement Act of 1963 (H.R. 3000, S. 580), would symbolize the essential unity of the nation's educational enterprise and would politically seek to unify the diverse education lobbies. Second, because college aid held the greatest promise of legislative success, and because in 1962 the college-aid bill had failed in conference primarily as a result of partisan (Republican) objection to scholarships and religious (Protestant) objections to grants to sectarian colleges, Kennedy dropped the student scholarship provision and called for construction *loans only* for public and private undergraduate colleges, while accepting grants for all other categories. Third, in light of the repeated failures of the Truman, Eisenhower, and Kennedy administrations to pass general, across-the-board aid, the 1963 message called for "selective, stimulative and, where possible, transitional" aid "aimed at strengthening, not weakening, the independence of existing school systems."[45] The previous fall's states' rights counterproposal—what the BOB had contemptuously called the leave-it-on-the-stump-and-run approach —which had tempted Sorensen and horrified the BOB, was jettisoned, along with the old across-the-board approach of general aid, in favor of an ambivalent salute to two ostensibly contradictory principles. On the one hand, federal funds were to be categorically targeted toward increasing starting and maximum teachers' salaries and average salaries in disadvantaged areas; constructing classrooms in areas of critical shortages; and initiating special projects to improve educational quality, especially in depressed rural and urban areas—all for public schools only. On the other hand, these funds were to be distributed through the states, to use for one or more of these purposes as *they* saw fit—or not to use at all. This inherent tension between the primacy of federal strings on categorical grants of treasury funds dedicated to overriding national purposes, and the states' rights "religion of local control," was to remain largely an abstraction at the elementary-secondary school level during the Kennedy administration, because the inherently controversial bill never got beyond the hearing stage. But it clearly heralded the tensions of the Johnsonian breakthrough after 1965.

On 1 February 1963 the *New York Times* editorially greeted the omnibus proposal with enthusiasm as "a radically new approach that concentrated on incentives for quality improvement," although it conceded that the call for transitional aid that would be phased out "runs counter to the realities of public life and may be nothing more than sugar-coating on the budgetary pill."[46] And on 6 February Fred Hechinger's column in the *Times* observed that "paradoxically, the message is, despite the omnibus range all over the educational landscape, far more pin-pointed in purpose than any previous proposal."[47] Hechinger recalled that the bill proposed earmarking funds for urban slums, much as had Kennedy's Hovde task force of 1960, and that it was the first major aid-to-education proposal since World War II that did not primarily hinge on the defense needs of the Cold War.

If the enthusiasm of the *Times*'s support for the omnibus bill was predictable, even more so was the immediate rejection by Monsignor Frederick G. Hochwalt, spokesman for the National Catholic Welfare Conference, of the exclusion of parochial schools as "totally unacceptable," and also the objections to their inclusion by the Protestant National Council of Churches. Members of Congress also complained that they were being inundated with too many proposals without any indication of the administration's priorities. Keppel recalled of the public-school aid proposal that "the Congress roared with laughter and had a lovely time chasing it around, saying, You don't really mean that there are no priorities—between higher education and the schools and between books and whatever!"[48]

But Keppel exaggerated, for a new and more mellow mood pervaded Congress in 1963. As James Sundquist observed in *Politics and Policy*, people *do* learn from painful experience.[49] The NEA had learned from its kamikaze telegram blitz of 1962, which had done so much to kill the higher education bill of that year, which in turn was the only education bill that had had any chance. The religious factions fenced more cautiously in 1963, and Kennedy's steadfast exclusion of parochial school aid greatly eased the fears of Protestants, and thereby also eased the path of categorical federal aid to sectarian colleges, most of which were Protestant. When Powell's committee broke the omnibus bill into four separate bills on 22 May—one each for aid to colleges, aid to impacted areas, aid to elementary-secondary education, and a catchall bill for the remainder—chances for passage of elementary-secondary aid were virtually dashed. But removal of that volatile element greatly strengthened the chances of the others. In response, the *Times* editorialized on 28 May that the omnibus breakup came as no surprise, that the omnibus vehicle had nevertheless served its purpose as a comprehensive White Paper to demonstrate the scope and interrelatedness of America's educational needs, and that the four-part breakup made sense. What was unfortunate, the *Times* complained, was that political priorities would thereby be placed on the least controversial and therefore the least critical areas of need—such as impacted areas, "with the loudest overtones of the pork barrel"—and that the crucial need to rebuild the house of education at its elementary-secondary foundation would be swept under the congressional rug. And this is largely what happened, although the result was far more positive than the original prediction of the *Times* suggested.[50]

THE CONGRESSIONAL RESPONSE

The agency and White House files for the spring and summer of 1963 reveal a different pattern from the previous two years, when congressional deadlocks had prompted intense bargaining and backdoor negotiations. But in 1963 the deadlock over public-school aid was taken as a given, a price to be paid for promising movement on the other fronts. So the executive branch, with Wilbur Cohen at the center of the DHEW effort, mainly monitored and nurtured Congress as it slowly worked its will, first on the difficult House side. There, senior Democrats Adam Clayton Powell, Carl Perkins, and Edith Green worked with diligence and skill, first on the college-aid bill, H.R. 6143; next on the combined vocational-NDEA-impacted-areas bill, H.R. 4955; then on the library bill and the catchall remainder of the twenty-five proposals in the original omnibus package, plus a few initiatives by Congress. The memo traffic reflects mostly tactical maneuvering: speculation, for example, about what modifications might induce Carl Elliott and Phil Landrum to help bring their fellow southern Democrats aboard, or how to persuade such swing Republicans as Albert Quie and Peter Frelinghuysen to help convince fellow Republicans. In the Senate, the administration torch was carried by Wayne Morse, who kept the omnibus bill intact until September, awaiting developments in the more volatile House. The details and timing of this complicated process are of less importance here than the nature of the most crucial congressional bargaining, especially in conference committee, and the results. Since the elementary-secondary bill was consensually dead, major attention was focused on the college-aid bill for classroom construction, H.R. 6143, which was sponsored by Edith Green, chairman of the higher education subcommittee. Green's bill was reported out of the full House Education and Labor Committee on 21 May by a bipartisan vote of twenty-five to five, and as in 1962, it added grants to the loans provisions for public and private academic facilities. On 14 August the House passed the five-year, $1,195,000,000 program (the funding was for only the first three years) by a bipartisan 287 to 113 roll-call vote (Democrats, 180 to 57; Republicans, 107 to 56).[51] Nevertheless, the reservations of southern Democrats about taxpayer aid to sectarian colleges were reflected in a regional breakdown, with northern Democrats voting for the bill 140 to 3 and southern Democrats voting against it 40 to 54.

In the Senate, the Labor and Public Welfare Committee reported H.R. 6143 with amendments on 7 October. The Senate version differed from the House bill primarily in amount and duration ($1,750,000,000 over five years, against the House's $1,195,000,000 over three years), and it earmarked the grants categorically for science, engineering, and library facilities only. After five days of floor debate and amendment, the Senate passed H.R. 6143 on 21 October by a roll-call vote of sixty to nineteen (Democrats, four to eleven; Republicans, nineteen to eight). As in the House, the most controversial aspect of the Senate debate concerned the religious issue.

JUDICIAL REVIEW AND TAXPAYER SUITS

During a similar debate in 1962, when the executive secretary of the Council of State School Officers, Edgar Fuller, had testified in both chambers on behalf of five national education organizations against broad federal grants to sectarian colleges, he had explained the opposition of these major public "lower" education lobbies in a reply to a critical editorial in the *St. Louis Post-Dispatch*.[52] Fuller, who was regarded with considerable irritation by the senior architects of education policy in both the Kennedy and Johnson administrations, explained why the public school constituencies viewed such aid not only as unwise public policy, but also as "probably unconstitutional." He concluded that "the current legislation would be declared unconstitutional, we believe, if it could be tested in court, but such a test of constitutionality is probably impossible for lack of jurisdiction under the decision of *Massachusetts* v. *Mellon* nearly 40 years ago."[53] Massachusetts v. Mellon was a case decided by the Supreme Court in 1923, in which Massachusetts challenged the constitutionality of the Sheppard-Towner Maternity Aid Act of 1921. That statute was a progressive-era measure based on a grant-in-aid inducement to states to cooperate with the newly created Children's Bureau in the Department of Labor to help reduce maternal and infant mortality and to protect the health of mothers and infants.[54] The Court never reached the merits of the case in 1923 but instead denied jurisdiction because the suit did not in reality arise between a state and citizens of another state, but rather was an attempt by Massachusetts to act as a representative of its state citizens against the national government. Justice Sutherland's decision also held that the constitutional questions raised by Massachusetts—that is, whether even such a voluntary grant-in-aid program wasn't coercive because the citizens of a nonparticipating state nevertheless had to pay federal taxes to support the program—were "abstract questions of political power." Because the case was decided with a companion case, Frothingham v. Mellon, in which the Court held that an individual taxpayer lacks standing to sue the national government for equitable remedy against objectionable treasury expenditures,[55] there seemed to be no timely and practical way to press for an early resolution by the Supreme Court on the hotly contested constitutionality of the broadening federal proposals for aid to religious schools.

In response to this dilemma, Congressman John B. Anderson (R., Ill.) offered a floor amendment to allow a college or university to enter a court suit to test the constitutionality of federal aid to sectarian colleges. But to the predictable Catholic objections were added arguments that such a provision might tie up the entire college-aid program and might even jeopardize the broad array of extant programs that aided private colleges, and Anderson's amendment was rejected on 14 August by a voice vote.[56] In the Senate, however, southern Democrats spoke with a stronger voice, and Senators Sam Ervin (D., N.C.) and John Sherman Cooper (D., Ky.) moved on the floor that all sectarian colleges should be excluded from the bill's aid. This was rejected by a twenty-seven to fifty-four roll-call vote. Then Ervin and Cooper offered an amendment that provided that an individual taxpayer could challenge the constitutionality of grants or loans to private colleges in federal district court. Morse argued against the amendment to his bill, insisting that the Supreme Court would likely follow precedent and rule unconstitutional the court test provision, and possibly therefore invalidate the entire bill; that such a provision promised to kill the bill in the House; that such a provision would prejudice the matter in the courts because it implied congressional doubt as to its constitutionality; and that it would surely delay the whole program far beyond its proposed beginning in fiscal year 1964. But the Senate accepted the Ervin-Cooper amendment by a roll-call vote of forty-five to thirty-three, and on 21 October the Senate sent the amended H.R. 6143 to conference committee.

This time around the pressure to compromise differences and avoid yet a third year of embarrassing failure and acrimony was so intense that the conferees did reach a compromise, one that was mainly skewed toward the House version. The Senate's controversial provision for judicial review was dropped, and the House version on funding was adopted, but the House's across-the-board approach to grants yielded to the Senate's categorical provisions based on defense and national security needs, which in turn were expanded from science and engineering and libraries to include mathematics and modern foreign languages. The conference report was agreed to by a lopsided roll-call vote in the House of 258 to 92 on 6 November, and it was safely on its way toward Senate approval when the president was assassinated on 22 November in Dallas (Senate approval came on 10 December by a roll-call vote of fifty-four to twenty-seven).

THE KENNEDY LEGACY

Although the fallen president never lived to witness the considerable fulfillment of his long and frustrating efforts in education, it was clear by mid-November that his major achievement, the college-aid bill, was going to be signed into law. Also well along toward almost certain passage was H.R. 4955, which combined extension of the popular NDEA and aid-to-impacted-areas programs with expansion of vocational aid. One key to the relative success of Kennedy's education program in 1963 had been the cooperative and indeed chastened behavior of the NEA, which that year had watched the public school-aid bill die with disciplined resignation, had even supported a college-aid bill that would aid sectarian colleges as long as there was a provision for a court test, and then had looked the other way when the conference had discarded the provision for judicial review. On 19 November Kennedy had called together the executive secretaries and senior staff of the NEA's state teachers associations in the White House Rose Garden. The group was led by the NEA's executive secretary, William G. Carr. The heart of Kennedy's address was direct and simple: "I want to thank you. Things don't happen; they are made to happen. And in the field of education they were made to happen by you and your members. So we are very grateful."[57] Commissioner Keppel's primary diplomatic assignment had been to prevent the religious war between the NEA and the NCWC over elementary-secondary school aid from again poisoning the well for aid to higher education, and, as Keppel later reflected, "the NEA, bless its beads, kept its word. Even though the higher education bill was going through, they didn't shoot it down because of anger that it wasn't an 'El-High' bill. They kept their word."[58]

President Johnson signed the Higher Education Facilities Act of 1963 into law on 16 December, and when, two days later, he signed into law the catchall bill that combined NDEA and impacted-areas extension with a broadened array of vocational programs, including aid to the handicapped, the immediate Kennedy legacy of 1963 was complete.[59] The box score for 1963 included, not surprisingly, more failed than successful initiatives from the original twenty-five-item omnibus bill. The casualties included, in addition to the major public-school-aid bill, proposals for federally insured college loans; work-study; graduate fellowships; educational research centers; adult literacy; modification of the aid-to-impacted-areas formula; and special programs to upgrade teacher preparation, special education, and the like. But the most significant change was the generation of a new momentum and mood, a new sense of dialogue and possibility, one greatly enhanced by the martyrdom of Kennedy's assassination.

In *John F. Kennedy and the Second Reconstruction*, Carl Brauer argues that President Kennedy's initial conservatism in civil rights, which belied his campaign rhetoric, was transformed by 1963 into a genuine commitment by the intransigence of southern resistance and the violence at Ole Miss and Birmingham.[60] Kennedy's persistence in pressing his badly battered education program clearly differed qualitatively from his belated commitment to civil rights, where a growing emotional consensus derived from the contemptuous defiance of such diehards as Governor Ross Barnett of Mississippi, and from the nationally televised brutality of "Bull" Connor in Birmingham. But the sheer stubbornness of Kennedy's drive to pass a Kennedy bill to aid education suggests less a maturing emotional or even intellectual commitment than a political determination to meet the expectations of the Democratic coalition that would be needed to re-elect him, and a resentment at the political embarrassment of repeated legislative defeats.

When President Johnson signed the new higher education bill into law in the Cabinet Room that 16 December, he acknowledged the Kennedy legacy in terms appropriate to the Kennedy myth: "President Kennedy fought hard for this legislation. No topic was closer to his heart. No bill was the object of more of his attention. Both his life and his death showed the importance and the value of sound education. The enactment of this measure is not only a monument to him, it is a monument to every person who participated in passing it, and most of you are in this room."[61] On that occasion, perhaps the former Texas schoolteacher's hyperbole may be forgiven: "A great former President of the Republic of my State said, 'The educated man is the guardian genius of democracy. It is the only dictator that free men recognize and the only ruler that free men desire.' So this new law is the most significant education bill passed by the Congress in the history of the Republic. In fact, this session of the Congress will go down in history as the Education Congress of 1963."[62] Like Kennedy before the NEA leaders in November, Johnson pledged to complete the crucial elementary and secondary component of the original Kennedy program in 1964: "I, therefore, strongly urge the Congress to take early, positive action on the unfinished portion of the National Education Improvement act, particularly those programs which will assist elementary and secondary schools."[63]

Johnson had stressed the same theme of national unity and continuity with Kennedy's legislative program when he first addressed a joint session of Congress as president five days after Kennedy's assassination, and he clearly meant it in relation to the Kennedy initiatives for a tax cut, a civil rights bill, and at least a skirmishing prelude to the war on poverty. But his pledge to press the fight for public school aid in 1964 was more rhetorical than real. For 1964 was an election year, *his* election year, and he had no intention of ensnarling himself in yet another bloody church-state fight while simultaneously battling for the civil rights bill. The school-aid drive would have to be postponed until 1965, while he concentrated in 1964 on passing the tax cut, civil rights, and antipoverty programs and forging a new and muscular Johnson mandate in the fall elections. In the meantime, he would seek a mechanism to create a bold new program, one that transcended the Kennedy legacy and heralded a great initiative of a distinctively Johnsonian brand.

3 / TASK FORCING TOWARD LYNDON JOHNSON'S GREAT SOCIETY

THE ANTIPOVERTY BANDWAGON

On 23 November, at the end of Lyndon Johnson's first day as president, he gave the Council of Economic Advisors chairman Walter W. Heller his enthusiastic authorization to "move full-speed ahead" with the "attack on Poverty. . . . That's my kind of program. It will help people."[1] The antipoverty program that Johnson and R. Sargent Shriver skillfully and quickly drove through Congress in 1964 rejected an income-transfer strategy in favor of a service strategy, which placed a premium on job-training and education, a "hand up" rather than a "handout." This, in turn, invited the keen interest of the departments of Labor and Health, Education, and Welfare. The substantial effort of the Department of Labor in greatly expanding the Bureau of the Budget's originally modest and cautiously experimental approach to fighting poverty led to a bold and inclusive strategy that created within the executive office of the president a new Office of Economic Opportunity. The OEO would launch a many-pronged assault on poverty that included the Job Corps; VISTA; a work-training program; a community action program; educational programs for adult literacy, migrant workers, and heads of welfare families; and a work-study program for needy college students. At DHEW, the chief legislative strategist, Wilbur Cohen, was quick to sense the new antipoverty momentum and sought to hitch to the rising new star the fate of the Office of Education's battered efforts to provide general aid for lower education.[2]

On 6 January 1964 Cohen proposed to the BOB's director, Kermit Gordon, that the administration repeat its 1963 elementary and secondary

education proposal for $400 million in grants to states for teachers' sala-
ries, construction, and special-formula-funded projects in the public
schools; and add a $140 million antipoverty package targeted toward
"pockets of poverty," with priority going to those with OEO-approved
community action programs. Cohen's proposal was forwarded by Gordon
to the bureau's Division of Labor and Welfare for comment, and on
8 January the division's director, Hirst Sutton, replied with several objections. DHEW's formula approach would spread the funds too thin, Sutton objected, whereas multipurpose project grants (including health as
well as educational components) would concentrate and coordinate
them. Furthermore, the DHEW proposal omitted funds for the handicapped and the gifted, and it was oriented too strongly toward the public
schools. Sutton conceded that the education proposal's new antipoverty
twist might give a "new face" to the school-aid proposals; but without it,
he argued, "there is nothing new in the education package, and the
President's proposals for strengthening elementary and secondary education rest on the same, old, tired aid recommendations that, in view of
the church-state issue, are generally recognized as having little chance
of enactment." Including such an antipoverty twist, however, ran the
risk that "the entire elementary-secondary education bill may go down
the drain and the Administration would not only lose this significant
education measure, but also a key element in its attack on poverty." Sutton concluded with three arguments for keeping all major antipoverty
proposals in the antipoverty bill that would assign them to be run by the
OEO, rather than scattering them about among the mission agencies.

1) Education is the key element in combating poverty and the
Administration's proposal for poverty would be greatly strengthened by inclusion of this measure in the poverty bill.

2) The proposal may have a better chance of enactment if [it
were] in the antipoverty bill.

3) Separation of the proposal from the usual education context
provides a better chance for freeing the measure from the restrictive "formula" grant and public school orientation which are undesirable limitations usually found in HEW education proposals.[3]

These arguments prevailed in large part because Sargent Shriver was
appointed by the president on 1 February to transform the Gordon-Heller
antipoverty task force planning into a legislative program that could be

passed before the fall elections. Shriver preferred to act quickly and directly through the community action program, with its emphasis on going around established institutions, rather than operating slowly and experimentally through the suspect educational establishment, including the USOE.

In his 21 January Budget Message, President Johnson rather ritually reiterated his support for the remaining items in Kennedy's omnibus education package, including the inherited proposals for grants to the states for teachers' salaries and school construction. But Johnson did not even bother to send Congress a general education message in 1964, and Congress not unexpectedly ignored the controversial teachers' salary and classroom-construction grants and instead cranked through extensions of the popular NDEA and aid-to-impacted-areas programs.[4] Congress did include adult literacy and work-study programs in the Economic Opportunity Act, largely at the insistence of the House Committee on Education and Labor, and over the initial objections of both the White House and Shriver, who feared (wrongly, as it turned out) that these two often-failed education measures might endanger the antipoverty bill. And while the administration and Congress were grappling with the antipoverty bill, the civil rights bill and its filibuster, and the tax cut during the spring and summer of 1964, the Johnson White House was secretly gearing up its comprehensive outside task force operation to plan for a distinctively Johnsonian Great Society.

THE TASK FORCES OF 1964

Early proponents of the task force device within the new Johnson administration were budget director Kermit Gordon and Chairman Walter Heller of the Council of Economic Advisers, together with presidential advisors Bill Moyers and Richard Goodwin.[5] In his "Great Society" speech at the University of Michigan commencement on 22 May, Johnson announced: "We are going to assemble the best thought and the broadest knowledge from all over the world. . . . I intend to establish working groups to prepare a series of White House conferences and meetings—on the cities, on natural beauty, on the quality of education and on other emerging challenges. And from these meetings and from these studies, we will begin to set our course toward the Great Society."[6]

On 30 May, Gordon and Heller sent Moyers a joint memo proposing fourteen task forces, and the first three echoed the Ann Arbor speech: metropolitan problems, education, and preservation of natural beauty. Gordon and Heller also suggested that "the Task Forces be composed mainly of technical experts who possess the gift of originality and imagination . . . the first systematic assault on these problems should be made quietly by people with specialized training and skills." They further urged that the task forces be kept quite small, and that their final reports should be submitted immediately after the presidential election.[7] On 2 July the president announced the task force operation to his cabinet, correctly anticipating an extraordinary political and economic opportunity in 1965 and summoning his administration "to think in bold terms and to strike out in new directions." Johnson emphasized that the task forces "will operate *without publicity. It is very important that this not become a public operation.*"[8] He attempted to reassure his cabinet officers that "the task forces are *not* a new 'planning group' in Government. Rather, their reports will provide the background for discussions among the Cabinet agencies and the White House in formulating the 1965 legislative program."[9] He outlined his approach:

> I am going to instruct each of the task forces to come up with *practical* program ideas. At the same time, I expect them to be imaginative, and not to be bound by tired, preconceived notions. You and I will have to exercise judgments later about what is feasible.
> I attach great importance to this effort. I believe you share my desire that this be an activist Administration, not a caretaker of past gains. I want to get the advice of the best brains in the country on the problems and challenges confronting America, and I want their help in devising the best approach to meeting them. I want these task forces to question what we now are doing and to suggest better ways of doing it. You and I will still have the final task of accepting and rejecting, of making the judgments as to what is feasible and what is not. But I want to start with no holds barred . . . in this first stage, let's set our sights too high rather than too low.[10]

Johnson's reassurances were somewhat disingenuous, for the task forces clearly *were* a new "planning group" in government, although in that pioneering summer of 1964 they were ad hoc, untried, unproven.

But the president's admonition that their sights must be set too high rather than too low, and his challenge to think in bold terms and strike out in new directions were taken at face value. Bill Moyers's files from those heady days contain various lists of striking new notions "under consideration." Although only one of the original task forces of 1964 centrally concerned international relations and foreign policy—Francis Bator's task force on foreign economic policy—several of the early and daring possibilities clustered there, among them the following: disarmament, and a UN peace force; outlawing chemical and bacteriological warfare; a reverse Peace Corps; a "hot line" to our allies as well as to our chief adversary; a "planetary" concept of the uses of the sea, with regulation for agriculture, husbandry, and habitation before national and commercial rivalries close in; world "area" administration; and desalination of the sea.

But most of Moyers's potential agenda items reflected the heavy task force concentration on domestic issues: discontinuance of immigration quotas; a "GI bill of rights for parents," providing tax deductions for college tuition payments; discontinuance of the draft, and the building of a well-paid voluntary enlisted armed forces; a presidential call for universal, voluntary service in time of peace; tax exemptions for donations to political parties; a new National Merit Scholarship for the poor; a nationwide, nonpartisan talent hunt for the best men and women, bolstered by the Equal Pay Act; an experimental service of urban extension agents; a cabinet-level Department of Science, Technology, and Automation; reform of the civil service system to reward good performance and facilitation of selecting out; a nationwide campaign against all forms of environmental pollution; a code of ethics and financial disclosure law for Congress, the judiciary, and the senior executive staff.

Clearly, such brainstorming was often more imaginative than practical; it suggested no priorities, little definition, and of course invited vigorous political culling. But it also testified, even in its naïveté, to the virtually uninhibited explorations of new policy possibilities that the president had proclaimed. Compromise would come later.

On 6 July, Moyers sent out his marching orders and the original fourteen task forces (see his official list of 22 July in table 1) were launched toward their 10 November deadline.[11] Moyers instructed the White House liaisons for each task force to form the task force "*at once* and then contact the relevant agency heads with responsibility in the area covered by

TABLE 1: 1965 Legislative Program Task Forces

Task Force	White House Liaison	Executive Secretary
Transportation	Feldman and Cater	Gordon Murray, BOB (Alternate: A. J. Read, BOB)
Natural Resources	White	Fenton Shepard, BOB (Alternate: Robert Teeters, BOB)
Education	Goodwin	William Cannon, BOB (Alternate: Emerson Elliott, BOB)
Health	Staats	Alex Greene, BOB (Alternate until 9/1, Walter Smith, BC Alternate after: Jim Falcon, BOB)
Metropolitan & Urban Problems	Goodwin	William Ross, BOB (Alternate: Phil Hanna, BOB)
Preservation of Natural Beauty	Goodwin	George Lamb, BOB (Alternate: Donald Lindholm, BOB)
Intergovernmental Fiscal Cooperation	Heller	Anita Wells, Treasury Department
Cost Reduction[1]	Jones	Ray Kitchell, BOB (Alternate: Gordon Osborn, BOB)
Government Reorganization[1]	Seidman	Herb Jasper, BOB
Sustaining Prosperity[2]	Ackley	Locke Anderson and Susan Lepper, CEA
Agriculture	Feldman and Schultze	Don Horton, BOB (Alternate: Richard Ottman, BOB)
Civil Rights	White	(Department of Justice to provide)
Foreign Economic Policy	Bator	Ed Hamilton, BOB (Alternate: task force member Dick Richardson, BOB, if necessary)
Income Maintenance	Schultze	Michael March, BOB (Alternate: Milton Turen, BOB)

SOURCE: Moyers file, LBJ Library, 22 July 1964.
1. Originally Task Force on Efficiency and Economy.
2. Originally Task Force on Antirecession policy.

Chairman

George Hilton
University of California

John W. Gardner
President
Carnegie Corporation

George James
Commissioner New York City Department
of Health

Joseph A. Pechman
Brookings Institution

Frederick J. Lawton
Former Director of the Budget

Don Price
Harvard University

Paul Samuelson
Massachusetts Institute of Technology

Charles Murphy
Department of Agriculture

Karl Kaysen
Harvard University

John Corson
Princeton University

your task force and bring him up to date on the makeup of the task force, the subject matter to be covered, and the time schedule involved"; and he alerted them to transmit the Bureau of the Budget's "issue papers" to the task force members.

THE BUREAU OF THE BUDGET'S "ISSUE PAPERS"

On 17 June Moyers sent the issue paper for the education task force to Richard Goodwin, the group's White House liaison.[12] This remarkably candid BOB document criticized the entrenched tradition of conceiving of education legislation in terms of the educational establishment, which had typically produced in recent years proposals to increase teachers' salaries, expand vocational education, build libraries and classrooms, and expand personnel in state departments of education—each with its highly organized interest group.

But group *interests often conflict*, with the result that their effectiveness is nullified. With the involvement of many dissimilar groups—such as the NEA, American Council on Education, National Catholic Welfare Council [*sic*], Council of Chief State School Officers, American Association of School Administrators, AFL-CIO, the Chamber of Commerce, NAACP, National Council of Churches and many others—it is no wonder that there have been diametrically opposed views on such perennial controversies as federal control, church-state relations, and racial segregation.[13]

Furthermore, many of the proposals are "*not very exciting*," such as giving teachers and teachers colleges more money. Also, predicted crises had not materialized, such as those reflected in the repeated presidential rhetoric bemoaning disastrous classroom shortages.

A crisis was forecast in the 1950's in meeting the burdens of the post World War II baby boom; yet State and local governments somehow increased their 1950 school expenditure of $6 billion to $16 billion in 1960 and to $20 billion in 1963. In 1957 a "shortage" of 336,000 classrooms was announced; after a year the estimate was revised to 159,000 and it has remained at about 125,000 for the past several years; yet classroom construction has approximated 70,000 units annually (despite annual predictions of a reduction).[14]

Finally, the BOB issue paper argued that small general-aid programs, in the range of $300 to $500 annually, were proposed in the vain hope that they could make much impact on annual state and local budgets of $20 billion. "It is no secret that recent Administration proposals earmarked as small a part of the Federal Budget for public school aid as possible (particularly on the expenditure side) so as not to inflate the total figures for a program that stood little chance of enactment."[15] As a result, Congress questioned whether the administration was really serious about recommending public-school aid. (Clearly, in 1964, it was *not.*)

The issue paper of course did not directly allude to President Johnson's pro forma recommendation of the failed leftovers from Kennedy's 1963 omnibus package, but it observed that "such proposals are worn thin from repetition" and are "unlikely to succeed." What was needed instead was a program characterized by *unity*, with a single comprehensive rallying point for all pressure groups, rather than a series of bills to be broken up into special and competing interest group measures; *direction*, concentrating financial resources on specific educational needs of people, such as those of the 30 percent of the school population that perform below the "average" pupil orientation of the school systems, rather than on just adding money to general-purpose school expenditures; *flexibility*; *stimulation*, rather than substitution; and *size*, perhaps a bold $2 billion annually increasing to $6 or $8 billion in four years, which "would demonstrate a strong national commitment to education and might well receive more serious consideration than a modest proposal." Above all, what was needed was a legislative approach "that will find appeal for the same reasons as the poverty program—because it *recognizes the value of developing human resources* as a step to advancement of social welfare and economic growth, and because it *meets the needs of people* (rather than of institutions or other levels of government)."[16] The critical posture and assumptions of the BOB veterans would heavily influence the range of discussion that awaited the convening of the new outside task force on education.

THE GARDNER TASK FORCE

The Johnson task forces have been especially interesting to academics, partly because professors were so heavily represented on them. On the thirteen original task forces for 1964 (excluding the civil rights task force, which was dropped after the passage of the Civil Rights Act on 2 July) sat 124 distinguished citizens (I am excluding the 13 who were White House liaisons and the 13 who were executive secretaries from the executive branch, although their roles were crucial). Forty-six of these 124 were professors, exactly half of them from the Ivy League plus the Massachusetts Institute of Technology (with Cambridge predominating, not surprisingly—in the spring of 1964 Goodwin had taken Moyers to Harvard to introduce him to prominent professors there), and a West Coast bloc of 10 represented the University of California campuses plus Stanford University.[17] Federal officials constituted the second largest bloc with 33 representatives, followed by municipal (8) and state (5) officials, commision, association, and foundation executives (10), and representatives from corporations and law firms (9), think tanks (6), and miscellaneous organizations (7). Only 5 members were women, even fewer were black, and there was no representation, oddly, from organized labor.

The Gardner task force on education was in most respects typical (see table 2). Its blue-ribbon representation included all levels of education: public and private, secular and parochial, black as well as white. The president met with the education task force on 21 July for a pep talk, and they were off and running—but running part time. They met only four times, and at long distance, for such busy luminaries. Clark Kerr attended *no* meetings. Occupying the strategic full-time, on-location spot was the task force's executive secretary, William B. Cannon, who was chief of the Bureau of the Budget's Division of Education, Manpower, and Sciences, and who drafted the issue paper that structured the task force's agenda. In early September Cannon sent a progress report to colleagues in the bureau, the CEA, and to Goodwin in the White House, in which he praised John Gardner as "being first class, and sure of what he is doing."[18] "I think that we have a good chance of producing a first class report," Cannon predicted, "although it will take some doing to meld the aspirations of the dreamers (Zacharias, Land, Riesman) with those of the practitioners (Commissioner Allen, Superintendant Marland, etc.)."

Also exercising unusual influence on the task force was Francis Keppel, who had served on its predecessor, the Hovde task force. He enjoyed a close relationship with John Gardner (Keppel's father had also been a president of Carnegie Corporation), he had helped recruit the other task force members, and he enjoyed a unique dual status as both outsider and insider—as the Kennedy administration's Harvard dean on an outside task force, yet also as the incumbent commissioner of education. Keppel shared Gardner's first priority: concentrating on the urban disadvantaged, especially if this could unify the divisive educational community. But his second priority was federal aid to strengthen state departments of education. If, from the elite viewpoint of the BOB, the Office of Education was a third-rate bureaucracy of report writers, statistics gatherers, and professional "educationists," the state departments of education were regarded by USOE and by many task force members with equal disdain.[19] Keppel recalled in his oral history interview that a good many of the people on the task force "felt that the state departments of education were the feeblest bunch of second-rate, or fifth-rate, educators who combined educational incompetence with bureaucratic immovability." He also noted that

> they were dead against Title V [aid to state departments of education]. Having sat on that educational bureaucracy in Washington, the last thing in the world I wanted was all those 25,000 school districts coming in with plans with my bureaucrats deciding whether to approve them or not. I wanted that stuff done out in the states. And to make it work in the states, you have to improve the state departments in making grants. . . . I think [James] Allen and I won the vote by one vote or something.

Keppel also wanted to aid "underfinanced colleges, particularly Negro colleges," and also needy college students. Finally, the Episcopalian Keppel got along well with those whom he called "the monsignors," and he wanted to find ways to aid the parochial schools.[20]

Cannon held a different perspective. His years of dealing with the education bureaucracy had made him somewhat cynical, not only about the general ability of USOE, but about the competence of the public schools as well.[21] Hence Cannon's first two priorities were supplementary educational centers and educational research and development laboratories, together with the extension network of regional demonstration and dissemination labs being pushed by Ralph Tyler.[22] These he viewed as almost subversive models for experiment and change, as new institutions that would not be hostage to the local educational establishments. For similar reasons Cannon had made important contributions to the design of the OEO's controversial community action program as a member

TABLE 2: Legislative Task Force on Education, 1964

Chairman	Executive Secretary
John W. Gardner President Carnegie Corporation New York City	William B. Cannon BOB (Alternate: Emerson J. Elliott)

Members

James E. Allen, Jr.
Commissioner
New York State
   Department of
   Education
Albany, N.Y.

Hedley W. Donovan
Editor
Time Magazine
New York City

Harold B. Gores
President
Educational Facilities
   Laboratory
New York City

Clark Kerr
President
University of California

Edwin H. Land
President
Polaroid Corporation
Cambridge, Mass.

Sidney P. Marland
Superintendent of Schools
Pittsburgh, Pa.

David Riesman
Professor
Department of Social
   Relations
Harvard University

The Reverend Paul C. Reinert
President
Saint Louis University

Raymond R. Tucker
Mayor
Saint Louis, Mo.

Ralph W. Tyler
Director
Center for the Advanced
   Study in the Behavioral
   Sciences
Stanford, Calif.

Stephen J. Wright
President
Fisk University

Jerrold R. Zacharias
Professor
Department of Physics
Massachusetts Institute
   of Technology

Francis Keppel
Commissioner of Education
DHEW

Richard Goodwin
White House Liaison

of the Kermit Gordon–Walter Heller task force on antipoverty. And his third priority reflected his dim view of USOE by calling for the creation of a new agency, a kind of educational OEO, located in the executive office of the president, to run the new programs.

On 24 September Gardner sent the task force members his draft of a nine-page statement reflecting their collective highest priorities.[23] First came the antipoverty theme: the "foremost challenge facing American education today is to equalize educational opportunity for the disadvantaged segments of our population," especially through a comprehensive attack on the educational deficiencies of urban slums. Then came the supplementary educational centers, which could serve students in parochial as well as public schools; and also the educational research and development laboratories, each linked to a university and including an experimental or demonstration school. For higher education, emphasis was on aiding the smaller and weaker colleges, especially through collaboration with strong universities. Financial aid for needy undergraduates was popular with Congress, and this invited a massive expansion of student loans. As for implementing the programs, state departments of education needed strengthening. And as for the Office of Education, "despite outstanding leadership by the present Commissioner of Education," the USOE at present was "incapable of meeting the requirements facing us." Gardner suggested creating a full-fledged *department* of education, *not* by simply pulling *E* out of DHEW, but by building a completely new department, pulling together education programs from all over the government.

When the final eighty-three-page secret report was delivered to the White House in early November, it contained eighteen recommendations that expanded on but did not significantly differ from the priorities reflected in Gardner's September draft, with one exception, and that was the one on the organization of the USOE, which I shall turn to shortly.[24] The first priority was the antipoverty emphasis on equal educational opportunity or "access" for children of disadvantaged background. The task force went on record as favoring general federal aid, especially for school construction; but it noted that if such aid (with an equalization formula favoring poorer areas) was politically infeasible, then it favored exploring other avenues of channeling federal funds into disadvantaged areas. It found especially "interesting" the proposed amendment to the program on impacted areas, which would create indexes of economic disadvantage to identify areas to receive funds by formula. This obviously was prefiguring Title I of ESEA, but not by inventing the wheel; the momentum of legislative planning in this direction was already considerable in DHEW and in Congress, especially through the efforts of Wilbur Cohen and Wayne Morse. But the prestigious (and semimysterious) Gardner task force was thereby giving powerful sanction to the planning convergence toward ESEA Title I.

Next came three major mechanisms to foster educational experiments, innovation, and service, especially for the urban poor. The first of these was the establishment of university-based *community extension programs*—the land-grant program for the cities, modeled on the Morrill Act's politically successful agricultural-extension service. Nor was this idea new; indeed, it was much in vogue in the early and middle sixties, and President Johnson had told an audience at the dedication of the new University of California campus at Irvine the previous June that "I forsee the day when an urban extension service, operated by universities across the country, will do for urban America what the Agricultural Extension Service has done for rural America."[25] Next came Cannon's subversive favorite, the *supplementary educational centers*. This was the Gardner task force's most original creation, and it was to translate directly into Title III of ESEA. The vague allusion to "supplementary services" was a facade, for what Cannon and Emerson Elliott (his BOB colleague and task force alternate) and the task force majority had in mind was a massive lever for change through federal grants, approved by nationally recognized panels of experts, for exemplary and innovative programs to bring a variety of *non*school influences, that is, universities, museums, artistic and musical organizations, and industry, into working concert with schools, both public *and* private, through broad-based consortia. The third program was also a Cannon favorite: the *national educational laboratories*, which would be research and development laboratories to support the supplementary educational centers, and an extension network of regional demonstration and dissemination labs. Neither were the R&D centers completely novel, for four already existed at the universities of Oregon, Pittsburgh, and Wisconsin, and at Harvard University. The task force of course knew this, and sought their expansion, to perhaps fifteen to twenty new regionally distributed laboratories.

Many of the eighteen recommendations in the report represented fairly standard fare for such a report, for example, support for the expansion of work-study programs, student loans, aid to the handicapped, and the like, although many of these presaged important future legislation, such as guaranteed student loans, equal opportunity grants, and the National Teacher Corps. But three of them in particular dealt with the high-priority issues discussed in Gardner's September draft. One was strengthening state departments of education, which was to become Title V of ESEA. Another was aid to "developing colleges," which became Title III of the companion Higher Education Act (HEA) of 1965. In the vision of Keppel, Gardner, and especially of Massachusetts Institute of Technology's Jerrold Zacharias, "developing colleges" was a euphemism for weak black colleges; Zacharias had been centrally involved in planning an American Council on Education program of summer institutes for black college faculty. Also, Edith Green's subcommittee had held hearings on the needs of such marginal colleges in 1964 and had pressed Keppel to assist them. But the third high-priority recommendation involved the thorny question of what to do with USOE, and there was spirited debate on this within the task force. Cannon, however, converted the majority to his view of the OEO model, so the report's majority recommendation was: "One solution—the *favored* solution as far as this Task Force is concerned—would be to establish an independent Office of Education at the Presidential level which, like the Office of Economic Opportunity, would have the responsibility to (a) coordinate Federal agency programs, (b) carry out new programs, and (c) develop national policy in the field of education."[26] But the report acknowledged that there was "vigorous" support for the "more orthodox" solution of creating a new cabinet-level department of education, but creating it anew rather than simply detaching the *E* in DHEW. The task force hinged its recommendation for a national humanities foundation to the resolution of the organizational problem, arguing that if the OEO model were adopted, then new humanities programs should be run from within the new agency like other new programs, to be coordinated and not split off. But failing that, a new national humanities foundation should be created, because further neglect of the humanities was intolerable.

POLITICS AND SECRECY

The Gardner report's support for a new national humanities foundation illustrates the partial truth of Philip Kearney's conclusion that the task force functioned as a "legitimating agent" for ideas already in existence. In this case the task force was responding supportively to an earlier initiative by the Commission for a National Foundation for the Humanities, chaired by Barnaby Keeney, president of Brown University.[27] But it raises also the political and partisan question of the Johnson administration's use of the task forces in the campaign against Goldwater. In September of 1964, President Johnson went to Providence, Rhode Island, to attend Brown University's celebration of its 200th anniversary, where he proclaimed, "I look with the greatest favor upon the proposal by your own able President Keeney's Commission for a National Foundation for the Humanities."[28] As in the Irvine speech, and in many others during the campaign, Johnson plucked the juiciest plums from the secret task force agendas and displayed them to the public. There has been no systematic archival study of the political role of the 1964 task forces, but the Gardner group's role is suggestive. When its White House liaison, Richard Goodwin, briefed the president on his 21 July meeting with the education task force, he began with a political caution: "This task force has been assembled on a non-partisan basis and includes Hedley Donovan of Time-Life. Therefore I would suggest the stress be on contribution to post-election program and references to campaign usefulness not be made. Of course, the work will be helpful in the campaign, and we will make use of the individual task force members."[29] Yet there is little evidence that individual task force members performed important partisan political tasks during the campaign. More probably, task force responsibilities dampened more active political participation by the large body of liberal Democratic university professors who dominated the task forces. And most important, Johnson didn't critically need them, because the Goldwater campaign was crippled from the beginning and by election eve was staggering "crushed and punch-drunk."[30]

Federal aid to education was an important campaign issue, however, and the 1964 Republican platform generally repudiated the GOP's 1960 platform, with its endorsement of federal aid for lower-school construction, and concentrated instead on "tax credits for those burdened by the expenses of college education." Parents paying expensive college tuitions were a natural Republican constituency, and the Johnson administration had been embarrassed early in 1964 when a tuition tax credit amendment was introduced by none other than Connecticut's freshman Democratic senator, the former DHEW secretary Abraham Ribicoff, who as governor had been an ex officio member of the Yale Corporation, and whose constituents were investing heavily in private schools. The strong latent support for a tuition tax credit was reflected in the Ribicoff amendment's narrow defeat on the Senate floor by a vote of forty-eight to forty-five on 4 February. Senator Goldwater soon offered a similar amendment, which Johnson attacked with gusto as a regressive measure to aid the wealthy.[31]

But word of Johnson's secret planning groups was bound to leak out, and they were equally bound to become a partisan dispute. University professors instinctively share information rather than shield it, and when on 14 July Douglass Cater complained to the president that "[Walter] Heller talks to the press too freely," which had led to "irresponsible" UPI stories about the task forces, Johnson instructed Moyers to remind all involved that "all conversations pertaining to task force matters be treated as privileged."[32] But this was Washington, and the intriguing task force story could not be contained. On 30 September, the *New York Times* reporter Tad Szulk ran a story describing the task force operation with fair accuracy, although he reported only eleven task forces and their chairmen (he missed the original task forces on health and on income maintenance). With perhaps equal inevitability, Republican spokesmen challenged the president's secret planning cabal, but because their party was sinking so disastrously that fall, it was to no avail. The Republican congressman Robert H. Michel of Illinois did subsequently attempt through repeated correspondence to pry from the White House the names of the education task force members, but presidential counselor Lee White successfully stonewalled. (He complained to Cater that "you guys have created yet another monster," and he received in reply Cater's suggestion that the answer to Michel's inquiries was always the same: "Nuts!")[33]

TOWARD A LEGISLATIVE STRATEGY FOR ESEA

President Johnson had been periodically briefed throughout the fall campaign on the progress of his task forces, and on 3 November, the national election day, Cater sent him summaries of their recommendations based on preliminary reports.[34] Cater noted that only the task force on agriculture seemed to be conflicting with Johnson's campaign commitments, that urban mass transit seemed to be an area of omission that would have to be remedied, and that most of the task forces were "reticent in giving cost estimates." Cater's two-page summary of the Gardner task force report reflected the main thrust of what were to become titles I, III, IV, and V of ESEA. The Gardner report was formally transmitted to the president on 15 November, and according to one account he personally read it through.[35] The week following Thanksgiving Day, Johnson met at the ranch with secretaries Celebrezze and Wirtz as well as with Moyers, Cohen, Keppel, and Cannon. There he gave a general green light to press ahead on the legislative strategy and program for education and stipulated that 4 January would be the date for the State of the Union Message, with the top-priority Education Message to follow on 12 January and the Budget Message on 25 January.

Goldwater's defeat on 3 November had brought the Johnson administration a crucial bonus of thirty-eight new Democratic seats in the House and two in the Senate. This meant, in the Senate, that the Democrat's previous and muscular majority of sixty-six to thirty-four was swollen to sixty-eight to thirty-two, so the Senate was even less likely to pose any serious obstacle to Great Society legislation, especially with a southern Democrat as president, and with the Civil Rights Act of 1964 out of the way. But much more important, the new House lineup offered a potential bloc switch of seventy-six votes to break the old Kennedy stalemate, which dictated a strategy of first passing the education bill in the House, then having the Senate pass it without amendment, thereby avoiding the perilous conference committee.

But what sort of bill might pass the House? The Civil Rights Act seemed at least temporarily to have deflected the racial issue, because its titles IV and VI already gave the federal government the desegregation club of civil suit and fund-withdrawal, which southerners had historically feared in a federal aid-to-education bill. But the other two troublesome issues, federal control and separation of church and state, seemed fiendishly designed to raise one another, and then to cancel one another out in a process that historically had canceled out federal aid to education also. The best way to avoid the charge of federal control was to provide general aid to the states in the form of what the Bureau of the Budget abhorred as the leave-it-on-the-stump-and-run variety. But if this aid was to be for public schools only, so as to keep church and state separate, it of course aroused the intense opposition of the Roman Catholic lobby and thereby split the Democratic constituency. This painful political dilemma was generally understood, but the Gardner report did not address it; indeed, it was not supposed to. But the legislative strategists at DHEW did.

On 1 December, at Moyers's request, Celebrezze sent to the White House a forty-page memo that contained Keppel's brief on the education program and a draft for the presidential message on education.[36] Celebrezze explained that he had discussed the education program with representatives of the National Education Association, the National Catholic Welfare Conference, the American Council on Education, the American Association of State Universities and Land-Grant Colleges, and the American Federation of Teachers (AFL-CIO). Within the administration, Keppel had consulted with Cater and Henry Wilson at the White House, Cannon at the BOB, Otto Eckstein of the Council of Economic Advisors, Director Donald Hornig of the Office of Science and Technology, Assistant Secretary Stanley Surrey of the Treasury Department, and Secretary Wirtz at the Department of Labor.

Keppel's remarkable memo was a candid political exploration of the basic strategies for passing a major education bill. The first strategic possibility was a renewed effort at the old goal of general aid for salaries and buildings for public schools only. This would embarrass the House leadership, prompt rigorous Catholic opposition, and rekindle the Catholics' bitter battle with the NEA and the Council of Chief State School Officers and other public-school bodies, which in turn would give their "delighted but largely ineffective support." Option 2 would provide general aid for *both* public and private schools. But this would be a "radical shift of policy" and would at least raise a serious constitutional issue, especially in view of the fact that so many state constitutions had such firm requirements on separation of church and state that federal aid to parochial schools would have to come directly from Washington. The NEA and public education groups would be in bitter opposition, and opposition could be expected from "Southern Congressmen combined with some liberals and many Republicans looking for a way to make trouble."[37]

There was a third way, however, that hinged on abandoning the quest for general aid as it was usually defined.

Such a program would satisfy no group entirely, but it would make opposition more difficult and would start down the road toward the ultimate goals for education a generation from now. To adopt this course may open the Administration to accusations of lack of nerve, unwillingness to bite the bullet, etc., etc., on the ground that the basic school problem is not being faced directly. But it seems possible to create a package in some ways more effective educationally—and larger fiscally—than previous "general aid" bills. Such a package would, therefore, be likely to be supported by the same groups which would back proposal number 1.

Keppel then advanced a five-part legislative program that would look remarkably similar to the five-title bill that the president would send to Congress ten weeks later. At its substantive heart (what would become Title I) was a program of *categorical* aid for the children of the poor in the slums and depressed rural areas, one that would reach children in both public and private schools. But its strategic political key was linkage to Public Law 874, the fourteen-year-old "impacted areas" aid program that enjoyed "tremendous Congressional support."

Using it as the vehicle to achieve a degree of "general aid" for public schools would be to continue down a well-traveled road. The National Catholic Welfare Conference, which in the past has been silent on this legislation, will object vigorously if its schools do not receive help under new amendments. But special grant programs of aid for certain types of materials and services especially relevant to their needs, if joined with the impacted areas approach, might avoid a political confrontation. It is not easy to oppose a combination of the existing impacted areas program and an added program for the poor.

Keppel proposed a vague formula based on the number of low-income children by school district so as to concentrate the funds on the intended antipoverty target, but he observed that "the great majority of all school districts in the Nation would receive payments under the proposal."[38] The political importance of this broad reach was difficult to miss.

Commissioner Keppel was careful to emphasize that the Task Force on Education supported this basic antipoverty proposal, and the task force had likewise supported what would become titles III (supplementary educational centers), IV (educational R&D laboratories), and V (aid to state departments of education). He did not invoke the sanction of the Gardner task force in regard to Title II (instructional materials, especially textbooks and library books, for both public and private schools), however, because the Gardner report said virtually nothing about it. Instead, Keppel cited the "lively interest" of Catholic Congressman Hugh Carey of New York. This was to be Keppel's "sweetener" for the Catholics, and it was a sensitive and volatile topic that Keppel knew much about, for he had been appointed commissioner by Kennedy and centrally charged with deflecting the Catholic lobby's attacks from Kennedy's college-aid bills. In this he had been partially successful. But this ongoing dialogue with "the monsignors" was soon to be intensified, and partly by his own design, because he had urged in his memo of 1 December that because "public education groups, most liberals, and many Southerners representing depressed rural constituencies will probably support" his third option, "the extent of Catholic opposition should be tested in advance of introducing the legislation."[39]

Two weeks later, Keppel met with a dozen Catholic monsignors to discuss the education program, and he relayed to Cater his report of a "convivial gathering" in which his relations were on a "good footing." Cater in turn reported to the president:

> 1. They [the monsignors] are not at all eager for a direct aid message which would lead unavoidably to a court test. They realize that this would only delay aid to education and heighten acrimony. (They may well be fearful of the verdict of such a head-on test.)
> 2. They stress the fact that they are not seeking aid to substitute for their own educational expenditures but to supplement them as a means of attaining better education. This offers encouragement for the "supplementary services" which are a strong part of the education package. Of course, Keppel avoided giving any hint of the content of the package.[40]

Cater also reported that two days later two of the monsignors, Hurley and Hochwalt, visited Keppel again to press for aid for their teachers' salaries, but that Keppel stalled them, because aid for teachers' salaries, public or private, was not contained in the legislative package. All major accounts agree that Keppel was the pivotal actor at this crucial stage. Bailey and Mosher write that "Keppel performed a key role as an intermediary broker of ideas, moving among various arenas: the task force, HEW and USOE planning staffs; the White House, the Congress; the Press; professional associations and interest groups."[41] Eidenberg and Morey concur: "In many ways the one man who was able to bridge the gaps that separated the various factions on this issue (church-state) was Francis Keppel."[42] But as Robert Hawkinson astutely observed, Keppel was not so much negotiating or bargaining as he was building a consensus toward a shared awareness of the mutual destructiveness of the rigidity and acrimony of previous years.[43]

THE PRESIDENT DECIDES

The important negotiating and specific bargaining, rather, was more internal than external, and on two important issues Keppel ended up losing. One involved the conflict between his keen personal interest in aid to state departments of education and the BOB's (and especially Cannon's) dim view of such aid, a view that Cater tended to share (or at best he rated it as a low priority). The other issue, which loomed much larger, involved abandoning the long quest for general aid in favor of categorical aid for poor districts. Keppel had withstood intense pressure from the public school professional associations and from within his own USOE bureaucracy to continue to press for general aid. So he had attached his Title I proposal to the popular aid-to-impacted-areas program, but he added a Title IB proviso that both P.L. 815 and P.L. 874 simultaneously be "reformed" so as to reduce their regressive impact, thereby generating annual savings in the $40 to $60 million range. Because few government installations were located in slums or remote rural depressed areas, much of the aid to impacted areas went instead to prosperous school districts, such as those in Maryland's wealthy Montgomery County, where government installations clustered around affluent Bethesda. The BOB and DHEW had long advocated such reforms, as had every president since Truman, but there had been little enthusiasm for them in the House, with the notable and powerful exception of Edith Green.[44] The politics of this decision were so crucial that ultimately only the president could decide.

Cater and Moyers reviewed the various task force and agency proposals during the first three weeks of December, which included their obtaining a Justice Department opinion that was mostly favorable on the church-state issue. The White House reading of the political climate was also basically favorable, as assessed by Cohen and Halperin at DHEW and by O'Brien's staff on the Hill. A similarly optimistic view of the economic outlook was reached by the Troika—the director of the Bureau of the Budget, the chairman of the Council of Economic Advisors, and the secretary of the Treasury. The archives reveal a stream of memorandums from Keppel to Cater in December that elaborated on cost projections and such sensitive issues as the amount of money and range of services likely to be available to parochial schools, and what the supplementary educational centers might do and for whom. The president spent an intense working Christmas at the ranch. Moyers brought down loose-leaf notebooks in which he had distilled the products of the task force recommendations, agency requests, and White House review.[45] They were joined by Gordon and Heller for consultations on fiscal prospects and budgetary evaluations, and they were frequently in touch by wire with Cater when education and health proposals were being discussed.

At one point Cater's wire to Moyers contained a strong plea by Keppel to retain the ESEA provision for aid to state departments of education.[46] Keppel was successful in retaining Title V, but its funding was drastically slashed from the $75 to $150 million range, which Keppel had requested, to a mere $17 million. But on the much more important question of aid-to-impacted-areas reform, virtually the entire senior bureaucracy of USOE and DHEW and the BOB, who favored such reform, lost out to Johnson's political instinct that risking it would jeopardize the entire education bill. So aid-to-impacted-areas reform was cut out by presidential directive, and with painful irony the nation's largest proposal for aid to educate the children of the poor was launched as an expansion of the unreformed impacted-areas law, which disproportionately aided the children of the middle class and even those who were well-to-do.[47]

THE ESEA OF 1965

President Johnson sent his Education Message to Congress on 12 January, and that same day the administration's bill (H.R. 2362) was introduced in the House by Carl Perkins, chairman of the general education subcommittee, and in the Senate (S. 370) by Wayne Morse, chairman of the education subcommittee of the Senate Labor and Public Welfare

Committee. The president's role throughout was vintage LBJ. Keppel re-counts a celebrated meeting in the Fish room of the White House that fateful January.

President Johnson came in, looking cheerful as can be, and said to the half-dozen or so people in the room who were respon-sible for various pieces of legislation. "Look, we've got to do this in a hurry. We've got in with this majority (of sixteen million votes) in the Congress," he said. "It doesn't make any difference what we do. We're going to lose them at the rate of about a mil-lion a month, and under those circumstances, get your subcom-mittee hearings going. Keppel, when are you starting yours?" And Cohen, who was handling the medical thing, "When are you starting yours?" "Get them through the sub-committee and through the full committee and past the rules committee and on to the floor of the House just as fast as you can get them going." And then he turned around with that characteristic jesture and said, "I want to see a whole bunch of coonskins on the wall!"[48]

Yet so extraordinary had been the preliminary planning for ESEA, through executive task forcing, negotiating, and consensus building with professional and private groups, that the congressional role was rendered unique. Eidenberg and Morey have commented on the "pecu-liar 'surrender' of congressional autonomy" over the policy planning phase of legislative formulation by a Congress desperate to avoid another "holy war."[49] As a result, Congress enjoyed the luxury of doing battle not over the hoary three Rs of Race, Reds, and Religion, but instead over the mundane but lucrative details of the distribution formula for Title I's pro-posed billion-dollar aid. As for the origin of the politically key formulaic approach itself, with its antipoverty rationale of aid to the child, not to the school, there have been many claimants. Keppel recalls wryly, "The NEA thinks they thought it up, and the Catholics think they thought it up, and I think I thought it up. I don't know. It just got put together."[50] Wilbur Cohen thinks that *he* thought it up:

Finally, during about 1964, Senator Morse introduced a bill that gave weight to several factors including unemployment, the number of children under aid to dependent children, and the bill was referred to the Department. And it was during that period of time that I finally said, "Why don't you use just a number of children in families under two-three thousand dollars? They're either public school children or in private school—and it doesn't make any difference. They're just disadvantaged children." Now, I had gotten the idea from my studies while I was at the University of Michigan that grew out of my book of which I was co-author, *Income and Welfare in the United States. . . .* Well, frankly I think and I say this with all humility here—I think that was the thing that everybody was looking for to try to come to some kind of solution to this problem that had vexed people for about twenty-five years.[51]

Eidenberg and Morey, as students of congressional behavior and as former congressional staff members, give primary credit to Wayne Morse and his senior subcommittee staffer, Charles Lee.[52] And Charles Lee recalled that Morse's formula approach owed much to Senator Taft's original initiatives on behalf of federal aid back in 1949, and this was a shrewd source of appeal to Senate Republicans. But Lee concluded, most convincingly of all, that the formula solution had multiple authors, and such was the only healthy source of legislative policy formulation in a democracy.[53]

The passage of ESEA into law in the spring of 1965 has been ably described by Eidenberg and Morey and others, and it needs no repeating here.[54] "In an astonishing piece of political artistry," observed Eric Goldman, "the Congress had passed a billion-dollar law, deeply affecting a fundamental institution of the nation, in a breath-taking eighty-seven days. The House had approved it with no amendments that mattered; the Senate had voted it through literally without a comma changed."[55] ESEA passed the House on 26 March by a roll-call vote of 263 to 153, and on 9 April the Senate approved the House bill by a huge 73 to 18 majority. The only near hitch in the strategy of avoiding a conference committee (and therefore any related complications with Judge Smith's House Rules graveyard) involved an amendment insisted upon by Senator Robert Kennedy. Again, Keppel recalls in his characteristic vernacular,

What happened was that that bill [ESEA], with some amendments—we managed to tack on a couple of Republican amendments just to make it smell good—went through the

House with a good solid vote on the floor. We had ridden the roller over Edith Green, who was having another one of her changes of life which seemed to go on forever, and got it through the House; and then it went by the Senate with Bobby Kennedy, and he said, "Look, I want to change this bill because it doesn't have any way of measuring those damned educators like you, Frank, and we really ought to have some evaluation in there, and some measurement as to whether any good is happening."

Wilbur Cohen and I were sitting there. Cohen said to me: "You want it?"

And I said, "Your're damned right I want it, but I haven't got the nerve to do it on the executive side, because all the educators will scream bloody-murder if anybody measures them. But if the *Congress* wants to put it on, that's my idea of how to deal with them."

So Kennedy grinned. And Cohen turned to him and said, "Senator, do you want this as a Kennedy amendment put on in the Senate so you get a [sic] publicity, or do you want this bill amended, because if so, we'll get it amended in the House and all you'll do is pat its fanny as it goes by in the Senate."

"Oh," said Kennedy, "I don't want a Kennedy amendment. I want the damned thing amended."

So we took his amendment down to the House, got a friend [Congressman John Brademas] to put it inside the committee in the House and the House voted it and it went by. Bobby patted its fanny enthusiastically and off it went.[56]

Off it went to Stonewall, Texas, where, at Cater's suggestion, President Johnson signed it on Sunday, 11 April, outside the former one-room schoolhouse where he began his own schooling, with his first teacher, Katherine Deadrich Loney, at his side. The ESEA was now law. In reality it was an elementary, not a secondary education law. Its passage was widely celebrated (even by the *Congressional Quarterly Almanac*) as a historic breakthrough for general aid, but every penny was categorical. The enormous implications of this were to become clear only gradually, and Senator Kennedy's amendment mandating evaluation would play a considerable role in these revelations.

THE HIGHER EDUCATION ACT OF 1965

As José Chavez has demonstrated in his able dissertation on the evolution of the HEA,[57] it shared with ESEA the generally tight executive control over the process of policy formulation, but it fundamentally differed in being more wide open, in both the formulation and especially in the congressional enactment phase, to a much broader array of external groups wishing to influence policy direction. In this sense it represented a far more normal process of legislative policy formulation than did the drive for ESEA. And this is partly because the administration's highest stakes rode with the ESEA breakthrough; higher education bills had passed before, and the Democrats' chief source of frustration—the inability since the Truman administration to pass a federal scholarship bill—had been blocked by House Republicans whose ranks had now been decimated by the Goldwater campaign.

The HEA's major titles (the first four of eight) reflect the composite character of its constituency base. Title I concerned the urban land-grant extension notion, which President Johnson had raised in his Irvine speech (which in turn was written by Cater, partly in response to initiatives by the American Council on Education, or ACE in Washington's acronymic jargon, which was the umbrella lobby for all of higher education). The ACE was worried that the land-grant extension model inherently concentrated on the rural and small-town land-grant campuses of the nineteenth century's two Morrill Acts, and hence it would be poorly related to the need for urban universities to help solve urban problems that were dramatized by waves of rioting in the 1960s. The concept of urban land-grant extension was not a new one; it had been under consideration at USOE and One Dupont Circle for many years, and it had found partial political expression in several bills that had been passed in the Senate. The ACE, which enjoyed a close client relationship with the Office of Education, feared the exclusion from the new urban-extension programs of public urban non-land-grant universities and major private urban universities—especially the latter, many of which (Columbia University and the universities of Chicago and Pittsburgh, for example) were located neck-deep in the urban turmoil of the sixties. So the ACE lobbied successfully for federal grants to go *not* automatically to land-grant universities (such as North Dakota State University in Fargo) exclusively, but for grants to *state* commissions with USOE-commissioner-approved plans that could include the urban public and also private universities. This sensible compromise pleased most combatants and represented ACE lobbying at its best. (At its worst, the public-versus-private, large-versus-small conflicts often internally neutralized the ACE.) So Title I went through the markup with rough consensus, but also with modest funding, because nobody really knew what urban land-grant extension meant.

Title II involved money for upgrading college and research university libraries. Here again the constituency-lobby tie with USOE was close and effective. The American Library Association and the Association of Research Libraries intensely lobbied USOE as well as the usual congressional subcommittees, and Keppel in turn pressed these claims successfully into the Gardner task force report. So the libraries were authorized $50 million annually in fiscal years 1966 through 1968 to upgrade their holdings and procedures. It was a modest amount, but it produced considerable constituent happiness—and it represented a camel's nose under the tent.

Title III was the section on aid to black colleges. It enjoyed the powerful support of Keppel, who had a blue-blooded Yankee's proper disdain for southern whites, and also the formidable support of Edith Green. In 1965, who could be against struggling black colleges? The Gardner report's endorsement reflected the particular pressure of Keppel and Zacharias, but also the generalized white liberal guilt of the entire task force. Title III's authorization for fiscal year 1966 was a modest $55 million. Public Jim Crow colleges for blacks and their private counterparts *had* clearly been financially starved for a century. But Title III's subsequent history has been troubled by three basic anomalies: The program had been conceived to aid weak black colleges; but most of the nation's marginal colleges, like most of the nation's poor, turned out to be white. In an era devoted to racial desegregation, Title III tended to reinforce the segregated racial identity of black colleges. Title III in operation ultimately produced some horror stories of mismanagement and corruption. I shall discuss this later.

Title IV brought out the main fight, which was over student financial assistance. The White House file bearing on the HEA generally reflects a monitoring and nurturing operation with Congress in control. O'Brien's status-reporting memos to the president generally reflect cooperation from the House leadership, but extreme frustration with the idiosyncracies of Adam Clayton Powell, who could be *very* effective when he was in command, but who too often preferred to dash off to the Bahamas on pleasure junkets.[58] Cater's reports to the president tended to reflect partisan problems with Republican attempts to torpedo scholarships in favor of tuition tax credits.[59] But HEA ultimately emerged as an artifact of congressional compromise, and Title IV's four-part package of student financial assistance represents this process in almost classic form. First, the Democrats finally got their scholarships through the antipoverty appeal: $70 million annually in fiscal year 1966–68 for Educational Opportunity Grants to colleges and universities (*not* directly to the students— this was to be a major battle of the Nixon years that the schools and the ACE would lose and the students and market choice would win) for scholarships for full-time students "of exceptional financial need." Pressed by the ACE, the Office of Education—with Keppel, Cohen, and Halperin working smoothly, as usual, with Cater in the White House and with congressional allies—lobbied hard and finally triumphed.

But in order to forestall tuition tax credits, which the Treasury Department especially opposed as both regressive and enormously expensive, Title IV offered a guaranteed student-loan program for the middle class, where the principal came from commercial lending institutions, and the interest was subsidized initially at a low 3 percent, with no needs test, and with the loan repayable in ten years. The low interest prompted an attack by the American Bankers' Association, and the threat of competition drew the fire of the United Student Aid Fund, but the assistant secretary of the treasury Stanley Surrey and Cater arranged a complicated compromise with the ABA and the USAF that, in the post–New Deal tradition of brokerage politics, satisfied them and isolated the outnumbered Republicans, so the bill went barreling through (streamrolling over Edith Green, as Keppel liked to chortle). Title IV's other two sections transferred OEO's college work-study program to USOE and extended the NDEA loan program (which was distinguishable from the new guaranteed student loan program in that NDEA loans required a needs test, the principal was a line item in the federal budget, and "forgiveness" incentives were included to attract graduates to areas where manpower was nationally needed).

Finally, Title V established the National Teacher Corps, but it was a shaky beginning. This represented no presidential initiative, no task force recommendation. Instead, the Teacher Corps was pushed by liberal senators Edward Kennedy (D., Mass.) and Gaylord Nelson (D., Wisc.), who attached it to the HEA bill in February when they failed to get it included in the ESEA bill. President Johnson signed on late, telling the NEA convention at Madison Square Garden on 2 July that he intended to propose a National Teacher Corps and asking Congress for it on 17 July. Johnson fought hard for federal scholarships and loans, for only a timely loan had allowed him to stay in Southwest Texas State University in the late 1920s. But the Teacher Corps was a Kennedy proposal, like John Kennedy's Peace Corps, and Johnson would not touch it until he knew that his congressional majorities were unstoppable. The Teacher Corps was indeed a potential albatross, because it symbolized the federal presence in the local classroom that conservatives and Republicans so deeply feared. But 1965 was not the conservatives' hour, so on 6 August the House passed H.R. 9567 by a roll-call vote of 368 to 22, and on 2 September the Senate passed H.R. 9567 with minor amendments by a thundering roll-call vote of 79 to 3 (only three conservative southern Democrats voted against it) and sent it to conference. On 20 October the House and Senate adopted the conference report and sent it to the White House. And on 8 November President Johnson signed the HEA at Southwest Texas State University in San Marcos, where he had graduated in 1930.[60]

This, then, was the "Education Congress," voting appropriations in 1965 for the Office of Education alone (for fiscal year 1966) of $3,032,585,000. But this complicated and relatively massive new aid program would have to be implemented by an agency, USOE, which the Gardner task force had found flatly incapable of measuring up to the new programmatic demands. The fundamental reorganization in structure and personnel that would be required to transform a primarily and historically report-writing and statistics-gathering office into a program-managing agency would be wrenching. And, given the president's fascination with the task force device, it not surprisingly would involve more task forcing.

4 / REORGANIZING THE GOVERNMENT

THE LEGACY OF BROWNLOW AND HOOVER

 The passage of ESEA was a legitimate triumph, but its implementation was destined to highlight the historic tensions within the executive branch over the relationship between the line agencies and their programs. This was primarily because USOE, which for a decade had been a frail member of a huge department dominated by health and welfare, was now simultaneously authorized to gain massive funds and yet was universally regarded as incapable of administering them unless some drastic transformation occurred. During the mid-1960s, when the Great Society breakthroughs became possible, that historic tension was briefly submerged in the euphoria of victory. But it remained a bedrock source of disagreement. The literature of public administration is characteristically dry fare, but within it can be detected the rational planner's inner scream that the nation's federal structure and political history had produced such tenaciously built-in administrative nightmares. How irrational it was that the earth's most powerful economy should governmentally organize itself not by major function—for example, with departments of human resources, natural resources, military resources, et cetera—but instead by political fiefdom and constituency turf, as is the case with the departments of Commerce, Agriculture, and Labor. Together these departments represented the economic lifeblood of the nation, yet they politically either made war upon one another or they serviced their powerful constituents with a single-minded political devotion that yielded little to any comprehensive view of a shared economic fate. As a result, the cabinet as a collective entity of policy guidance was virtually useless.

All modern presidents had initially tried to engage the cabinet as a council in the broad governing enterprise and had quickly given up in despair (though this is less true of Eisenhower than of his successors). Kennedy and Johnson were exemplars of this rule, and the archives bulge with evidence of rather pathetic and doomed attempts to find some common purpose and practical utility for the cabinet. Bill Moyers told Time-Life's Hugh Sidey in 1969 that he believed that the cabinet as a collective policy-making institution was archaic, too formalized, and virtually useless to the modern presidency.

> There's nothing in the Constitution that establishes a Cabinet. The Cabinet was an effort by early Presidents to assemble around them men who could help them run the government. Their functions were institutionalized to the extent that future Presidents became ensnared in that formal, institutionalized process. But I think that it does not make sense to have a system, or tradition, to which you feel obligated to conform. If a Secretary feels excluded from a Cabinet meeting his feelings are ruffled and his pride is damaged. And so you have him there. Very often, as a consequence, nothing happens at Cabinet meetings of any significance. They become charades.[1]

Moyers, not surprisingly, preferred a muscular White House staff of special assistants and *their* staffs, and his replacement, Joseph Califano, vigorously sought to implement this alternative model. But I will treat that transition in the next chapter. Here we must begin with a brief recapitulation of the organizational groping toward the concept of a modern executive since Franklin D. Roosevelt's administration.

Despite the legacy of Watergate and the reaction against the Imperial Presidency, the history of the modern domestic presidency has been more typically characterized by institutional weakness, especially in contrast to chief executives in parliamentary systems. Roosevelt squandered a precious opportunity, which he had inherited from Herbert Hoover, to strenghen his office substantially during the emergency crisis of 1933–36. But he was too busy, and he had so little help, and he could not decide what he wanted to do until it was too late. Then in 1936, when his early authority to reorganize the government had expired, Roosevelt appointed the President's Committee on Administrative Management, headed by Louis Brownlow and including Charles E. Merriam and Luther Gulick. Early in 1937 the committee boldly called for consolidating all ninety-seven sprawling and uncoordinated government agencies under twelve cabinet departments, the addition of six administrative assistants to the presidency, and a "clearinghouse" planning agency. But Roosevelt's reorganization request to Congress coincided with his ham-handed attempt to pack the Supreme Court, and instinctive congressional resistance to strengthening the executive branch was reinforced by conservative howls of dictatorship. So in the end Roosevelt got only his six aides "with a passion for anonymity," and an Executive Office of the President (the Bureau of the Budget had been created in 1921 but had been located within the Treasury Department). Agency consolidation went nowhere, to the great pleasure of Congress and the great relief of a refractory civil service.

Over the intervening years, there was some modest, occasional accretion of presidential power, but it was more notably effective in strengthening the national security apparatus in a Cold War climate, where the president was manifestly commander-in-chief, than in shoring up presidential control over the domestic agencies, where congressional committees jealously safeguarded their inherited jurisdictions. Thus Congress in 1946 gave the president his three-economist Council of Economic Advisors but thoroughly defanged the celebrated Employment Act of 1946. (Congress even dropped the word "full" from the title and smashed the threatening proposal for a comprehensive planning device, the National Production and Employment Budget.) But the following year the president got his National Security Council. Located in the White House, it was to make the State Department down in Foggy Bottom forever miserable.

Then came the two Hoover commissions of 1947–49 and 1953–55, both of which stemmed from congressional concern that the war-swollen executive branch was too big, too wasteful, and too inefficient (the charge had a familiar conservative Republican ring, but it also had some truth to it, as even Truman conceded). Following Truman's surprise victory in 1948, commission chairman Herbert Hoover made a statesmanlike decision not to try to use the commission to repeal the hated New Deal, but to concentrate on promoting government efficiency instead. The result in 1949 was a two-million-word report containing 174 recommended reforms generated by twenty-three task forces. The first Hoover report recognized the primacy of functional rather than constituency-based grouping but then shrank from grasping the nettle. It did see a need for one new department—something combining welfare and social security and education—and suggested some marginal consolidations and transfers involving transportation. But twelve politically powerful and independent agencies, such as the AEC, TVA, and the Veteran's Administration, were left outside departmental boundaries.[2] Otis Graham has observed that the litmus test for any rational reorganization of the federal government is whether the Army Corps of Engineers has its pork barrel civil works functions (which have virtually nothing to do with the army) relocated so the president could coordinate them with similar activities involving domestic waterways and soil erosion and the like.[3] The first Hoover report actually toyed with the radical idea that the Corps's dam building might have some more rational purpose in Interior but then backed away from the idea. Otis Graham concluded that the Hoover commission members "found the situation desperate, but not serious." So nothing fundamental was changed, although some useful marginal reforms were implemented.

The second Hoover commission of 1953–55 was less cautious. This time the Republicans controlled both the White House and Congress, at least when the commission's deliberations began. But by 1955, when the 3.3-million-word report was issued, with its 314 recommendations accompanied by partisan horror stories of a "sprawling and voracious bureaucracy, of monumental waste, excesses and extravagances, of red tape, confusion, and disheartening frustrations, of loose management, regulatory irresponsibilities, and colossal largess to special segments of the public,"[4] it was too late again. Hoover seemed always to be cheated by the capricious timing of history. The Democrats had recaptured Congress, and President Eisenhower had lost interest in epic battles over government reorganization or repeal of the New Deal. He settled for the creation of the new Department of Health, Education, and Welfare in 1953, which was fashioned around FDR's old Federal Security Agency of 1939, which in turn had housed, in somewhat illogical catchall fashion, the Public Health Service, the Social Security Board, and that poor latchkey child, the Office of Education, which had been desperate to bail out of the hostile Department of the Interior.[5] And that, essentially, was the legacy of bureaucratic inertia and partial reform that Lyndon Johnson would inherit.

THE PRICE TASK FORCE ON GOVERNMENT
REORGANIZATION

One of the original task forces set up by Bill Moyers in the summer of 1964 was the legislative task force on government reorganization, chaired by Dean Don K. Price of the Harvard Graduate School of Public Administration. Price, who had chaired a task force for the second Hoover commission, was joined by five other academics with expertise in government and public administration, including Stephen K. Bailey of the Maxwell School at Syracuse University and Richard E. Neustadt of Columbia University. Five federal officials participated on the task force, including Harold Seidman as White House liaison and Herbert N. Jasper as executive secretary (both of these men were from the Bureau of the Budget). Finally, the private sector was represented by Sydney Stein, Jr., of the investment firm of Stein, Roe, and Farnham.[6]

The Price task force explored the troubled realm of federal education policy in a major working paper prepared by the BOB staff. This identified such problems as the familiar program inconsistencies, duplication and inefficient sprawl and lack of coordination, and a program imbalance that loaded federal support toward the sciences and starved the humanities. The secretary of DHEW had responsibility for the direction of the Office of Education but curiously had no real line control over its functions. As for the benighted USOE itself,

> There is widespread dissatisfaction both in and out of Government concerning the functioning of the Office of Education. In addition to operational shortcomings, it is alleged that the Office suffers from an almost complete lack of creativity and innovative capacity in planning for American education in the 60's. Historically, the Office has been loath to assume major policy-formulating responsibilities, and has been generally viewed as the willing captive of school administrators and education associations.[7]

Ultimately the Price task force, like the Brownlow committee but unlike the two Hoover commissions, recommended a thoroughgoing reorganization of the executive branch according to function rather than constituency. It would create five new departments. First priority was a department of transportation. Second was a department of education. Because "research and education are likely to be the key to new policy

developments and new domestic policy opportunities," the new education department should include the Office of Education, the newly proposed humanities foundation, the National Science Foundation, the education and basic research programs of the National Institutes of Health,
and such miscellany as the National Bureau of Standards, the Smithsonian Institution (including the John F. Kennedy Center for the Perform-
ing Arts), the National Council of the Arts, plus Gallaudet College and
Howard University. The remaining three new departments would be a
department of housing and community development; a department of
economic development (including nontransportation elements of the
Department of Commerce, the OEO—which as a program-running operation the Price task force wanted to *eject* from the policy-planning and
program-monitoring Executive Office of the Presidency—the Small
Business Administration, and maybe the Department of Labor); and finally a department of natural resources (essentially a merger of the departments of Agriculture and Interior).[8]

The lean, twenty-one page Price report (excluding appendixes) was a
bold stroke. It consistently spoke from a comprehensive presidential perspective, saying of the president that "he alone is the General Manager"
and rejecting the creation of some sort of administrative supermanager
under the president. But its proposed reorganization was political dyna-
mite, because it would radically scramble the traditional network of
congressional subcommittee–executive agency symbiosis and thereby
threaten to deflect the new administration's mandate and energy away
from Great Society legislation into jurisdictional squabbles. And unlike
the Brownlow and Hoover reports, the Price report was secret. Lyndon
Johnson wanted to build the Great Society, not strangle it in a major
reorganization dogfight with a Congress whose votes he needed and
whose territorial instincts he knew so well. In their administrative history of the Johnson administration, Emmette S. Redford and Marlan
Blissett observe that "comprehensive reorganization was not part of the
Johnson strategy. When the [Price] task force met with him after submission of the study, he said nothing about the report and for most of the
evening talked about the Vietnam War."[9] Redford and Blissett reasonably
conclude of the Price report's call for radical functional reorganization
that "for Johnson at this point it would have made no sense whatever."
Johnson instead would take his reorganizations on one at a time, after
first building a policy consensus. He would create the Department of

Housing and Urban Development (HUD) in 1965 and the Department of Transportation (DOT) in 1966, thereby partially vindicating the Price recommendations and thereby also avoiding the bureaucratic carnage that would inevitably stem from an attempt to dismember and merge such historic, congressionally comfortable, and constituency-captured agencies as the departments of Agriculture, Commerce, Interior, and Labor.

But in January of 1965 the Bureau of the Budget had been asked by Senator Hill to comment on S. 100, a perennial bill to establish a department of education by combining all educational programs scattered throughout forty or more federal agencies. The bureau's formal response was a carefully hedged conclusion that "consideration of S. 100 at this time would be premature," and that the first priority should be to "explore thoroughly other possible approaches and to resolve the complex and difficult organizational issues resulting from the close interrelationship of education with training, defense, science, health and other major purposes of Government."[10] But the bureau's internal dialogue in responding to the Senate is most revealing of its view of the question of reorganization in relation to educational programs.[11] First, there was the basic dichotomy between *institutional* and *instrumental* programs in education. Institutional programs were

> designed primarily to strengthen schools and colleges as such: i.e., as *institutions* whose overall quality and service to society is a matter of national concern. Nearly all the programs of the Office of Education fall into this category. The personnel training and education aspects of the National Science Foundation, the preschool program of the Office of Economic Opportunity, the programs directly aimed at medical education in the National Institutes of Health, and the College Housing program in the Department of Urban Affairs could be put in the same category. The Community Action Programs of the Office of Economic Opportunity, VISTA, and parts of its Youth Corps, are more doubtful but could be so categorized. The total in this category for FY 1966 is approximately $4 billion.[12]

The second federal educational category involved programs in which schools and colleges were used by federal agencies "as necessary *instruments* to carry out their particular missions." Virtually all federal agencies sponsored such programs, for example, the vast network of military service schools, the educational programs for agriculture, forestry, mine safety, drug abuse, highway safety, and nutrition, down to the mountain-climbing school for the Marine Corps at Pickle Meadows, California. The list seemed endless, and the bureau estimated the fiscal year 1966 budget for such programs at over $4.5 billion. Should the Marines' Pickle Meadows be turned over to the Office of Education, in the interest of functionalist logic? If so, was it politically feasible? The Bureau of the Budget didn't actually ask about Pickle Meadows, but both questions were implicit at the margin, and both (especially the latter) answered themselves with a thundering negative. The bureau staff added an additional and intriguing pluralist argument against a massive functionalist reorganization in federal education:

> A basic goal of Federal activities in education is to strengthen schools and colleges and universities so that they have the internal strength to preserve their own freedoms. In the judgment of the institution, preservation of this freedom may mean refusal to take part in a particular program of a particular Government agency. To put *all* programs under one head, both "institutional" and "instrumental," might lead to some hesitation to take such action in fear of reprisal. Higher education may complain now about the plethora of governmental interests and programs, and the attendant confusion. But it is a reasonable guess that it is learning fast that there is advantage to playing off one agency against the other.
>
> The complaints of undue Federal control under centralized management could be expected to increase rapidly. It has been pointed out that institutional freedom lies in part in the interstices between Government agencies.[13]

So for a sound combination of political, practical, and theoretical reasons, the Johnson administration was not prepared to push for a department of education.

THE PROBLEM OF THE OFFICE OF EDUCATION

But if there was to be no new department of education, or superdepartment of human resources or whatever, then what was to be done about the sorry state of affairs at USOE, which was about to inherit a massive new brace of programs, and which was generally regarded as so thoroughly captured by its clientele groups that innovation was impossible? To the Bureau of the Budget, the prospects looked grim. The bureau's Science and Education Branch reviewed DHEW's preliminary proposals for new education legislation in September of 1964 and reported to Hirst Sutton with dismay that although DHEW officials had earlier discussed some provocative ideas (for example, tuition-free junior colleges and formula grants for public schools for shared-time programs with private school students), what DHEW was formally asking for was essentially the tired and rejected remnants of the Kennedy omnibus bill, centering on aid for teachers' salaries and school construction.[14] When the Gardner task force report broke new ground in November, its alternate executive secretary (to William Cannon), Emerson J. Elliott, reported for the BOB's Division of Labor and Welfare that "we view the Task Force recommendations as inadequate to the magnitude of the problems."[15]

When in early December of 1964 USOE sent up to the Bureau of the Budget its package of legislative proposals in response to the Gardner report, William Cannon expressed his general disgust in a bureau staff memorandum: "There seems to be a serious possibility that the Office of Education's legislative program will end up as an unsorted grab bag of items with priority given to the most ineffective, second order, or trivial." USOE's first five priorities were aid to impacted areas, free textbooks, aid to state departments of education, university extension, and student loans; "everything else is a distant second—the supplementary education centers; the national educational laboratories; the college development programs, etc.—and are probably thought of as a cover, to be peeled off, as the program moves through the Executive Branch and Congress." Cannon complained that the USOE approach had "no substantive connection among the OE items, no rationale, no theory about education. . . . In fact, they probably were not selected with any regard toward the substantive problems of education. Their real connection is that most of them have the support of powerful groups; the NEA, the State School Superintendents, the Land Grant Colleges, and the American Council on Education—the silent partners in the administration of the Office of Education." Cannon regarded the aid-to-impacted-areas approach as only "a vehicle and stratagem for obtaining general aid, particularly for teachers' salaries," and as such it "suffers from the smell of deception, blackmail, and cynicism" and would represent "the first move to exploit the poor for purposes that have very little to do with them." Furthermore, the USOE proposal to provide "free textbooks for all schools is a straightforward attempt to buy parochial school aid for the impacted areas program." Aid to state departments of education was "a long-range and questionable program in its best light, and a 'patronage' program for OE at its worst." Cannon concluded gloomily that "the existing situation seems pretty hopeless. The Office of Education has again confirmed the long-standing, wide-spread view that it is an incompetent stodgy agency with no program except that furnished by outside bureaucracies." [16]

Yet when the Price task force report came in, its recommendation for a new department of education, which would reward this "incompetent" and "stodgy" and "hopeless" agency with elevation to cabinet status, did not square with the preference of the majority of the Gardner task force, which was to follow the OEO model and place the new education programs in the Executive Office of the President rather than in USOE. Given this dissonance, the Bureau of the Budget hedged. The Division of Labor and Welfare reported to Harold Seidman that it saw some merit in the Price report's recommendation that USOE be joined to the highly regarded NSF. But they sounded a note of warning: "It is our view that NSF programs could actually be harmed if they were brought into the kind of environment which now exists in HEW and the Office of Education. NSF enjoys a higher professional standing than the Office of Education and it has administrative and program flexibility to a degree not found in HEW." [17] The Office of Education, in fact, was something of a tar baby:

> The Office of Education . . . lacks vigor and stature, although we do not believe that this is necessarily due to its location in HEW. For too many years, the Office of Education has not exercised a leadership role nor was it being urged to assume such a role. Too many senior personnel of the Office have not been suited for a role of leadership. Also, the Office of the Secretary of HEW has been hesitant about pushing the Office of Education, or any of its other constituents for that matter, to assume roles not sought by the constituents. The Office of the Secretary has almost totally

failed to assume a leadership role itself, and it lacks staff for program planning and development and for effectively coordinating and managing the Department's business.[18]

In March of 1965, in response to Keppel's calls urging internal reorganization, Hirst Sutton wrote Elmer Staats that because the White House wanted to handle only one new department at a time, and in 1965 that new department was Housing and Urban Development, and because USOE was "not well equipped to administer effectively its many new responsibilities and that it does not get strong support from the Secretary's office in solving its administrative problems," the best immediate response would seem to be the internal reorganization of USOE itself.[19]

Lest the bureau's role vis-à-vis the Office of Education be regarded as largely confined to hectoring the hapless agency, it should be acknowledged that BOB correspondence over USOE during the 1960s constantly urged shoring up the sagging agency, starting at the top. Here are some typical observations and recommendations.

The commissioner of education was too low in rank. At level V he was outranked by the assistant secretary of education (who had no line authority) as well as by the heads of such agencies as the National Science Foundation (level III) and the chairmen of the Arts Endowment and the Humanities Endowment (both level III).

Correspondingly, the commissioner was embarrassingly underpaid, making a lower salary than many local school superintendents in the Washington metropolitan area.

OE was grossly understaffed at the supergrade level, having about 1.5 percent of staff at supergrade, which was about a fifth of the level of NSF staffing.

OE staffing was rapidly falling behind rapid program and budget growth. Between 1961 and 1966 there occurred a 500 percent increase in OE's budget, a 150 percent increase in the number of OE programs, but only a 90 percent increase in OE staff.

In 1961 OE grant dollars divided out to $537 thousand per employee. By 1966 that figure had grown *three times*, to $1.7 million per employee.

Programs requiring individual project-by-project approval climbed from $50 million in 1961 to $1.2 billion in 1966. This alone amounted to $500,000 per employee. But beyond this, about $2 billion in "pass-the-money-out" formula grant programs also had to be administered.

Less than 9 percent of OE employees were stationed in the field, yet 99 percent of OE funds were spent in the field.

Whenever OE would manage to achieve some measure of consolidation of function through internal reorganization, Congress would refragment the agency by authorizing new programs mandating separate organizational structures.

The Brownlow report had insisted that the president "needs help." Throughout the 1960s, the BOB sniped at the inappropriate "educationist" skew of the USOE staff in a new age of program management. But the bureau also kept up a steady call for a modern management structure equal to the new demands.

So the BOB in 1965 recommended that USOE remain in DHEW, but that internal reorganization and staffing up at the senior level were badly needed immediately. The bureau's candid internal memorandums frequently exempted the energetic and uncaptured Commissioner Keppel from their complaints, because he was highly regarded for his political acumen and diplomatic skill and, indeed, charm; unlike most of his predecessors, Commissioner Keppel had not "married the natives." But Secretary Celebrezze, whom the BOB did not attack directly, was clearly regarded as a caretaker waiting for a judgeship whose time had come, at least by the summer of 1965, when the ESEA had sailed through Congress and the Higher Education Act was pending. On 1 July Cater wrote the president that "if and when you are considering a new Secretary of HEW, I suggest the following candidates. (1) John Gardner—my top choice . . . the task force he headed produced the basic ideas which emerged so successfully in your education program."[20] President Johnson had persuaded Gardner to head the White House Conference on Education that was held 20–21 June, and the following month Gardner was persuaded to replace Celebrezze as secretary of DHEW. But at the same time, Keppel's relationship with the president had seriously deteriorated, and that story is intimately linked to the question of reorganizing the Office of Education.

KEPPEL, LOOMIS, AND THE INK TASK FORCE

Since the winter of 1963 Commissioner Keppel, who had concentrated his talents on negotiating the legislative program, and who was not regarded by himself or by others as a gifted manager, had been consulting with Kermit Gordon and John Macy in an attempt to recruit a high-powered manager to replace his inherited career deputy of the old school, Wayne Reed. In 1964 Keppel settled on trying to recruit Henry Loomis, a former Harvard colleague who was director of the Voice of America in USIA, and who earlier had built a strong managerial reputation in senior appointments in the Department of Defense, the NSC, the Office of Science and Technology, and at Massachusetts Institute of Technology. The Loomis oral history in the LBJ Library reflects the brusque, judgmental tone of a no-nonsense manager, essentially Trumanesque in his profanity.[21] Loomis at first refused Keppel's offer, which was extended in 1964 by an old bureaucratic friend and competitor, DHEW's assistant secretary for administration Rufus Miles, to which Loomis replied: "Jesus Christ, not me! What the Hell, I don't know anything about education." But by early 1965, Loomis was chafing under the "totally inept" leadership of USIA director Carl Rowan and hence was "getting madder by the minute and less effective by the minute." So when Keppel tried again, Loomis was curious enough to poke about USOE, was appalled by what he found, and said to himself, "The question is whether to leave Government and to say, 'The Hell with it, anyway'; and do this on the way out, and it was so horrible that it sounded that it would be pretty good fun." Loomis was also pressed to take on the herculean task by a strategically positioned old friend, John Gardner. Loomis told Keppel that the key to his accepting the post would be the removal of Deputy Commissioner Wayne Reed, so Keppel found a way to remove Reed through a lateral shuffle that at least minimally saved face for a man Loomis regarded as "a very nice guy" but one with "no backbone or managerial drive." So in March Loomis quit VOA and signed on as Keppel's deputy.

When President Johnson heard about the new arrangement he was furious, because upon leaving USIA, Loomis had held a press conference, and in his remarks, he implied that political interference was being imposed by the Johnson administration on the Voice of America, and the story appeared in Mary McGrory's column in the *Washington Star*.[22] Loomis later insisted that he was complaining about the State Department, not the president or the White House, but the damaging appearance of bad judgment and disloyalty prompted the enraged Johnson to call Keppel, have the White House operator break in on a telephone conversation between Keppel and a southern governor, and demand that he rescind the appointment.[23] Keppel stood by his guns in insisting on a deputy of his choice, and Celebrezze backed him up, but Keppel recalls that virtually every time he saw the president thereafter, Johnson would greet him by demanding, "Have you fired that son-of-a-bitch yet?"[24]

Deputy Commissioner Loomis brought along from USIA his reconstruction team—his secretary; his researcher; and, most notorious of all from the viewpoint of the threatened old-line staff, his "hatchet-man," Walter Mylecraine, who quickly earned the sobriquet "the Terrible Turk," and who even Loomis admitted was "ruthless." Loomis regarded the professional "educators" at USOE with searing contempt, as second-rate men who not only were managerially incompetent, but who were "emotionally, almost religiously against the act which they were trying to administer." Keppel promptly appointed Loomis chairman of the new executive group of less than a dozen senior staff members, and they first met on 2 April, and thereafter twice weekly on Monday and Thursday, beginning at 10 A.M., in Loomis's office throughout the subsequent year of reorganization. Most of the executive group's energies during 1965–66 were devoted to implementing the ESEA and the HEA, as well as Title VI of the Civil Rights Act of 1964. As described in some detail by Bailey and Mosher in *ESEA*, this involved a planning group to coordinate task forces on the various new titles. But the earliest and most dramatic attention was paid to reorganizing USOE. The executive group minutes are essentially action summaries, and they reveal a crisp, get-cracking action agenda that began on 2 April with an order for a "quick, first-cut evaluation by numercial scale of all USOE employees against their specialty co-equals and by their supervisors, bottom to top, with the Commissioner rating the bureau and office chiefs."[25] The executive group ordained that up to fifty new supergrades "will be recruited and added NOW," to become "a management and substantive core within two or three years."

In a parallel development, Cater was conferring with Gordon, Staats, Keppel, and Cohen about setting up a short-term ad hoc task force of three men working for three intensive months to help Keppel reorganize USOE. Johnson approved this on 12 April, and two days later Cater reported that Gordon and Staats had recommended borrowing as task force chairman Dwight Ink from the AEC—"He is an able organization man who did a first rate job last year on the Alaskan crisis"—plus Herbert Jasper of BOB and Nicholas Oganovic from the Civil Service Commission (he was replaced almost immediately with Gilbert Schulkind from the same agency).[26] The next day, 15 April, Cater informed Celebrezze of the Ink task force, reminding him that two days earlier, at the reception for Congress on the occasion of the passage of ESEA, that the president had announced, "I am asking Secretary Celebrezze and Commissioner Keppel to move immediately to prepare the Office of Education for the big job that it has to do, just as soon as the funds are appropriated. Upon their recommendation, I am notifying the Secretary that I am going to appoint a task force to carry out his recommendation to assist him in the next 60 days on organizational and personnel problems in this area to administer this bill."[27] The Ink task force worked intimately with Loomis's executive group, frequently sitting with them (and occasionally joined by Keppel) in late April and early June, and clearly formed a consensus, which was reported to the president on 15 June in a forty-one-page report entitled "Recommendations of the White House Task Force on Education."

The Ink report's eight sections dealt variously with strengthening USOE in personnel and financial administration, planning and evaluation, management, and contracting and grants, but at its heart was an organizational critique and a theory of reform. It observed that the present organization of USOE had been established by former Commissioner Sterling McMurrin in 1962 based on the Homer Babbidge report of 1961, entitled "A Federal Agency for the Future," which in turn reflected a study conducted in 1960, when USOE ran twenty programs on less than $500 million annually and with only 1,100 employees (the Ink report did not mention the names; they are supplied). Now USOE faced managing more than forty programs costing more than $3 billion, with perhaps $300 million more in pending legislation, and hence was confronted by a need for at least 2,300 employees. But beyond size there was that familiar structural problem, which was inherent in an organization like USOE, that is, whether to organize by *function* (research, international education, statistics collection, contracts and grants) or by *level* (elementary-secondary, higher, adult education), or by some combination of both. The McMurrin reorganization of 1962 had leaned toward the functional principle, but in a rather schizophrenic way, with functional bureaus presiding over divisions and branches that reflected groupings by level.[28]

Finally, in addition to size and the function-versus-level tension, there was the fragmenting congressional habit of establishing a "separate organizational unit for each new statute."[29] So with the recent program growth had come excessive fragmentation and layering with consequent delays in action—USOE alone had thirty-six units in 1965, with major expansion on the way. Although the Ink report reflected discreetly on the political and public administration problem, it was well known that this fragmentation was reinforced by the tendency of program managers to form strong ties with strategic congressional subcommittees, and this in turn was reinforced by political alliances with clientele groups. So the Ink report opted to combat this program fragmentation by reorganizing according to level, with a bureau each for elementary-secondary education, higher education, and adult plus vocational education, but also with a crosscutting functional bureau for research—all of this, of course, in the hallowed name of efficiency and couched in sanitized government prose. But as Bailey and Mosher observed, "What they did not say was that it would also greatly facilitate the reassignment or the phasing out of old-timers who had developed both internal and external centers of power around isolated functional units" and begin the transformation of branch management from the traditional specialist to generalist hands.[30]

So with the reorganizational program in hand and presidentially blessed, Keppel and his hatchet man Loomis and *his* hatchet man Mylecraine all went at it with gusto. Bailey and Mosher, who interviewed survivors and, presumably, nonsurvivors when the carnage was fresh in their minds, describe the results:

> The speed of action and the fact that the plan was shattering to
> *all* vested interests, produced a reaction of numbed, bewildered,
> bitter acquiescence. . . . The anguish can only be imagined. The
> ensuing, if temporary, administrative chaos was shattering. For
> days and weeks, people could not find each other's offices—
> sometimes not even their own. Telephone extensions connected
> appropriate parties only by coincidence. A large number of key
> positions in the new order were vacant or were occupied by act-
> ing directors who were frequently demoralized by status ambigu-
> ity and eventual status loss. Those who could not live with the
> status loss resigned. And all of this came at a time of maximum
> work load.[31]

But Loomis and Mylecraine were trying to save USOE through radical surgery, not kill it. They demanded from the White House fifty new supergrades, and when Cater balked, Loomis attacked with his customary instinct to go for the jugular: "I said: 'I don't give a goddamn how many there are in government, and you know it. You know you can't make it otherwise; you want this thing to fail? You want the President to be discredited? You're going to tell me, sitting here, that you can't get fifty? That's absurd.'—That was done deliberately to be a shocker, to say that this wasn't business as usual."[32] This was the usual Loomis tough talk, but the Johnson White House wasn't used to that kind of flak—from Congress, perhaps, and from the public and the media, but not from their own troops. Loomis received only twenty-three supergrades, which was a compromise in the low range. Within a year he was on his way to the private sector.[33]

In his oral history interview, Dwight Ink was asked if the reorganization was carried out to his satisfaction. He responded, "Not to my satisfaction. . . . Both Frank Keppel, the head of the office, and his deputy Henry Loomis left the office within three or four months, and so the continuity was gone. By the time they were able to replace that team, the momentum had been lost."[34] In November of 1965 Secretary Gardner sensed that Keppel's political capital had been used up—at USOE, where the Ink-Keppel-Loomis reorganization had shattered morale; on the Hill, where both the reorganization and Keppel's aggressive enforcement of the school desegregation guidelines was stiffening resistance; and in the White House, where the president's resentment at the Loomis appointment was massively exacerbated by Mayor Daley's rage at Keppel's threat to cut off federal funds to Chicago's schools.[35] So Keppel was kicked upstairs to assume the newly created staff position of assistant secretary for education, and he was replaced as commissioner in January 1966 by "Doc" Harold Howe II.

THE ORGANIZATIONAL PROBLEM OF DHEW—AND THE GREAT SOCIETY

In the next chapter we will return to the narrative beyond the watershed year of 1965, but the intractable question of how best to organize the federal government to implement the Great Society programs continued to vex the Johnson administration throughout its tenure. The problem of internally reorganizing USOE dominated the structural agenda during the summer of 1965, but earlier in the spring, Cater had sent the president a memo addressed to the larger question of the future organization of DHEW, which "unfortunately," he observed, the Price task force had failed to deal with, other than to recommend a separate department of education.[36] Cater attached a memo that he had received from Mike O'Neill, a veteran reporter for the *New York Daily News* who covered DHEW and was a stringer for *Medical World News*.

O'Neill began with the sober observation that "HEW's high command structure is an administrative mess which has been inadequate to the Department's mission for more than 10 years and will collapse completely under the weight of its new Great Society responsibilities."[37] First priority was to find "a great HEW Secretary . . . a la McNamara." Next was reorganization, preferably along the lines of the Department of Defense model, with separate secretaries of health, education, and welfare under an HEW secretary and undersecretary, underpinned by seven or eight assistant secretaries with backup staffs.

> It is utterly ridiculous to be trying to run a $6 and $7 billion business with only a handful of people. HEW is actually being run now by only three guys—Cohen, Quigley, and Dempsey [assistant secretary James M. Quigley and Edward Dempsey, special assistant for health and medical affairs]. Congress originally refused to give the Department any real staff because of its alleged fears about empire-building in the important health-education-welfare field. The result has been administrative chaos. The Secretary—and therefore the White House—has never been able to achieve any real control over the agencies. They have gone their own merry way for years, even in the old Federal Security Agency.[38]

O'Neill then added a laundry list of examples of two or three different agencies taking off in different directions on the same problem, launching rival and conflicting programs, with never so much as a by-your-leave:

> The Children's Bureau, for example, is running a flock of health programs without any reference to PHS. FDA and PHS have both been mucking around in the environmental health field without either one getting any place. The Welfare Administration is launching huge new health care programs without so much as a

nod to PHS which, theoretically, should have a good deal to say in the matter. The Office of Education wrote some provisions into some of its legislation that cut across NIH programs—but it only belatedly consulted NIH. It also proposed aid for medical libraries without coordinating with the National Library of Medicine.[39]

Cater asked for and received from Johnson permission to form a small working group composed of himself, Kermit Gordon, John Macy, and a deputy representing the secretary of health, education, and welfare to begin planning for a broad reorganization of DHEW.

Shortly thereafter, Gordon left the BOB to become president of the Brookings Institution, but his successor as budget director, Charles Schultze, promptly appointed an ad hoc task force of BOB consultants, chaired by Stephen Bailey and charged with recommending solutions to the government's growing problems of intergovernmental program coordination. Formed in August of 1965 and working closely (for three months) with BOB's Harold Seidman and his Office of Management and Organization staff, the Bailey task force identified "an increasing lack of structural and policy coherence within the Federal establishment and a series of administrative strains upon state and local governments." The report's first page illustrated the growing "maze of interagency and intergovernmental procedures, overlaps, delays, and jurisdictional disputes": [40]

Anti-poverty and economic development programs are being carried out by a dozen Federal agencies which relate to each other imperfectly and intermittently in Washington and the field.

Four Federal agencies handle in different ways closely similar grants and loans for local water and waste disposal facilities.

Community planning bodies and processes assisted by the Federal Government in the several aspects of community development—physical, economic, and social—are frequently unrelated to one another.

Federal grants-in-aid to states and localities vary needlessly and widely in requirements for matching money, in overhead allowances, and in standards of review and enforcement.

Gross inequalities exist in the capacity of states and localities to develop proposals for Federal aid and to negotiate the maze of Federal program review.

Previous attempts at program coordination through interdepartmental committees had proved too weak and cumbersome; and lateral coordination, with one department assigned to coordinate others in a particular field, had failed because departments would not submit to coordination by other departments of equal rank. The solution, then, lay not at the departmental or cabinet level, but only at the level of the presidency, where the executive office needed either a reinforced new Bureau of the Budget or a new Office of Community Program Coordination.

The Bailey report of 1965 anticipated the Heineman report of 1967 not only in calling for muscular program coordination at the presidential level, but also in simultaneously advocating administrative *de*centralization, preferably through "common regional boundaries and headquarter cities for related Federal agencies—particularly HUD, HEW, OEO, and Labor." In response, in the summer of 1966 Schultze appointed William D. Carey as a noncareer assistant director of the bureau in charge of troubleshooting interagency and intergovernmental problems on a largely ad hoc basis; and he directed the bureau's Office of Management and Organization to conduct fact-finding surveys to discover what worked and what didn't and why.[41] In November of 1966, Schultze forwarded a summary of the field surveys to Senator Edmund S. Muskie, whose subcommittee on intergovernmental relations was holding hearings on "Creative Federalism." (This was a letter to "Dear Ed" signed "Charlie" for his "personal use," and it explained that its frankness and candor "obviously would pose quite a problem if the document were released or quoted from.")[42] Muskie had succinctly observed that the core of the problem was "the difficulty of managing 170 grants-in-aid programs in the 21 different Federal departments and agencies in over 92,000 units of government throughout our 50 states."

Schultze's summary to Senator Muskie conceded that part of the problem was caused by weakness at the state and local levels—that is, the basic fragmentation of local government units made it extremely difficult for state, county, or city chief executives to administer a given geographic area. Typically these executives faced severe constraints and statutory limits on their taxing, budgetary, and appointment powers; most governors were institutionally weak; city governments were hostile to state interference, and most faced severe financial problems. But most of the problems were *federal* in origin:[43]

Over 20 agencies and numerous congressional committees with differing jurisdictions, clients, and methods of approaching a problem are involved in intergovernmental programs characterized by overlapping and duplication.

Federal assistance is provided through a series of increasingly narrow and complex categorical grant and loan programs. This fragmentation reinforces the structural duplication and overlap, and is characterized by an excessive number of small grants, pressure on states and localities to go for the "easy money," no rational pattern of matching requirements or consistent pattern on equalization in terms of fiscal capacity and tax effort.

Pressure to get federal matching funds in narrow categorical grant programs tends to distort state and local budgets, and federal planning requirements are too complex, inconsistent, and based on differing standards and data.

Federal field structure prevents effective coordination, with most federal agencies either lacking field organization or lacking common regional field locations. Narrow categorical programs increasingly lead federal agencies to deal directly with local governments and organizations, thereby angering state levels and often by-passing federal field offices entirely.

Late appropriations and delays in project approval make state and local planning and budgeting difficult.

Federal action is often taken and regulations are prescribed without regard for state and local laws, government structure, financial and administrative capabilities, and on-going programs.

By the fall of 1966 there was growing concern among the president's senior staff that Great Society legislation was piling up, but that their administration was in increasing trouble. Both Moyers and Califano recognized the pressing priority of improved administrative structure, and Charles Schultze, Secretary Gardner, and OEO director Shriver proposed a variety of alternative organizational reforms. These included a domestic council patterned after the NSC (Shriver); conversion of DHEW into a triple-based superdepartment patterned after the Department of Defense (Gardner); a new department of economic development that recombined the Department of Labor with what little was left of the Department of Commerce after it lost 80 percent of its annual budget, its trust funds, and 15 percent of its personnel to DOT (a combination of Price, Macy, Califano, and Schultze); and a new office for program management in the executive office, with regional and even major city field offices (Schultze).[44] This array of proposals from the subpresidency constituted a rich (and politically explosive) agenda for the president's second, and final, outside task force on government organization.

THE HEINEMAN TASK FORCE

Benjamin W. Heineman was a lawyer-businessman who, as chairman and president of the profitable Chicago and North Western Railway Company, had first come to President Johnson's attention when he helped negotiate the threatened Illinois Central Railroad strike in the summer of 1964. That September he helped form a National Independent Committee for Election of Johnson and Humphrey. In 1965 he sat on Robert Wood's outside task force on Urban Affairs and Housing, and in 1966 he chaired the volatile White House Conference on Civil Rights. Both Johnson's confidence in him and the strength of his independence is suggested by Heineman's report, in his oral history, that he variously rejected the secretaryships of HUD and the Department of Commerce, the Bureau of the Budget directorship, and in 1968, DHEW (which then went to Wilbur Cohen)—Heineman claimed that he was interested only in being attorney general.[45] In October of 1966 he was persuaded to head the Task Force on Government Organization. Its distinguished membership initially included Hale Champion, director of finance for California; Mayor Richard Lee of New Haven; William Capron of the Brookings Institution; Kermit Gordon, now a vice-president at Brookings; Yale political scientist Herbert Kaufman; Dean Bayless Manning of the Stanford Law School; and Chancellor Harry Ransom of the University of Texas— with Joe Califano as White House representative, and Fred Bohen of Califano's staff as staff director.

The presidential importance of the task force is indicated by Johnson's personal approval of ten of the twelve names originally suggested by Califano, and especially by Johnson's addition of the Ford Foundation president McGeorge Bundy and, later, Secretary McNamara and budget director Schultze. The task force met three times with the president in the White House, and in total it met seven times for twelve days between 12 November 1966 and 7 May 1967. Its initial working papers included the

Price task force report, statements on organizational problems from the Wood task force report, testimony by government officials to the Muskie subcommittee on intergovernmental relations, and submissions related to the Shriver and Gardner proposals for executive reorganization.[46]

The Heineman report was not due until the middle of June 1967, but so high-powered was its membership and so broad was its charge that it sent the president periodic recommendations both before and after mid-June—on topics that ranged beyond the structural concerns for administering Great Society programs, to include national economic policy and even foreign affairs. But the succinct, ten-page "final" report of 15 June 1967 clearly falls in the high tradition of Brownlow, Hoover, and Price—in fact, its bold vision was closest in spirit to Brownlow. All four reports embraced a firm presidential perspective, and the Heineman report was quick to identify both the problem and the enemy.

> Insofar as its aim is responsive and efficient management, the Federal Government is badly organized. Top political executives—the President and Cabinet Secretaries—preside over agencies which they never own and only rarely command. *Their managerial authority is constantly challenged by powerful legislative committees, well-organized interest groups, entrenched bureau chiefs with narrow program mandates, and the career civil service.*[47]

The very legislative success of the Great Society had made the administrative problems worse: "*The target problems—poverty, discrimination, urban blight, dirty air and water—are not the sole concern of any one Federal department; they will not yield to a series of isolated program efforts.*" Federal social programs remained badly coordinated; the social problems were in the field, but the administration of domestic programs was "*centralized excessively in Washington . . .* in autonomous bureaus and administrations *below the Presidential and departmental level.*"[48]

The report conceded at the outset that some, but not all, of the "severe attack" being mounted against the president's social programs stemmed from political and ideological partisanship, and "*some criticism stems from deflated hopes,* with current funding levels well below ultimate need and demand." But because the task force members could scarcely attack the president's budget decisions, they concentrated on three basic structural remedies. First, they would strengthen the executive office of the presidency by creating two new well-staffed offices within it: an office of program development located within a reorganized Bureau of the Budget, with clear responsibility for domestic program formulation; and an office of program coordination, with a permanent field force, located parallel to but outside the Bureau of the Budget.[49]

Second, they would "presidentialize" the department and agency structure—to force it to look *upward* for guidance, primarily through unification in "superdepartments." The report urged continued efforts to reduce, through merger and realignment, *"the number of departments substantially in the grip of parochial interests* (Labor, Commerce, Interior, and Agriculture), *and resist proposals to create additional departments* by narrow, specialized interests or professional clienteles (Health or Education)."[50]

Finally, the task force would balance this steepening of central executive control with decentralized regional administration, primarily through consolidating the different and uncoordinated regional zones and offices of DHEW, HUD, the Department of Labor, and OEO into ten common regions with collocated field offices in common regional cities. Heineman preferred DHEW's nine regions but would split its large western region in two (the last page of the report was a foldout map suggesting the ten common regions and regional headquarter cities).

As for DHEW, the report conceded that despite recent organizational improvements, HEW *"continues as a holding company for highly independent administrations and bureaus. While its program burdens are enormous, the department is grossly understaffed at the top."* So first priority in HEW was strengthening the authority of the secretary over entrenched program operators. Only then should existing line administrations (such as PHS, USOE, Welfare, etcetera) be consolidated into "two or three multi-functional staff agencies in HEW (such as Health and Welfare and Education and Manpower), *led by political executives of Under Secretary rank."* With such an aggrandized future in mind, the Heineman report recommended consolidating all manpower programs in DHEW—ripping them away from the Department of Labor and OEO. Its vision of DHEW's future was as a grand model of presidential guidance, departmental consolidation, and coordinated decentralized administration: *"In many ways HEW is the Department of the Great Society. It administers the majority of Federal social legislation—old and new. It has the potential to become a superdepartment* for social services and human resource development *and thereby to coordinate a vast array of social programs short of the President.*"[51]

The Heineman report's grand model, with its intriguing and perhaps inherently contradictory built-in tensions between centralization and decentralization, was never to be tested during the Johnson administration. It simply came too late. Enthusiasm for the Great Society was becoming engulfed by antiwar turmoil, ghetto rioting, and soaring inflation. Only six months after the Heineman task force's last report had been submitted, Johnson stunned both the American public and his own administration by announcing that he would not seek reelection. In November of 1968, when President-elect Nixon's transition representative asked Charles S. Murphy, Johnson's transition coordinator, for a copy of the secret Heineman reports, Murphy asked Johnson whether he should forward copies and added that "Joe Califano's feeling is that you should not make the report available to the President-elect but should keep it for your own use."[52] This memo is one of the favorites of researchers in the Johnson archives, because the president, who was normally not very communicative in replying in writing to his staff memorandums, checked the "no" box on the approval sheet and then scrawled, "Hell no. And tell him I'm not going to publish my wife's love letters either."[53]

But it was to no avail. Johnson, who had been extraordinarily successful in leak-prone Washington at keeping his six-score-and-a-baker's-dozen task force reports secret, was too much of a lame duck to contain an extraordinary report that the new president wanted and the old president had not used. Later, when Nixon appointed the President's Advisory Council on Executive Organization under the chairmanship of businessman Roy L. Ash, Heineman made his task force reports available at their request.[54] As Redford and Blissett note in their history of the Johnson administration, "The imprint of the Heineman task force reports on the Nixon administration is unmistakable":[55] the attack on fragmentation; the call for larger, consolidated departments; the quest for a balanced combination of presidential direction, agency integration, and administrative decentralization; and the radical restructuring of the Bureau of the Budget into the Office of Management and Budget.

But that major transition is of course beyond my purview here. I left the narrative with the triumph of the Great Society breakthrough in 1965, and it was accompanied not only by a reorganization within DHEW, but also by an important internal transition in the Johnson White House, one symbolized by the departure of Bill Moyers as ranking White House aide and his replacement by Joseph Califano. The implications of this transition were not immediately apparent in late 1965, but they were soon to become so. And that transformation would first be reflected in the changed pace and rhythm of the task force operations themselves.

5 / EXPANDING THE
TASK FORCE DEVICE
From Moyers to Califano

When Goodwin's suggestion and President Johnson's enthusiasm led Bill Moyers to mount the impressive task force operation in 1964 that paid off so handsomely in 1965, Moyers had regarded the task force operation as primarily an ad hoc, one-shot planning operation. He hoped it would produce a distinctively Johnsonian legislative program for the Eighty-ninth Congress. The subsequent evolution, primarily under Califano, of a more systematic rhythm, and on a much larger scale, of customarily six-to-eight-month (and often one-year) outside and four-month interagency task forces, has obscured Moyers's distinctively hybrid vision of his original secret task forces. As Moyers explained to Hugh Sidey,

> I think the reason that those 14 task forces were so successful lies in the awareness—among those of us who were working on them, of the opposition that would develop if certain groups were not participating in their work. So instead of setting up a totally independent, outside, non-government task force which we knew the Bureau of the Budget and the Cabinet departments would resist, we made hybrid operations out of them. We put on them outside experts from the universities around the country, we put on them representatives of the bureaucracy, we picked the best men from within government to go on a particular task force with these outside experts.[1]

Moyers was especially keen to involve the Bureau of the Budget with its institutional memory, experience in legislative reference, broad overview of the federal enterprise, and keen loyalty to the president:

> No policy can ever be considered apart from its budgetary relationship, so we put on there a representative of the Budget Bureau. In fact, we made the executive secretary of each task force a staff officer of the Bureau of the Budget. You had, therefore, the best of three worlds—the world of the bureaucracy, which would be finally responsible for implementing the ideas; you had the world of expertise outside of government; and you had a White House special assistant who was in charge of several different task forces. We anticipated the reactions of different constituencies that would be served or alienated by the recommendations of that task force and made them a part of the process in developing the programs. I think that was the most essential, crucial decision that was ever made about these task forces.[2]

Actually, of Moyers's original fourteen task forces, only eleven drew their executive secretary (and therefore logistical staff) from the BOB; one executive secretary was provided by the CEA, one by the Treasury Department, and one task force, on civil rights, was stillborn (or rather, was mooted by the passage of the Civil Rights Act of 1964). Furthermore, only seven task forces had White House liaisons who were White House aides; the other seven White House liaisons were split between senior executive office staffers from the BOB and the CEA. But Moyers's main point is largely sustained: the thirteen executive secretaries and the thirteen White House liaisons were joined by thirty-three other federal officials to constitute a substantial *third* of these original "outside" task force members, with academics accounting for roughly another third. But by 1967–68, at the height of the Califano task force operation, half of the personnel on the outside task forces had typically academic backgrounds and only a fifth of them had federal backgrounds. The federal slack was to be taken up by small *interagency* task forces, customarily composed exclusively of senior federal personnel. A prime example is the Keppel interagency task force on education of 1965, which marks the transition from Moyers to Califano.

Califano's arrival was, in part, at Moyers's own insistence—and also Harry McPherson's, and clearly and most insistently Lyndon Johnson's.

In his exceptionally rich and detailed oral history, McPherson recalls in late 1968,

> The President had heard from Moyers that Califano was the ablest of all the Special Assistants to the Secretaries that he had known—that he was a real can-do man. When Moyers moved to Press Secretary in July 1965, that task of being the President's man on domestic programs and of putting together the legislative program was left vacant. The President, for a time, thought that he would put me in there. . . . I thought that I would not be the best engineer of that operation. And I—when he said he was also thinking about Califano [I] strongly recommended that he get Califano here. And . . . after a long struggle with McNamara, he was able to get him over. Califano has developed in the last two-and-one-half years the most coherent organization for the preparation of the legislative program that I believe any President has ever had in the White House.[3]

Moyers's appointment as press secretary in July 1965 astonished all observers, including Moyers.[4] But Johnson's raid on McNamara for "Whiz Kid" Califano did not. A native of Brooklyn who attended Catholic parochial schools and the College of the Holy Cross, graduated magna cum laude from Harvard Law School, did a brief legal tour for the navy in the Pentagon, and then got "bored with splitting stocks for Tom Dewey's [Wall Street] law firm,"[5] Califano linked himself to Cyrus Vance's climb upward through the Pentagon labyrinth and emerged as McNamara's top troubleshooter.

In the spring of 1965 the Bureau of the Budget began its routine solicitation of central clearance bids from the agencies for the 1966 legislative program, but so great was Johnson's enthusiasm for the creative and short-circuiting device of the task forces that the machinery was cranked up again for the summer's new beginning in virtually all major policy areas. In education policy, however, clearly no new outside brainstorming was needed in light of the early triumphs of ESEA and the almost certain autumn triumph of HEA. What *was* needed was internal consolidation, and for four basic reasons. First and most obviously, the burden of administering the massive new education programs in the midst of radical reorganization was more than sufficient challenge to the understaffed and poorly prepared USOE and DHEW. Second, the vigor with which commissioners Keppel and, subsequently, Howe enforced the school desegregation guidelines severely strained the ephemeral North-South coalition of Democrats that had pushed ESEA through. Third, the secret White House task forcing had bruised agency and congressional egos that had been long accustomed to the routine deference and agency-subcommittee tradeoffs of central clearance. Finally, the legislative calendar of expirations and renewals was fairly crowded for 1966. Most important, ESEA itself had been authorized for only one year in 1965. Also scheduled for renewal were the popular school-construction and operation grants for federally impacted areas, the Higher Education Facilities Act of 1963, and the Library Services and Construction Act of 1964.

The shift from the brainstorming outside task forces of 1964 to the consolidating and coordinating interagency task forces of 1965 was a dramatic one. The 1964 operation witnessed (ultimately) fifteen outside and no interagency task forces. In 1965, there were only four outside task forces and thirteen interagency task forces. Of the four outside groups, only one, Robert Wood's task force on urban problems, represented a major substantive exploration of solutions to domestic problems in the spirit of 1964. Indeed Wood, a political scientist from Massachusetts Institute of Technology, had chaired a similar task force in 1964, and in 1965 President Johnson and Califano clearly planned their major domestic push toward urban problems and transportation, including the Model Cities program and the establishment of the departments of HUD and DOT.[6] The other three outside task forces were Stephen Bailey's previously discussed task force on intergovernmental program coordination, Clark Clifford's on foreign aid, and Dean Rusk's ill-starred task force on international education.

The fate of the Rusk task force is especially instructive because like Wood's urban task force of 1965, it enjoyed a large and powerful membership and strong presidential backing, and unlike Wood's task force, it ultimately went nowhere. In addition to five university presidents, its membership included such ranking federal officials as cabinet secretaries Rusk and Gardner and Commissioner Keppel; directors Sargent Shriver of the Peace Corps, David Bell of AID, Leonard Marks of USIA, and Leland Haworth of NSF; senior presidential aides Cater and McPherson; and Charles Frankel, who as assistant secretary for educational and cultural affairs was de facto chairman of the task force.[7] Johnson's domestic successes with ESEA and HEA contrasted sharply to his growing entanglement in Vietnam, and applying the magic of education to international turmoil clearly struck the president as a natural and beneficent extension of his sure domestic touch—especially because, like foreign aid, most of its expenditures would be invested in this country, primarily to increase international understanding among American college students, and to bring foreign nationals to America to better understand the United States. Johnson was to get his International Education Act passed and its programs authorized in 1966, but just barely, and without a penny of appropriation.[8] The bill was passed on 29 October, just one day before the second session of the Eighty-ninth Congress adjourned, and the delay was to prove fatal. Following the elections of 1966, the Ninetieth Congress was to prove far more resistant to President Johnson's submissions, partly because his "Goldwater majority" was considerably reduced, but also because of fundamentally altered fiscal and budgetary circumstances. But in the meantime, outside task forces were to take a decided back seat as Califano mounted his formidable array of interagency task forces in the fall of 1965, looking toward the January State of the Union and Budget messages and the legislative agenda for 1966.

THE KEPPEL INTERAGENCY TASK FORCE ON EDUCATION OF 1965

Of Califano's thirteen interagency task forces of 1965, most linked a senior executive as chairman to problem and coordination areas under his jurisdiction, for example, Secretary Orville Freeman on agriculture, Wirtz on labor, Weaver on urban problems and housing, Commissioner Keppel on education.[9] Two were ad hoc: Ink on reorganizing USOE, and Attorney General Ramsey Clark on the Watts riot; and two were special projects: Staats on adult work programs and Ackley on pollution abatement. Moyers took the initiative in establishing Keppel's task force, inviting Cater on 23 July to meet with him and Keppel on 27 July to discuss the 1966 legislative program for the second session of the Eighty-ninth Congress. But the day after that meeting, Califano took over, informing Secretary Celebrezze of the new Keppel task force and adding to it Cater and Cannon. Shortly thereafter the task force was completed with the addition of Phillip DesMarais, deputy assistant secretary of DHEW, and Stanley Surrey, assistant secretary of the Treasury Department. The task force was small, but it was genuinely *inter*agency and hence relatively free of the USOE hierarchy and of central clearance routines.

Califano instructed the Keppel task force to prepare position papers addressed to eight problem and potential program areas:

(1) Relieve the doctor, nurse, and medical technician shortage, especially in light of the new Medicare demands. (2) Expand financial aid to middle class college students. (3) Develop a year-round preschool education program. (4) Refine the hastily developed ESEA Title I so as to reach more disadvantaged children and concentrate more heavily on their remediation. (5) Devise a grant program for quality improvement to selected institutions of higher learning, especially predominantly Negro colleges. (6) Explore how best to transfer NDEA student loans, which were line items in the federal budget, to such off-budget devices as an "Educational Development Bank." (7) Improve drop-out prevention for talented students. (8) Develop a program of international education.[10]

Califano also asked for a list by 10 August of priority needs as seen by the task force.

On 10 August, Keppel sent Califano *his* list of priorities, and right at the top was his favorite, a program of national assessment of educational progress. Keppel and Gardner and the Carnegie Corporation had been promoting the rational utility of generating a reasonable national benchmark of learning progress against which to measure gains and losses, especially in light of the ESEA. But to those imbued with the religion of local control, the concept of a national assessment was as ominous as a national ministry of education, and as un-American. Keppel admitted as much to Califano.

Many educators, perhaps even the majority, are dubious about any kind of national testing on the grounds that it would restrict imaginative teaching, that results will discriminate in favor of students from advantaged homes at the expense of the disadvantaged, that comparison will be made unfairly of one school system to another, and fairly on those who do not care for competition, and that the ultimate result will be a rigid national curriculum and the loss of local initiative and control.[11]

This was a fair summary of the objections. Nevertheless, Keppel was determined to proceed, albeit cautiously, through samples and small nibbles, while awaiting what was to be called the Coleman report on schools and learning, which the Civil Rights Act of 1964 had ordered up by July of 1966. Keppel's remaining three priority items were less novel: shoring up the base of education in personnel and buildings; more R&D in higher education, and special efforts in international education (this was preempted by the Rusk task force); and concentrating on such specific problems and areas as construction aid to reduce northern de facto segregation, an "educational TVA" for the backward southeast, a larger effort on behalf of the handicapped and the delinquent, and retraining for workers displaced by technological advance. Barring the dispute over a national assessment it was a sensible list but not a very moving one—in the spirit of the large reach of the Gardner task force.

But if Keppel's education agenda for 1966 legislation for fiscal year 1967 represented mostly marginal consolidation and fine tuning, Califano reported to the president on 11 August that his thirteen interagency task forces were expected to report that fall on such novel ideas as a "Marshall Plan" to purge crime and blight and make America's cities safe, healthy, and comfortable; new welfare programs to provide the training and incentive to induce the "unemployable unemployed" to become tax-producing, not tax-consuming citizens; a "medicare" program for children; a frontal attack on accidental highway death. Little of this was achieved, or even seriously tried, in 1965, for earlier priorities and contemporary political realities dictated otherwise. It was probably inherent in the nature of interagency task forces, as distinguished from outside task forces, to consolidate, rationalize, and expand at the margins rather than to reach boldly ahead (and let the line bureaucrats catch the attendant flak). Besides, Johnson had charged the newly arrived, thirty-four-year-old Califano with three basic legislative tasks for 1966: orchestrate the creation of a department of transportation, "totally rebuild the ghettos," and forge an open housing bill.[12] So Keppel's task force sensibly sought to consolidate recent gains and necessarily sought also to deal in reverse order from the normal planning scenario by assessing the initial effects and defects of the program that they had politically ramrodded through in 1965, so as to fine-tune and tinker in 1966.

During August and September Cannon reported to budget director Schultze (through Phillip S. Hughes, head of Legislative Reference) on the progress of the Keppel task force. Most attention was being devoted, Cannon observed, to the concept of an education development bank to provide off-budget, private bank-financed loans to college students. Off-budget loans promised a dual advantage: "They offer an opportunity for getting around budgetary constraints and providing large sums of money for desired programs; and they provide a way of trading off administrative budget reductions on existing programs for budget increases in new programs." As for ESEA, attention centered on the proposal of Otto Eckstein of the CEA to raise the annual family income cutoff from $2,000 to $3,000. This promised to increase the number of disadvantaged children covered from 5.5 to 8.1 million, and it would bring the ESEA definition of economically disadvantaged into closer alignment with the antipoverty war's definition. But it would also cost perhaps $350 million more. Here Cannon inserted an "*Editorial comment:*"

> The Commissioner of Education is taking an extreme laissez-faire approach in handing out the money, so he will not be able to give any assurances that the States and localities are being monitored in a way which would assure effective use of the funds. The Commissioner of Education probably will try to meet these problems by pointing to his efforts to develop a series of national standards for evaluating performance of schools. However, this move has politically explosive implications.[13]

When Keppel sent his final task force report to Califano on 8 October, he emphasized dedicating the 1966 legislative year to improved executive action and coordination of recently enacted legislation.[14] The report's recommendations repeatedly shied away from major new financial commitments, even while identifying pressing national needs: de facto segregation in the North (with an estimated backlog of $15 billion in school construction), tuition for middle-class college students (study the feasibility of an educational development bank), strengthening education in the southeast and training professional personnel to run the Great Society programs ("within existing appropriations"), and exploring the possibility of nationwide kindergarten for poor five-year-olds. Program considerations in international and health education would be deferred to the Rusk and Cohen task forces. Even raising the poverty income line from $2,000 to $3,000 would add 2.6 million more students at a cost of only $350 million (that figure turned out to be an extremely low estimate). Best of all, for Keppel, the report's first recommendation, that the federal government undertake a systematic national assessment of educational progress, could be couched in the rhetoric of "Planning and Cost Analysis" that was so dear to Califano. Secrecy and speed were also dear to Califano, who on 9 September reminded his task force chairmen that "even if [a] Cabinet officer or Agency head is on the committee, he should *not* be provided with a copy of the report," and who on 27 October ordered the new secretary of health, education, and welfare, John Gardner, to have the education task force prepare eight additional studies and submit them by 12 November.[15] These qualities did not endear the brash Califano to cabinet secretaries in general, or to the lofty Gardner in particular, although Gardner accorded Califano's intellect and energy the respect it clearly deserved.

THE POLITICS OF THE SECOND SESSION OF THE EIGHTY-NINTH CONGRESS

When the first session of the Eighty-ninth Congress convened in January of 1965, the United States had 25,000 troops in Vietnam. One year later, there were upwards of 200,000. In addition to the expanding war and its attendant inflationary pressures, the intensifying cycle of summer race rioting and the acceleration of federal enforcement of school desegregation guidelines had considerably soured the euphoric mood of 1965. President Johnson's State of the Union Message of 12 January pledged both to persevere in Vietnam and to expand the Great Society at home, and to do so within a lean, "anti-inflationary," yet record $112.8 billion budget. This budgetary and programmatic tension set the essential tone of the curious second congressional session, wherein the president's partisan "Goldwater majority" budgetarily boomeranged on him. Liberal Democratic majorities on the authorizing committees repeatedly voted "budget-busting" increases over the administration's recommendations. The growing tendency of substantive legislative authorizing committees to vote large amounts for pet projects to please clientele groups, thereby requiring the more conservative appropriations committees to take the heat for reducing expenditures, had its origin as far back as the Civil War, when the old monopoly of the House and Senate appropriations committees was broken.[16] Over the years the authorizing committees had proliferated, especially in the House, and their powerful chairs were strengthened by the seniority system. But congressional logic also suggested the proliferation of subcommittees and their staffs, and even the Legislative Reorganization Act of 1946 could not successfully throttle them back, as the number of subcommittees on the Hill surged to over 140 by the 1970s. This process was unusually accelerated in the middle 1960s in the committees handling education legislation, although in different ways and for different reasons in the two chambers.[17]

In the House, the Education and Labor Committee had evolved as essentially a *labor* committee, dominated by liberal Democrats from the urban-industrial northeast and midwest. On this partisan, ideological battlefield, education programs were favored but were ancillary to such labor priorities as repealing Taft-Hartley's Section 14(b) permitting state "right-to-work" laws, and allowing common situs picketing. Unlike most congressional committees, Education and Labor contained few southerners, and since 1959 committee Republicans had remained hopelessly outnumbered. Pro-labor and education bills were usually reported with lopsided majorities but then were often killed or rewritten on the floor. Chairman Graham Barden (D., N.C.) had ruled with firm seniority and with ideological moderation in the 1950s, but in the middle 1960s, Chairman Adam Clayton Powell had unleashed the subcommittees to roam free, hiring their own permanent staffs on their own budgets.[18] A member of the dominant liberal-Democratic coalition (unlike Barden), Powell wanted to share credit for the large number of liberal bills passed, and when his energies were concentrated, he could be very persuasive. But Powell's erratic and frequently bizarre behavior eventually destroyed the good will that he had generated by granting subcommittee automony. In addition to his widely publicized public escapades—his drinking and womanizing on taxpayer-funded pleasure jaunts, his losing jousts with the courts, hiring his wife to perform committee services that were never rendered—Powell was variously described by his committee colleagues as unreliable, inattentive, unfathomable, and given to quixotic unpredictability.[19] Worse, from a policy perspective, Powell frequently used his disappearing act to prevent committee action, and on three major occasions in the Eighty-ninth Congress he delayed transmittal to Rules of bills that were dear to the hearts of the liberal-Democratic coalition, his purpose being to hold them hostage in bargaining for greater benefits exclusively for black people (such as FEPC, black hiring in construction, and anti-poverty money for Harlem—the liberal bills were repeal of 14(b) in 1965, and in 1966 the common situs picketing bill and the antipoverty amendments). As White House aide Henry Hall Wilson wrote President Johnson during crucial House committee markup sessions in mid-July, "The final hurdle will be Powell who is out of town this week. I am sure we can expect blackmail here, but we'll cross that bridge when we get to it."[20]

In the Senate, the chairman of the Labor and Public Welfare Committee was Lister Hill of Alabama. Hill had been an early champion of education legislation, but as resistance to school desegregation came to dominate Alabama politics, Hill concentrated almost exclusively on his primary interest, which was health (Hill chaired his own subcommittee on health, and he was named after the renowned English surgeon, Joseph Lister). This left a free reign to subcommittee chairman Wayne Morse, much as it had the year before—but with two radical differences. First, in 1965, Morse had dutifully supported the administration position and the House bill on ESEA down to the last comma. But in 1966, the president wanted to consolidate, reform, and moderate the growth of the Great Society's education programs; whereas Morse and his subcommittee and its clientele allies wanted to expand it. Second, in 1965 Morse had been willing to separate his antiwar views from his sponsorship of the administration's education program; but by 1966 he viewed the Vietnam escalation as a bitter tradeoff, with defense buildups and inflation directly competing for educational dollars. Such were the altered political, ideological, and personal circumstances of 1966.

THE CASE FOR BUDGETARY AND PROGRAMMATIC RESTRAINT

As expected, the president's State of the Union Message of January 1966 set domestic priorities on creating a new department of transportation from thirty-five existing agencies, concentrating on urban and environmental pollution problems, and seeking prohibition against racial discrimination in the sale and rental of housing. Although President Johnson promised to carry forward with "full vigor" the previous year's landmark programs in health and education, his Budget Message of 24 January called for expenditures at a level of $2 billion *less* than Congress had authorized for Great Society programs in 1965, and his Health and Education Message was not sent to Congress until 1 March.[21] Johnson did budget significant increases for educating the disadvantaged, but this was counterbalanced by reductions in aid for federally impacted areas and needy college students, reductions that were bound to prompt objections in Congress.

Johnson's Budget Message of 1965 had emphasized Great Society programs and deemphasized defense. But his dilemma in 1966 was primarily war induced, with excess-demand inflation soaring dangerously after a recovery through 1965 that had been essentially inflation free, and the dilemma was to prove increasingly intractable. The president's rhetorical solution, of course, was to insist that America could afford both guns and butter, and in theory at least he was quite right, as James Tobin has observed:

> [T]he society could well afford both. Vietnam War spending was never a large fraction of GNP, and at its height the total defense budget was smaller relative to the economy than in the 1950s. But in 1966 the economy could not finance both without an increase in taxes. Deficit financing overheated the economy and began the era of inflation and instability still afflicting us.
>
> The President's motive was to save his domestic programs from the cuts which a request for higher taxes would, as experience later showed, surely have invited.[22]

But in practice, Johnson sought to minimize and obscure the extent of war spending, and his budget estimates invariably underestimated defense outlays. (In January of 1965 he estimated defense spending for fiscal year 1966 at $49 billion, but it exceeded $55 billion.)[23] He also sought to minimize domestic budget estimates through such devices to reduce net government outlays as accelerated sale of government assets; savings estimates to be derived from program funding "reforms," such as in aid to federally impacted areas, which Congress was unlikely to accept; and shifting from line-item to off-budget accounts, as in proposing to fund future NDEA scholarship loans through federally guaranteed private loans. Lyndon Johnson did not invent these devices of budgetary legerdemain, but his early manipulations to hold the fiscal year 1965 budget under $100 million had gained him a notoriety that was both earned and sustained throughout his administration.

But as the Keppel task force had concluded, there were compelling practical reasons for program rationalization and consolidation in 1966 that operated quite independently of the president's fiscal and budgetary constraints. The crux of the matter was that too much money was being spent too fast in too many places and under too many categorical programs. For the administration to propose and Congress to assent to pouring more money into the new programs and also create even newer ones, or new categories of beneficiaries for inclusion in the old ones, would only compound the already severe problems of implementation. The chaos of a radically reorganized USOE has already been described, from the viewpoint of Washington insiders. But hearings before Carl Perkins's subcommittee on elementary and secondary education in the spring of 1966 elicited testimony from throughout the nation's school districts about the problems encountered in implementing ESEA. One of the most thoughtful and searching criticisms came from political scientist George LaNoue of Columbia Teachers College, who together with Dean Kelley had written what remains the most penetrating analysis of the church-state settlement in ESEA.[24]

In his congressional testimony LaNoue concentrated on general problems of administration in Title I and on church-state problems in Title II. First, he argued that the political attractiveness of setting Title I eligibility standards so low that 95 percent of the nation's 30,000 school districts could qualify clearly attracted broad support in Congress, but concomitantly spread the funds too thin. At the same time, it unwisely benefited suburban school districts that combined their little pockets of poverty with superior advantages in applying for grants and in attracting teachers with rare skills in remediation. LaNoue cited his own affluent system in suburban New Jersey, which had been awarded $44,600 under Title I "presumably because a few more than 100 of the roughly 7,000 children in the system meet the [disadvantaged] formula standards." He testified that

> with these funds, 10 teachers who have special skills have been hired for the second semester to work with the "educationally deprived" children of this already affluent and superior school system. Now you may say that this situation wasn't exactly what Congress had in mind when Title I was passed but no harm is done. Unfortunately this is not true. Teachers with these special skills are in very short supply. Wealthy suburban communities already have great advantages in hiring. The Title I funds in-

creased the "have" school system's ability to take still more of the best teachers from the "have not" schools in the urban and rural depressed areas.[25]

LaNoue's objection to the implementation of Title II was that Everson's narrowly circumscribed child-benefit theory upon which it was constitutionally based, and upon which Congress had insisted, had been abandoned by the Office of Education in its haste to write implementing guidelines that would maximize efficiency of administration. In the process, aid-to-the-child theory—which would require, for instance, a demonstration that private school children were being ill served by the community public libraries—was implicitly abandoned in favor of aid-to-the-institution practice, whereby private school administrators were invited to submit project applications for public funds to order books with which to permanently and unconstitutionally stock their private libraries. LaNoue saw the root of the problem to lie not primarily in a hectic drive for maximum efficiency and speed in implementing ESEA, but more fundamentally in a basic confusion of principle, one that required recognition that an emerging administrative commitment not to aid children who were demonstrably ill served by public facilities as required by Everson, but rather to strengthen both public *and private* (which would hence include religious) institutions as such would have to be abandoned.

The massive tomes that faithfully record the long line of witnesses' testimony before the education subcommittee hearings in the spring of 1966 differ from those of the immediately previous years, however, in that the hoary church-state issue was consciously downplayed. This made LaNoue's testimony somewhat lonely (testifying in association with the American Civil Liberties Union was often a lonely endeavor), although Halperin privately conceded to Howe, Keppel, and Cohen that "LaNoue's argument is brilliant and I am now convinced that we will soon be in serious trouble over the administration of Title II."[26] Most of the 1966 testimony, as was customary, was from the same groups that had testified the year before, was offered by the same spokesmen, and hence tended to be repetitive and predictable. But the attention by LaNoue and others to problems of program design and implementation was welcomed and echoed by agency spokesmen who were quick to acknowledge that the demonstrable problems encountered in implementation demanded greater program coordination and consolidation, rather than simply more funding and new categories of aid. Commissioner Howe, who was received with increasing hostility on the Hill, both by southerners who resented DHEW enforcement of the school desegregation guidelines, and by northerners who resented increased busing to reduce de facto segregation (Congressman Paul Fina, a Republican from the Bronx, publicly denounced Howe as a "sociological quack"), vigorously resisted increased funding for Title I, which would only produce "wasted funds [and] inadequately planned expenditures" because the nation lacked the trained manpower to absorb Title I, which in turn had led to the stockpiling of electronic apparatus bought with federal funds rather than to direct service to disadvantaged pupils by new trained personnel.[27]

To speak of 1966, then, in terms of emerging "iron triangles" in education is premature, because at this early stage of implementation the aggressive opposition of DHEW and USOE to liberal expansion of funding and programs blunted the tendency toward a logrolling, triangular relationship with the clientele groups and the authorizing subcommittees. But unlike the executive agencies, the latter two groups felt little bound by the administration's constraints. Given a liberal Democratic Congress, an extraordinarily healthy economy through 1965, and both the rhetoric and the achievements of the Great Society thus far, it was no surprise that 1966 should witness a scramble among clientele groups for expansion of benefits.

THE 1966 COALITION FOR INCREASED EDUCATION PROGRAMS

As soon as the president's cautious budget for education began to circulate on the Hill and among the nest of education lobbies on DuPont Circle, a coalition of dissenters began to form, and its complaints, demands, and momentum were regularly reported to the White House during the late winter and early spring of 1966 by Ralph Huitt, who was DHEW's assistant secretary for legislation. On 18 February Huitt described the renewed activities of a spectrum of education associations, ranging from the most unhappy to the merely disgruntled, as follows: the impacted areas superintendents, who were confident that "they have the votes and need make no concessions" on expanding rather than halving impacted aid. The American Vocational Association, which was "disgruntled" because the fiscal year 1967 budget requested the appropriation of only $250.8 million of $319 million authorized; it demanded "its own" work-study program, because the old vocational work-study program was being phased out and absorbed by Labor's Neighborhood Youth Corps. The "well financed and ably led" National Audio-Visual Association, which joined producers of scientific instruments and encyclopedias in attacking the administration's call for appropriations for teaching equipment and college library materials at only half the level of authorizations. The handicapped children's lobby, which enjoyed "the most complete bipartisan support, particularly in the Senate. . . . Because the church state issue doesn't seem to arise in this area, this interest is tooling up to get benefits, including grants to parochial schools for the handicapped, which could scarcely be contemplated by many sponsors for *regular* school programs. The Catholics, naturally, are standing by, enthusiastic, waiting to help. So this may be the year for a big handicapped children's educational aid provision." The American Library Association, which called for a doubling of its recommended appropriations, and which enjoyed the one-two, lower-*and*-higher education punch of its two main constituent associations, the "big and articulate" Association of School Librarians and the "influential" Association of Research Libraries.[28] Huitt reported the special resentment of the higher education community: "They are hurt and resentful at the Administration because they were not consulted last fall about the program. They resent the anonymous 'task forces,' and especially the fact that they do not know how to get their ideas into the task forces. Most of all, they have deep-seated distrust of the Administration because the NDEA loan conversion was sprung on them without warning and without adequate time to try to carry it out." Huitt concluded rather bluntly that "the Administration's failure in this and other attempted changes and reductions has hurt its prestige with this group. . . . We may be approaching a time when we really will need them again."[29] On the somewhat more positive side, Huitt acknowledged with relief that the million-member NEA was busy trying to get ESEA off the ground, but neither could they be expected to help the administration hold the line against budget busting and program proliferation, because their top leadership still rankled over the failure to get classroom construction aid. The best news was that Edgar Fuller's querulous Council of Chief State School Officers, "usually a dissenter from Administration legislative plans, is now most quiescent" (they had their hands full trying to run the new ESEA's Title I and spending Title V's $17 million dollars), and this was generally true of the usually like-minded American Association of School Administrators. But if 1965 had been a year of fulfillment for the old general-interest line organizations of teachers and administrators (no group of equivalent power represented the students), 1966 promised to galvanize the special-interest groups for inclusion and expansion. And in such an unusually predominantly liberal-Democratic congress, it was going to be difficult to spurn pleas to extend aid to children who were handicapped, orphans, delinquents, or living in foster homes, in addition to including the children of Indians and migrant workers, as the president had requested.

At the end of March Huitt sent Cater and Wilson an analysis of the congressional mood and anticipated political response to the administration's education proposals that Halperin had prepared. Its essence was that Congress would forget the old holy wars and concentrate on fattening the administration's inadequate budget.

> On committees handling our legislation there is scarcely a Democratic Member who is interested in "holding the line." Rather, a substantial majority seeks new programs with rather expensive price tags. Some Members, particularly in the Senate, feel that the President's budget for education is totally inadequate in a host of areas. The most prevalent view on the authorizing committees is that the Members should do "what is right" by authorizing substantially more than is in the President's budget. Then, some of these Members would not feel too badly if the appropriations committees did not fully fund these new programs. (Of course, the appropriations committees are not happy about being made the "goats" by failing to appropriate what the majority of the Congress has authorized.)[30]

Specifically, Halperin reported that "not a single member believes we have the votes to pass the cuts [on impacted areas] proposed by the Administration." Given the administration's modest increase for library services and construction, "no key member 'takes them seriously.'" The Council of Chief State School Officers regarded the ESEA Title V budget as a "cut" and was confident of getting $8 million more from Congress. As for Title I, 1966 looked like "the year of the big push" for federal aid for the handicapped, especially in the Senate, where a bipartisan committee looked "probably unanimous"; and in the House Congressman Carey was pushing it as another way for increasing federal aid to Catholic schools. Also, a major fight over the Title I formula was assured, with "Mrs. Green, the Republican leadership, and certain Democrats from poorer States (e.g., Yarborough, Hathaway) talk[ing] about the necessity of 'correcting' the formula before it is extended for 3–4 years and thus becomes 'frozen' into local educational finance." On the other side, urban Democrats and Senator Javits (New York and California being over-represented on the education committees) demanded that funding be based on census estimates of welfare (AFDC) children updated to 1965; the retention of the incentive grants that politically sweetened ESEA in 1965, but that regressively rewarded affluent suburbs; raising the poverty definition from $2,000 to $3,000 in fiscal year 1967, *not* in fiscal year 1968 as the administration requested; and including institutionalized orphans and delinquents.[31]

THE REVOLT OF SENATOR MORSE

Holding the budget line in the House was difficult given the congressional spending mood, but the behavior of the key personalities seemed familiar—at least from the perspective of the White House. Chairman Powell was relatively cooperative when he was not in absentia; Perkins remained a "loyal soldier"; Mrs. Green was "deviously stirring the discontent of the Southerners."[32] In late July Powell's committee voted the education bill out by a twenty-to-nothing vote (with two abstentions) that doubled the administration's requested authorization for aid to impacted areas and added $128 million in new authorization to Title I, mainly to facilitate a compromise over the distribution formula by providing more money for both poor southern states and northern urban areas. But Cater told Johnson that it was "a surprisingly responsible result 'considering the Morse subcommittee's behavior' in the Senate." He went on to note that

> our real trouble is in the Senate Committee. Senator Morse made it clear at the opening of the hearings that he would accept Administration arguments on the educational merits of various amendments, but not on budgetary grounds. His staff man, Charlie Lee, has been blissfully compiling one expensive amend-

ment after another for the subcommittee's consideration. They have already knocked out your cutback on impacted areas and have indeed added a few extensions. . . .

There is no reasoning with Morse. I have talked with Senator Hill and urged his assistance in holding the line. So far, he has failed to attend the subcommittee sessions.

I would recommend that you call Hill to the White House for a visit, remind him of his responsibilities as the committee chairman, and urge that he produce a bill you will not have to veto. (Lee talks about the bill as being "veto proof.")[33]

Henry Hall Wilson wrote the president that "Senator Morse's attitude appears to be [that] budgetary considerations are meaningless and that you should save money by cutting down spending in Vietnam,"[34] and Wilson appended a recommendation from budget director Schultze recommending a veto threat in response to "the anarchy of Senator Morse's subcommittee," which would add $1.5 billion to the budget, an amount Cater called "preposterous."[35] When on 15 July the Morse committee reported out just such a bill, Cater advised Johnson of the particulars of the case in a memo entitled "Talking Points with Senator Hill." Hill had been summoned to meet with the president the following day. His angry language was highly unusual for the normally restrained Cater:

1. Wayne Morse has declared war on his President and is trying to use education legislation as his weapon. Two days ago in the higher education hearing he announced to the witnesses that he was going "to place the responsibility for the Vietnam war where it belongs—on the doorstep of the White House." . . . Morse has badgered witnesses, not only from HEW but from the American Council on Education who sought to support the Administration's proposals.

2. Yesterday, Morse reported out of subcommittee the Elementary and Secondary Education Act containing more than twice the amount the Administration requested. This was despite the fact that Secretary Gardner called on him and presented a strong supporting letter arguing against the proposed increases.

3. Your education advisors tell you this will lead to waste and ultimately to scandal in the education program. Your economic

advisors tell you that to ignore this will contribute to inflation. You are being strongly urged to veto such a bill if it comes out of Congress.

4. To veto an education bill would be like killing one of your own children. It will not help you and it will not help members of Congress who are standing for re-election this fall.[36]

The upshot of the late summer and early fall maneuvering was that the president was able to exert enough pressure through his personal and partisan influence over the congressional leadership, including its committee chairmen, to extract a compromise that greatly stretched his budget and considerably modified his legislative program but gave him enough to permit a 3 November signing of eight Great Society bills authorizing nearly $15 billion for new and expanded programs in education, urban renewal, antipollution, health care, and consumer protection—just five days before the crucial off-year elections of 1966.[37]

In elementary and secondary education (H.R. 13161 became P.L. 89–750), the administration was successful in holding off until fiscal year 1968 its proposed increase of Title I's family poverty floor from $2,000 to $3,000 annually, which would require funds for an additional 300,000 children. When Congress insisted on allowing states to use the national rather than their state averages in per-pupil expenditure as a basis for Title I grants (thereby benefiting the poorer states by an estimated $343 million), the administration was able to postpone its implementation until fiscal year 1968 also. The administration also was successful in repealing ESEA's original incentive grant program and in including the children of Indians and migratory workers. On the other hand, Congress ignored Johnson's plea for cutback and reform of aid to impacted areas; added a new title for handicapped children; included orphans and neglected, delinquent, and children in foster homes; and generally boomed the budget to $6.1 billion for two years. (Johnson had asked for a four-year authorization but wanted only $4.4 billion for the first two years.)

In higher education, less was at stake, but Johnson got most of what he requested *except* for phasing out the NDEA's existing direct-student-loan program in favor of the HEA's formula for federally subsidized and guaranteed private loans, with most of their cost appearing off-budget. H.R. 14644 (P.L. 89–752) authorized $3.6 billion over three years, and the International Education Act (H.R. 14643 - P.L. 89–698) was passed with an authorization of $131 million, none of which was ever appropriated.[38] Overall, the first session of the Eighty-ninth Congress had been a triumph, and the second had certainly avoided disaster. On 8 November the voters would render their quadrennial, off-year judgment on the first half of the incumbent administration's term.

THE QUIET SEA CHANGE OF 1966

The fall elections of 1966 occurred against a backdrop of budding disaffection with war and inflation and urban riots that was dimly perceived at the time, but that looms large in hindsight. The ghetto riots of 1966 more closely approximated the widespread and sporadic pattern of 1964 than the megariot of Watts in 1965 (or of Detroit in 1967). But in the summer of 1965 a fateful decision had been made, and its consequences were becoming clearer by the fall of 1966. On 7 June 1965, General Westmoreland requested that his American troop strength in Vietnam be increased from 75,000 to 175,000. On 28 July, President Johnson announced his decision to grant the increase *and* to provide additional forces as required by the field commander. In *Planning a Tragedy*, Larry Berman concluded that Johnson took that fateful step because he believed "that losing Vietnam in the summer of 1965 would wreck his plans for a truly Great Society. In doing so, he apparently gave very little attention to where he would be six months or one year down the road. . . . Thus did Lyndon Johnson commit slow political suicide."[39] But sixteen months down the road, the United States was fighting a ground war in Asia with a draftee army in an age of television and a period of surging inflation and domestic race riots. Even Republicans who patriotically supported the president's war effort, as most of them did, nevertheless stood to benefit from the same kind of growing public disaffection that had turned on the Truman administration in the Korean War.

In elegant testimony to the staying power of the equilibrium tendency in American politics, the Grand Old Party, which was feared near death after the crash with Goldwater in 1964, came roaring back in the fall of 1966 to recapture forty-seven seats in the House, three in the Senate, and also eight governor's chairs (which gave them an even twenty-five/twenty-five statehouse split, and their twenty-five states contained a majority of the nation's population, especially with Rockefeller still in

New York State and the new governor Ronald Reagan in California). Democrats still could claim a substantial lead in the Senate (64 to 36) and in the House (248 to 187), but the Republican resurgence clearly spelled trouble for the Ninetieth Congress and the presidential election of 1968. Midterm losses by incumbent administrations are of course standard fare, and by late 1966 the Republicans enjoyed numerous comeback advantages: the Vietnam War and Johnson's falling popularity and "credibility gap," rising inflation, surging ghetto riots and crime, plus lots of Republican money ($1.6 million to the Democrats' $250,000 spent at the national party level) and fresh new candidates who were not cast in the Goldwater mold.

Such results would seem to suggest for 1967 and the Ninetieth Congress a continuation and even intensification of the 1966 mood of prudent caution. By the end of 1966 there were 389,000 United States troops in Vietnam, and the accompanying surge of Great Society/Vietnam inflation was widely recognized and deplored. Would President Johnson accordingly consolidate his formidable achievements in building the Great Society in order to concentrate resources on turning back communist aggression in Vietnam? No. There is a hint about the future of Great Society programming in the disappearance at midchapter of Joseph Califano, who was replaced in the frenetic world of White House and agency memo traffic by the likes of Cater, Wilson, Schultze, Cohen, Huitt, and Halperin; and this is because we shifted from planning programs to passing bills. Now we shall shift back to legislative agenda formulation for the new and problematic Ninetieth Congress, and to Califano's burgeoning White House staff, which was to approximate the NSC as a kind of domestic council and was to engage in brainstorming campus visits and task force formation that would dwarf the celebrated efforts of Moyers and his colleagues in 1964.

6 / FORGING THE CALIFANO SYSTEM 1966–1967

When Joe Califano joined the White House staff in July of 1965, he was charged by the president not only with the broad duties that attended the replacement of Bill Moyers, but also with the specific tasks of orchestrating the combination of major parts of thirty-five autonomous or semiautonomous federal agencies into a coherent Department of Transportation, and of putting together the Model Cities program. This appealed to Califano's preference for a planner's "total approach" to problem solving, much as did the PPBS system of cost-benefit analysis that he had imported from the Pentagon. The administration's legislative success with both DOT and Model Cities was testimony to Califano's extraordinary skill and drive.[1] Similarly, his disdain for the normal modes of central-clearance program formulation led him to embrace and elaborate upon the task force device he had inherited.[2] But to do this he needed to build a tightly knit domestic staff similar to the National Security Council (and to Nixon's subsequent and formally designated Domestic Council). Califano's closest assistant was his Harvard Law School classmate, deputy special counsel Lawrence E. Levinson, whose role as Califano's alter ego was similar to Feldman's relationship to Sorensen. Joining Califano in 1966 was James Gaither, who had led his law class at Stanford and had clerked for Chief Justice Warren, and who was to become Califano's chief liaison with the task forces.[3] By 1967 Califano had added Fred Bohen, a political scientist who came to the White House by way of Princeton's Woodrow Wilson School (Califano recruited Bohen from the Heineman task force, where he was executive director); and Matthew Nimetz, who had led his law class at Harvard, studied at Oxford University, and clerked for Justice Harlan. Their average age in 1967 was thirty-two.

Two men who did not report to Califano were to function closely with him and his staff of Young Turks in formulating educational policy, although for quite different reasons. One was the veteran Douglass Cater, who would retain his oversight of health and education policy in a vaguely defined relationship with Califano, who nevertheless remained *primus inter pares* on the domestic White House staff and who admitted to Hawkinson that he had "moved in on Cater." The other senior aide was Harry McPherson, who early in 1966 had replaced Lee White as special counsel to the president. McPherson was a native of Tyler, Texas. In 1965 he was thirty-five. He had graduated from the University of the South (Sewanee), studied at Columbia University, and after service in the air force, he had earned a law degree from the University of Texas. He had worked with Lyndon Johnson as counsel to the Democratic policy committee of the Senate from 1956 to 1963, and he was widely regarded as one of the most cultured, learned, and reflective members of the White House staff. In this capacity he had inherited the departed Moyers's mantle as resident Texan brainy humanitarian.

McPherson's recollection of his move from a senior State Department post to the White House staff is revealing. He had earlier declined a Moyers offer to become Lee White's deputy: "I was looking out for myself, very specifically, as a matter of my place on the greasy pole. Coming from Assistant Secretary of State, a position that required Senate confirmation, over to be a deputy to somebody on the White House staff didn't strike me as the right thing to do for an upward mobile youth." So Moyers offered him a trial-on-loan arrangement looking toward appointment as special assistant, "which would give me the clout that I felt I needed." So I said, "Okay, I'd like to come." He recalls:

> I remember Bill looked at me for a long time and said,
> "Really?" He couldn't quite believe it, because even though he
> was enjoying power, he also was suffering from it and from his
> proximity to the President. Both of us know the President very
> well, and we knew his problems. I think what Moyers was re-
> flecting was his own sense of loss of personal freedom here in the
> White House. While he was already a person of very great conse-

quence in the Administration and had the power of the White House under the Presidency behind him when he spoke, he maintained a genuine sense of loss, I think, throughout his time here that he was not back in the Peace Corps or in some other organization in which he had freedom to run the thing as he chose—freedom from the white telephone of President Johnson. And he knew that I had that freedom in the State Department and was a little incredulous that I would want to give it up. But I'm afraid, to be entirely candid, that I was very much like Moyers.[4]

Unlike Cater, McPherson's policy concerns were as wide ranging as the presidency, and hence he normally would have had relatively little connection with the development of education policy. But in 1966 the Vietnam War was heating up, and Johnson's popularity was falling, especially on the university campuses that had been the mainstays of the 1964–65 task forces. If task forcing was to be greatly expanded, then so would university contacts, and McPherson, like Moyers before him, would be a visible reminder that Texas Democrats in high administrative positions could still speak with the voice of urbane liberalism, corn pone accents notwithstanding.

THE CAMPUS VISITS OF 1966

In early May of 1966, Johnson received a confidential memo from Robert E. Kintner, a friend of the president who had joined the White House staff in March, ostensibly as secretary of the cabinet. Both as a former Washington columnist and later president of both ABC and NBC, Kintner's main task was to cultivate contacts in the news media and to improve Johnson's image.[5] Kintner said that he had been wracking his brains as to how an academic atmosphere could be created around the president, so he proposed monthly White House dinner meetings "to discuss ideas and to get reactions from academic circles." Invited would be either the presidents of two colleges covering six regions of the country, or "a very bright professor in his late 30's" selected by the college presidents.

There is a potential for good ideas coming from such a group, but more importantly, I think, a potential for creating an affirmative public impression. To some degree, it resembles the New Deal Brain Trust that Roosevelt used very informally, to wit: Frankfurter, Corcoran, Cohen, Hopkins, Moley.

Perhaps I am reaching too much, but I hear on all sides that the "intellectual community" and "youth" are areas of the public influence where some affirmative, remedial action should be taken by you.[6]

Johnson checked the "yes" box and scribbled, "I like this."

Kintner had conceded at the outset that "this may sound like a very wild idea," and Walt Rostow, who had been sent a copy, thought that indeed it was. On 11 May he wrote Johnson that "the problem with the college presidents is that discussions will tend to be diffuse, unprepared, and unconnected with actions you are undertaking." Rostow recommended instead that the outside task forces, whose members were carefully screened and whose deliberations were focused, be brought in to discuss their reports.[7] But because this was often done anyway, there were so few outside task forces scheduled that summer, and in any event such discussions reached out only minimally to the campuses, Johnson decided instead to send the three-man team of Califano, Cater, and McPherson to visit five regional campuses for academic dinners and discussions in June and early July to test the political waters.

The academic trips began early in June with a Columbia University-centered trip that included historian William Leuchtenburg, who had published an approving article on the original Johnson task forces in the *Reporter* the previous April. The New York group also included officials from the Ford Foundation, IBM, and *Scientific American*. Next came a Cambridge trip that combined eleven professors from Harvard University, three from the Massachusetts Institute of Technology, and Wesleyan University's Daniel Patrick Moynihan. (Harvard's contingent included Don Price, James Q. Wilson, Thomas Pettigrew, Otto Eckstein, and Dean Theodore Sizer of the Graduate School of Education; MIT's included economists Paul Samuelson and Robert Solow, and political scientist Myron Weiner.) The White House trio visited with twelve University of Texas professors in Austin in mid-June, then on to Los Angeles to combine nine academicians from the University of California at Los Angeles and the University of California at Berkeley, five from Stanford University, and four from California Institute of Technology. The last visit, to

Chicago, came on 12 July, where University of Chicago provost Edward Levi was joined by fourteen campus colleagues, plus small professorial delegations from the University of Illinois, the University of Michigan, the University of Minnesota, Northwestern University, the University of Notre Dame, and the University of Wisconsin.

On all five visits the three senior White House staffers asked three questions: (1) Where does the Great Society go from here? (2) What are the needs still left unmet? and (3) What are the new problems we create by our solutions to old problems? On 9 August Califano reported to the president that over the summer his group had seen a total of eighty-one professors and experts from sixteen universities, plus some representatives from major foundations and firms; and that his staff, under the direction of the newcomer James Gaither, had compiled an "idea book" three inches thick, from which they would cull the best for Johnson's night reading the following day.[8] Califano attached a list of the attendees and their institutional affiliations, and four sample "Dear Joe" letters. These averaged four single-spaced typed pages and were written in response to Califano's follow-up thank-you letters, which had invited further comments and suggestions. Because the campus visits were repeated in 1967 on a more systematic and planned basis, I shall analyze their apparent relationship to the mature Califano system of program formulation later, especially regarding two of the campus visits' main purposes: the solicitation of new program ideas, and the maintenance of a sympathetic White House presence on prestigious campuses during a period of rising campus unrest. The third purpose of the academic dinners, recruiting talent, is somewhat easier to trace, especially in relationship to the large new battalion of outside task forces that Califano was simultaneously recruiting.

THE CALIFANO TASK FORCE OPERATION OF 1966

Compared to the previous year's four outside task forces that had been established by Moyers, in 1966 Califano launched eleven.[9] Califano met for two four-hour sessions in his office with Schultze and his deputy, Phillip (Sam) Hughes, Cater, McPherson, and Gaither to eliminate unpromising ideas and to construct a list of new task forces (by topic, not by membership) for presidential approval. Gaither recalls that Johnson's approval was almost always granted, although Johnson often objected to specific members, especially when he complained about regional (that is, Ivy League) imbalance. Six of the eleven outside task forces of 1966 were six-month efforts designed to deal with fairly specific problem areas, such as American Indians, campaign finance, career development, emergency labor disputes, intergovernmental personnel, nursing homes and the elderly. Their reporting dates were in December of 1966, but the remaining five involved broad policy areas and were asked to report the following year, most of them a full year later, in the midsummer of 1967. On the eleven outside task forces of 1966 sat 112 members (again exclusive of the executive secretaries and White House liaisons), 51 of whom were university based. A dozen of the latter were drawn from the academic dinners (and doubtless many more were recruited through that network), and these were highly concentrated on the five broad-policy task forces. One of these was discussed before: Ben Heineman's task force on government reorganization. On it sat Dean Bayless Manning of the Stanford University Law School and Chancellor Harry Ransom of the University of Texas, men who had dined with Califano on the California and Texas trips. Paul Ylvisaker of the Ford Foundation chaired the major task force on cities, where he was joined by fellow academic dinner veterans Julian Levi, the task force vice chairman from the University of Chicago, and economist John Dunlop and education dean Theodore Sizer from Harvard University. Joseph Hunt's important task force on child development contained, surprisingly, no veterans from the academic dinners, but George Schultz's task force on urban employment opportunities involved Texas law professor Jerre Williams. Finally, William Friday's high-powered task force on education—the only successor to the Gardner outside task force—included Levi of Chicago and Pettigrew of Harvard.

But the legislative and policy recommendations of these groups could not be considered until a year hence, when they would be fed in midsummer 1967 to short-term interagency task forces for winnowing and costing out, looking toward the president's ultimate pre-Christmas decisions down at the ranch, and then the State of the Union and Budget messages in January 1968. Meanwhile, the president and his domestic staff faced the likely prospect of a more Republican and hostile Congress in January of 1967, and toward this end Califano appointed an unprecedented thirty-four interagency task forces (compared to thirteen the previous year). Most of these once again linked a cabinet or subcabinet agency head to a policy area that obviously fell under his or her jurisdiction, for example, Katzenbach and Clark on civil rights, Weaver on housing and urban development, Schultze on economic growth, Macy on government personnel, and Esther Peterson on consumer protection. Some were highly specialized, such as Lee White's on pipeline safety, Willard Wirtz's on wage garnishment, Orville Freeman's on meat inspection, Ramsey Clark's on compensation for real property. The chief virtue of all of them was the forcing of interagency dialogue, if not necessarily cooperation, and the setting of deadlines for the legislative program and budget cycle. No agency head got more heavily assigned by Califano than John Gardner, who not only drew health (which he shared with Phillip Lee), education (which he bucked down to Commissioner Howe), and older Americans (which he passed along to Wilbur Cohen), but also, and rather oddly, accident prevention.

Reporting on the last day of October, the Gardner interagency task force on education of 1966 was of little consequence, and its final report was a rather formless jumble. As Cannon reported to the budget director, it nibbled at the margins to the modest tune of perhaps $125 million in new obligational authority (NOA), and administratively sought to tidy up loose ends, consistent with the generalized mood that 1966 was a year of consolidation, and 1967 was a year of unknowns with a new Congress.[10] But Cannon's director, Charles Schultze, was growing alarmed in the fall of 1966 about the way rising inflation and the cost of the Vietnam War were whipsawing the administration, and he wrote the president to warn about one budget problem that stood out above all others:

> That problem is simply that *we are not able to fund adequately the new Great Society programs.* At the same time, States, cities, depressed areas and individuals have been led to expect immediate delivery of benefits from Great Society programs to a degree that is not realistic. This leads to *frustration, loss of credibility, and even deterioration* of State and local services as they hang back on making normal commitments in order to apply for Federal aid which does not materialize. *Backlog, queuing,* and *griping* build up steadily.[11]

Schultze was especially concerned because Califano's burgeoning staff had cranked up the task force machinery to a fever pitch, thereby generating a profusion of new legislative proposals that would attract congressional and clientele support in a period of increasing fiscal deterioration that was certain to underfund even the existing Great Society programs.

> [W]e are now in the process of developing a wide range of *new legislative proposals*. . . . Adequate funding will be a very tough problem *even if there are no new programs*. . . . In the present budget situation I see very little hope of any *significant* expenditure buildup on *existing* Great Society programs. . . . As I see it, the situation will get *worse instead of better* unless we decide to *digest what we already have on our plate* before reaching for more. We should be *extremely selective* in adopting *new* Task Force recommendations.[12]

On the following day the midterm elections with their Republican boost in the House added their bellwether burden to the administration's more cautious mood.

THE TASK FORCES VERSUS THE BUDGET

One final element of confusion surfaced late and unexpectedly that fall as the administration looked toward placing before the uncertain Ninetieth Congress its 1967 legislative proposals for fiscal year 1968. During that hectic December, when the disparate proposals from approximately forty task forces were being culled, pruned, blended, winnowed out, and forged into some theoretically coherent and affordable legislative package for the president's use in January's State of the Union, Economic, and Budget (and subsequent special legislative) messages, it was discovered that the new legislative program and the budget didn't mesh. As Gaither candidly admitted, "One of the most serious problems was that we had not paid much attention to the budget in the development of the legislative program for 1967. And while we had everything priced out and showed all the dollar figures on the outline and in the presentation to the President, we never really checked to make sure that all those dollars were in the budget." The result was that they weren't, not by a long shot. "So in January we found out that we had a beautiful legislative program and no money in the budget, and the budget had already been printed.

So [on 4 or 5 January] we had a wild six or eight hour meeting with Califano and Schultze and me to try to put some money into the budget for
the key elements of the President's program in 1967."[13]

The Bureau of the Budget's administrative history assesses the problem in drier official prose, but without fundamental disagreement.

> The program proposals and the budget add-ons being generated
> by the task force reports involved large resources, often totaling
> many billions for the first year and with occasional individual pro-
> posals on a multi-billion dollar scale.

> Task forces were generating new ideas and program proposals
> *without any guidance with respect to fiscal resource constraints*
> *while such constraints were a large element in regular budget*
> *planning, particularly under the tight budget guidelines necessi-*
> *tated by the growing costs of the Vietnam conflict.* Moreover, no
> specific arrangement existed for obtaining the judgment of a task
> force on the relative priority of its various proposals.

> As task force efforts broadened it became clear that there was a
> substantial overlap between task force proposals and those being
> considered in the regular budget process. The task force reports
> often included recommendations for expansion of existing pro-
> grams and these proposals were frequently at a variance with
> those that were submitted to the Bureau through regular chan-
> nels. Proposals were being made to the White House that an
> agency could not accommodate in its budget requests.

> The *ad hoc* costing of task forces and legislative proposals was
> not being carried on in a uniform basis and frequently with no pro-
> visions for exploring costs several years ahead. This left a sub-
> stantial gap in data necessary for decision making on national
> programs.[14]

This meant a frenetically scrambled beginning for the first session of the
Ninetieth Congress, but in the longer run, and especially in light of
Schultze's ominous warning that the administration was starving the old
Great Society programs while developing new ones, it boded ill for the
crucial working relationship between the Bureau of the Budget and the
White House.

In 1967 Schultze and Califano worked hard to establish a more systematic feedback relationship between the BOB, the agencies, and the increasingly White House-centered planning operation for the legislative program. But part of this very process was the enlargement of Califano's program staff in the spring of 1967 through the addition of Fred Bohen, to specialize in housing and urban development, and Matthew Nimetz, who covered crime and conservation. This left Gaither, whose skills had been spread far too thin, coordinating more than forty task forces in 1966, to concentrate on manpower, health, education, and poverty. But the increased staff allowed Califano's team to launch thirty-five new task forces in 1967 (eleven outside and twenty-four interagency) while processing the five outside reports that were due that year. This meant that an energetic and increasingly efficient engine had been created to pass new laws and create new programs, and then to propose even newer ones and spend and commit the new funds that this inevitably required, all of this while the fiscal and budgetary pressures generated by inflation and war were pressing ever harder in the opposite direction. Caught in the middle was the Bureau of the Budget, and Schultze was moved to confront an unwilling president with this worsening dilemma as early as the fall of 1966. But the severity and danger of the coming crunch were not yet generally recognized. Most attention was turned more immediately to the Great Society's prospects with the new Ninetieth Congress.

THE HUNT TASK FORCE ON CHILD DEVELOPMENT

The increasing tension between task force brainstorming toward new Great Society programs on the one hand, and the tightening constraints of war, inflation, ghetto riots, and partisan political arithmetic on the other hand, is nicely illustrated by the brief but lively career of the outside task force on child development of 1966–67. Its origin lay in the 1966 campus visits of Califano's academic dinner circuit, as recalled by Jim Gaither.

When Califano and I and other members of the White House staff traveled around the country talking to academics in the early summer of '66, everybody kept saying, "One of the problems which you're missing is child development." By the time kids get into Head Start at age five or six, as they were then doing, it was too late. They were saying that a child's ultimate capacity was fifty percent developed by the time he was five or six; and by the time he was eight, it was eighty percent established; and that the most rapid point of growth was before, really between two and four, and some were suggesting that it was sooner. And they pointed to an awful lot of the federal efforts where indeed what we were doing was coming in at a late stage and trying to compensate for the handicaps which these disadvantaged children had already developed. So that basically was the question we asked this outside group. What are the critical phases of a child's development and what can we do about it? What should the federal role be? [15]

Califano urged the task force on Cater, who in turn discussed it with Wilbur Cohen within the context of a current series of articles on national day care needs in the *Ladies Home Journal*. Cohen in turn discussed it with Cannon, and they suggested an interagency task force with Cater as chairman, joined by representatives from BOB (Cannon), DHEW (Lisle Carter), OEO (Jules Sugarman), and CEA (Ben Okner).[16] But Califano, fresh from his academic tours, wanted to tap the universities, so he formed an outside task force, one that was parallel to the Friday task force on education, but that focused its attention exclusively on children, roughly from their prenatal phase through kindergarten. Appointed to head the task force was psychologist Joseph McV. Hunt of the University of Illinois, and joining him on the distinguished sixteen-member group were such academic notables as Jerome Bruner of Harvard University, Nicholas Hobbs of Stanford University, Urie Bronfenbrenner of Cornell University, and Oscar Lewis of the University of Illinois.[17]

Like the Friday task force and indeed most outside task forces, the Hunt group was originally given a year to report. But according to Gaither, "Then the President said, no, he thought this was too important; that they ought to get their recommendations in and have a program ready for 1967." The academics, however, were accustomed to unhurried, scholarly deliberation, especially on such important matters, and they stoutly resisted the new forced-march timetable—to Gaither's considerable dismay: "They rebelled and at one point were on the verge of resigning. They basically said, "We can never get any consensus by mid-December; we don't know enough facts; we may know a little about helping really disadvantaged children, but we don't know, once you pass a certain stage, what you can really do that can help semi-disadvantaged children or well-to-do children—just too many questions." But John Gardner came to the rescue, according to Gaither.

> Well, when they threw up their hands I guess probably around the first of November after they'd been at work for roughly a month and had had two or three meetings, John Gardner happened to come to the meeting where they threw up their hands. And it was very interesting to see John get up, having had the experience of running a task force in '64 as well as some experience as the Secretary of HEW, stand up before this group and in effect lecture and challenge them.

Gaither recalls Gardner's reprimand in paraphrase:

> "Basically there isn't a man in this room who hasn't spent at least fifteen years in this field, and there isn't anyone in this room who hasn't for most of that time written or lectured and told the American people all of the problems that they saw in this field; what a terrible job that we were doing in terms of meeting the needs of disadvantaged children and the importance of early childhood education and development; and then when the President asks you for a recommendation, you throw up your hands and say, Oh, I don't know what the answer is . . . the President and this country doesn't have to be one hundred percent sure in a field as complicated as child development; you never will be one hundred percent sure that the solution you're recommending is the right one, but when you're seventy-five percent sure and you know that there are virtually no risks attached to that proposal, then you ought to recommend that it be done." [18]

So they did. By the end of November their basic recommendations were crystalized, and Hunt submitted their formal report on 14 January.

Entitled "A Bill of Rights for Children," the Hunt Report was a bold, cohesive, and moving treatise on the massive and tragic waste of human potential that flowed from disastrous child-rearing patterns in poverty, especially among urban "Negroes." It included a nice historical section, observing with appropriate irony that almost immediately after the establishment of the Children's Bureau in 1912, which was sponsored by Republican senator William E. Borah and signed into law by Republican president Taft, the old progressive era solicitude for child welfare began to fade. The opposing forces included social Darwinism and genetic determinism, as transmitted into America's nascent social science by Francis Galton and G. Stanley Hall. Modern biological and social science had learned that the early environment was crucial in snow mosquitoes and salamanders and geese and mammals alike, but it became ever more crucial as one ascended the phylogenetic scale. Clearly slum rearing guaranteed severely stunted potential in its wasted and dangerous children. Head Start was splendid (although it was disturbingly devoid of successful male role models), but it began far too late (the years of maximum atrophy were from two to four) and was too short-lived.[19]

A FEDERAL OMBUDSMAN FOR CHILDREN?

The Hunt report generated enormous excitement in the White House, moreso even than the famous Gardner report; and its substantive recommendations, which centered on earlier intervention and Head Start follow-through, were greeted with enthusiasm.[20] But its chief procedural and symbolic recommendations were politically explosive. The report dryly observed that "children do not vote" and bitterly commented that whereas in 1967 federal benefits and services for the 19 million people over sixty-five who were very good at voting would total $25.7 billion, averaging $1,350 per person, for the 24 million children under six, the total was only $2 billion, or $85 per child (equivalent federal health expenditures were $234 per elderly person against "a paltry $8 a child"). Worse, the weak existing federal efforts were confusingly and often contradictorily fragmented in the customary bureaucratic fashion.[21]

But the report's leading structural recommendation sounded starkly Orwellian, especially with a more Republican Ninetieth Congress leading toward a presidential election in 1968: establish a Federal Office for Children in the DHEW, administered by an officer for children equivalent in rank to the chief officers for health, education, and welfare, to act as the federal "ombudsman" for children. New federal grants would fund at the city or county level community commissions for children, which in turn would organize neighborhood centers for children and parents. The neighborhood centers would be permanent and funded by federal grants from the commissions. They would provide a single-stop, integrated array of services: economic, family planning, medical, and social, including day care and preschool facilities, counseling for parents, and educational entertainment. The task force suggested that they might also experiment with such income maintenance proposals as "children's allowances and paying mothers for 'services' as mothers" so they would not have to work, and they should provide information and devices for family planning. The centers might best begin on a moderate pilot scale of perhaps 100. "Yet, in the end," the report concluded, "the financial commitment must be massive. . . . If we choose now not to mount the effort and meet the cost, we shall eventually pay a far higher price in human misery, and even a higher price in economic cost and loss. Nor can we refuse to mount the effort if we are true to our heritage, for we are confronted not merely with the needs of America's children, but with their inalienable rights.[22]

Hunt's group of professors was comfortable with the federal presence and leadership, but to the politically sensitive White House staff the recommendations conjured up visions of a federal commissar for children and predictable conservative and Republican alarums, especially in light of growing political problems with federally funded community action groups attacking city hall in the antipoverty war. Besides, the Heineman task force was considering structural change. Best of all, the formidable array of education and antipoverty laws passed since 1963 provided broad discretionary authority for most of the major Hunt substantive recommendations without new legislation. In this instance, sentiment within USOE strongly reinforced the White House reservations. Nolan Estes responded to a December draft of the Hunt report by praising it as "imaginative" and agreeing that its substantive recommendations were "badly needed." But he attacked the failure to spell out the administrative machinery of the governing bodies, the commissions and especially the neighborhood centers, which sounded to him like "a combination of the interagency coordinating committee approach and the CAP [Community Action Program] election of representatives-of-the poor approach—in short, an administrative monstrosity." As deputy associate commissioner for elementary and secondary education, Estes was "bothered by the scant mention of States involvement" and complained that "the schools are given short shrift in the Task Force report. . . . I think the failure to give the schools adequate mention reflects the perennial problem of trying, on the one hand, to strengthen the role of the school in the community, and on the other, bypassing it because it won't perform in the specific manner desired. This impatience is natural but, really, we ought to give the schools a chance!"[23]

William Cannon reported for the Bureau of the Budget to Gaither that DHEW opposed giving a federal children's office "a status equivalent to USOE or PHS, or locating—in any permanent way—an operating office at the Secretary's level." DHEW welcomed the proposal to transfer Head Start to DHEW from the Office for Equal Opportunity, but OEO was "ambivalent" through "fear that Head Start would turn into an uninspired State-administered program," and BOB agreed. Both DHEW and OEO favored a major follow-through program, but Cannon urged strongly for the BOB, in response to the Hunt report's major structural recommendations: "that we limit our approach to a pilot-demonstration attack, that we get as much mileage out of existing programs as possible, and that we keep any new legislation in narrow bounds."[24] So the Hunt ombudsman for children was quietly buried, together with the massive federal commitment to create commissions and centers to offer one-stop comprehensive nurturance to the children of the poor.

But President Johnson did propose, in his State of the Union Message of 26 January, to launch a major Follow-Through program as a supplement to an expanded Head Start, and on 8 February in his "Special Message on Children and Youth," he attacked the ravages of poverty on children in language that strikingly mirrored the indictment of the Hunt report. The Hunt task force's pivotal role in DHEW's subsequent comprehensive expansion of the preschool nurturance of the children of the poor remains a proud and honorable legacy. But Johnson's Budget Message of 24 January revealed his basic strategy in education for the Ninetieth Congress, which was generally to avoid seeking new legislation and to wring the maximum mileage out of the broad authority granted by the Eighty-ninth Congress, especially the ESEA and HEA of 1965. "Our task now," Johnson concluded, "is to use this authority in an imaginative, creative, and responsible way."[25]

LEGISLATIVE STRATEGY IN THE NINETIETH CONGRESS

The administration's cautious strategy for education in 1967 was most pronounced in higher education, although numerous hearings were held and preliminary votes were taken (the Education Professions Development Act is not here defined as major; see note 7). Most controversy centered on Senator Ribicoff's perennial call for tuition tax credits, which promised to attract stronger support in 1967 because the rise in both inflation and college enrollments was coinciding with rising interest rates. This in turn discouraged the banks' participation in the low-interest guaranteed student loan program that had been created in 1965. But Ribicoff's call for tuition tax credits was also strengthened because so many Democratic senators faced reelection campaigns in 1968, which represented for the administration an ironic penalty for the lopsided Democratic dominance of the Senate. President Johnson attempted to deflect this pressure by appointing a cabinet-level committee to study the tuition problem, but on 14 April the Ribicoff proposal, which had failed the year before on a Senate roll-call vote of thirty-seven to forty-seven, carried by a solid vote of fifty-three to twenty-six. The margin of reversal was provided by northern Democrats, who switched from a eleven-to-twenty-six opposition in 1966 to a twenty-two-to-twelve margin of support in 1967.[26] Administration forces were able to bottle up the Ribicoff amendment, chiefly by pressing the fiscally more conservative Senate Finance and House Ways and Means committees to oppose it as Treasury busting, but it signaled an unavoidable battle for 1968, when authorization for most existing higher education programs would expire.[27]

But on elementary and secondary education, the president's Budget Message of 24 January revealed that he would request appropriations of only $1.2 billion for aid to disadvantaged children, which was only half of the $2.3 billion authorized by the outgoing Eighty-ninth Congress. This prompted Charles Lee, Morse's chief education staffer, to call USOE and complain loudly that the administration had not been educationally honest in its earlier authorization requests, which it now proposed to cut by a half, and that its justifications were "not educationally sound but were 'rationalizations' to justify budget cuts because of defense commitments."[28] On 28 February Johnson presented Congress with a modest educational package that included state and local planning and evaluation grants; aid extension for adults, the handicapped, vocational-training and career counseling; expansion of the National Foundation for the Arts and Humanities; and, finally, a request for an expanded National Teacher Corps and for earlier appropriations to enable realistic school planning. The first several items represented routine adjustments, but behind the latter two lay crucial political considerations.[29]

First, Teacher Corps authorization was to expire on 30 June, and without timely reauthorization and funding it would die—to the delight of most Hill Republicans. But the Teacher Corps was a title of the HEA of 1965, and here it was proposed as a new Part B of Title I of the Elementary and Secondary Amendments of 1967, which meant that it would expire as part of HEA and be reenacted in the amended ESEA. Administration spokesmen explained that the NTC volunteers taught almost exclusively at the lower level, and that hence such a packaging was more logical. This was true, but it was not the main reason for the switch. The primary strategic concern was the reshuffling of the House Committee on Education and Labor, which was occasioned by congressional refusal to seat former chairman Adam Clayton Powell. This in turn elevated loyalist Carl Perkins to the chairmanship and would leave higher education, including the NTC, under the subcommittee jurisdiction of Edith Green, who had never been sympathetic to the Teacher Corps. As Huitt advised Cater, the switch would leave Perkins, "who intends to chair a subcommittee having jurisdiction over the ESEA . . . to guard the NTC from Mrs. Green's opposition."[30]

Second, behind the question of timing for federal aid programs lay legitimate and widespread complaints from the states and the school districts that annual funding occurred too late for realistic planning or effective use. Testimony before the Perkins committee by DHEW, USOE, and numerous school officials was overwhelmingly in agreement on the need for longer-range funding cycles. The relentless annual rhythm of the school calendar gave schools a powerful argument here, but schools are by no means unique in preferring longer-range funding. Moreover, Congress, and especially the House, has customarily been unsympathetic to such pleas, preferring instead to exercise the power of budget decisions on an annual basis. But Congress also tends to enjoy ducking no-win controversies in an election year. In 1967 an amendment proposed by an amiable and highly regarded moderate Republican, Albert H. Quie, who had been a steady friend of federal aid to education on the House Education and Labor Committee, so fiercely rekindled the still-warm embers of discord over religion and race and federal control that two largely unanticipated results occurred. First, Congress was thrown into a turmoil over fundamental strategies of categorical versus block grants, not only in education, but by implication in every field of Great Society endeavor. Second, after a year of brutal infighting, Congress funded the ESEA amendments through fiscal 1969, which nicely neutralized the volatile issue for the 1968 election year.

THE BATTLE OVER THE QUIE AMENDMENT

In *Education in National Politics*, Norman C. Thomas ably traces the convoluted path of the Johnson administration's education legislation through the mine fields of the Ninetieth Congress. From the perspective of the 1980s and the Reagan administration, or even of the Nixon administration, consolidating the Great Society's proliferation of categorical programs into block grants to the states would appear to represent a typically conservative attempt to dismantle the Great Society. And that is the way the *New York Times* reporter Marjorie Hunter saw it in 1967, as she reported on the brewing storm over the Quie amendment (H.R. 8983), which would shift $3 billion in federal school aid funds to the states in fiscal 1969.

> Deeply concerned, House Democratic leaders are holding almost daily meetings, seeking to map their strategy. For there is far more at stake than the future course of Federal school aid. Administration aides say that President Johnson's entire legislative program will be squarely on the line.
>
> The reasoning is, that if Republicans win this first big legislative fight of the session, in the House, they will have established their ability to call the signals on such other Great Society legislation as antipoverty, model cities and rent supplements for the poor.[31]

But Albert Quie had never been lumped into the GOP's conservative bloc.[32] As ranking minority member on Edith Green's special subcommittee on education, he had long been regarded as a moderate to liberal Minnesota Republican and a staunch advocate of federal aid to education.[33] Quie explained his motives in his oral history.

> I have felt that we are proliferating federal efforts in education—in other places, too—but in education where many of the large school systems had to hire a person just to concern themselves with federal programs, hunt them up and see if they could qualify to receive money under them. You could greatly simplify all of the red tape and give more flexibility to the local schools if we consolidated programs, and we used the term "block grant." When we did, of course, we caused all the special interests in their specific protected program to oppose it because then they'd

have to compete for the money. But I had as a rule of thumb that after a categorical program had been in operation for five years it ought to then be consolidated with other ones and give this greater flexibility.[34]

Because the timing question had generated proposals to fund education programs through 1970, which would be five years after the passage of ESEA, Quie offered his amendment on 20 May. His recollection of the White House reaction is abundantly confirmed by the spring storm of executive branch memorandums: "For some reason or another, it caught fire down in the White House," Quie said. "They thought they were more endangered than I thought they were. You know, there weren't that many Republicans around. Then, the flames of the church-state issue were fanned, and we really got into hot water."[35]

The problem here was primarily that thirty-five state constitutions prohibited public funding of any private school activities, which would mean that the politically crucial ESEA formula for indirect federal aid to parochial schools would be largely short-circuited. So the powerful Roman Catholic lobby attacked the Quie amendment, to the delight of the White House. The concept of block grants to the states with minimal federal strings attached threatened every categorical program in the federal bureaucracy, so the White House and the executive agencies were powerfully united in their highly partisan counterattack. Quie's chief political vulnerability was his need to woo both affluent Republican constituencies, like his own, and conservative southern Democrats from poor states whose main attraction to the block-grant concept was its states' rights promise of avoiding DHEW's desegregation guidelines (although it also appealed to their more conservative political philosophy generally). Cater quickly reported to President Johnson on this partisan vulnerability, ticking off the Quie amendment's multiple flaws:

1. The House committee of jurisdiction had held no hearings on the Quie substitute, which was not supported by the "world of education."
2. Administratively, the amendment would throw American education into chaos.
3. It would launch a new church-state Holy War.
4. The states were not yet ready to handle the job, and ESEA had

been passed in large part because the states had neglected the cities, the educationally deprived, and the handicapped. The beauty of the present ESEA is that *Congress*, not the state departments, *guarantee that certain essential jobs will be done* that were formerly neglected by the states.

5. No school districts would know their entitlement under the Quie bill.

But Cater's most politically telling criticism was that the Quie formula "takes from the poorer States and gives to the wealthier." Cater noted the loss of $359 million that the eleven southern and three border states would incur under the Quie bill, as opposed to how they would fare under the administration-backed committee bill (H.R. 7819) and urged Johnson to use his influence on three key southern Democrats: Wilbur Mills, Phil Landrum, and Olin Teague.[36] On 26 April Secretary Gardner blasted the Quie proposal in a public statement attacking the "disastrous" Quie proposal, which would "strike at the very heart" of the ESEA consensus, and on 27 April President Johnson drove across town to the Washington suburb of Camp Springs, Maryland, to praise the achievements of the Crossland Vocational Center and to attack the Quie substitute for stabbing the ESEA consensus in the back, to the detriment of poor states, poor children, and the cities. Quie's senior minority staff member, Charles Radcliffe, who had originally drafted the Quie bill, joined Quie and Gerald Ford in an exhausting series of negotiating sessions with the contending interests, especially the Catholics, in a vain attempt to shape a compromise that would not fatally violate the block grant principle.[37] But despite the enthusiastic support of Edgar Fuller and the Council of Chief State School Officers, Quie was facing formidable odds. In mid-May the White House imported 150 big-city school superintendents to reinforce urban fears over the Quie amendment, and Johnson mustered not only the partisan artillery of congressmen Perkins, Albert, Brademas, O'Hara, Carey, Gibbons, and Landrum, with all of the attendant implications of Democratic, big-city, Catholic, and southern poor-state support, but also bipartisan support from Republican Congressmen Ogden Reid (N.Y.) and Alphonzo Bell (Calif.). In the ensuing crunch Albert Quie was crushed. But the big winner was not really Lyndon Johnson; it was Edith Green.

THE TRIUMPH OF EDITH GREEN

Although she was an Oregon Democrat and shared the putatively liberal persuasions common to northern and western Democrats, Congresswoman Green maintained an alert liaison with more conservative southern Democrats and with Republicans as well. Oddly, the latter connection was easier than the former on the labor-stacked House Education and Labor Committee, where southerners were rare. As Henry Hall Wilson told the president (who didn't need the explanation),

> As you know, the House Committee itself possesses built-in problems on legislation. For 20 years or more the organized labor has with complete success managed to stack the Democratic side of the Committee so that now only one southerner, Sam Gibbons of Florida, remains among the Democrats. The result of this is that every bill emerging from Committee fails to reflect the general balance of the House and is wide open to challenge on the floor.[38]

Green convinced Perkins that the Quie substitute would fail on a floor vote (it was rejected by a teller vote of 168 to 197 on 24 May) but that the committee's bill might also fail unless her amendments were added. One of them, which called for desegregation guidelines to "be uniformly applied and enforced throughout the 50 states," clearly appealed to the southerners and was adopted by voice vote on 23 May after three hours of confused debate over what its precise legal implications were. Another Green amendment would strip the commissioner of education—the unpopular, desegregation-enforcing Doc Howe—of his 15 percent discretionary set-aside of Title V funds to strengthen state departments of education. This carried by a standing vote of 133 to 104. But Mrs. Green's most significant amendment was to strip the commissioner of all Title III authority and turn the program entirely over to the states. This would mean that USOE's direct grants of $500 million to local school districts to sponsor innovative programs would instead be channeled directly to the states—in effect, into the clutches of Edgar Fuller's hostile Council of Chief State School Officers.

William Cannon, who had fought so hard and so successfully for Title III on the original Gardner task force, was predictably appalled. Secretary Gardner and Commissioner Howe dutifully testified against the amendment, but Cannon knew that Gardner and Howe had earlier sought a compromise to permit a phased-in state participation leading toward state takeover. Howe emphasizes the point in his oral history interview, but his conclusion is the opposite of Cannon's.

> There's an interesting story that hasn't been told. In January of 1967 I proposed to the Secretary, and he and I together proposed over in the White House, that we make a compromise in our new legislation that year, and that we seek state participation in Title III. What we wanted was a system under which the states would phase into a responsibility for growing percentages of these funds over a period of three years or something of that kind. We wanted to keep some federal component of the funds but develop gradually a major state component. I don't know if the President ever got involved in this, but the combination of the White House staff and the Bureau of the Budget said, "No, let's go for Title III as it has been. This will be the President's program."
>
> And so we fought for it up on the Hill and we got licked. I think that if we had been able to go with our compromise program, we would have so spiked their guns by showing a willingness to compromise that we would have come out with a much better balanced kind of situation in the new elementary-secondary legislation that year.[39]

Cannon was disgusted: "The Office of Education *excreted* Title III as if it were a foreign body."[40] The roll-call vote was 230 to 185, with Republicans supporting Mrs. Green 154 to 26, northern Democrats opposing her 8 to 139, and southern Democrats providing the margin of victory: 68 to 20. The House then easily passed the amended bill by a roll-call vote of 294 to 122, with a majority of Republicans for the first time in support.

Edith Green had won, and she had protected the administration's basic commitments to link federal school aid to an antipoverty rationale (Title I), and to preserve the aid-to-the-child mode of spending taxpayers' money on religious schools (Title II). But she had also, in Cannon's view, "wrecked" Title III by shipping it off to the states, and in the process she even managed to have jurisdiction over the Teacher Corps remanded to her special subcommittee on education (the amendment was sponsored by Republican John Erlenborn of Illinois), thereby foiling the administration's strategy of including it in the ESEA amendments and maximizing her bargaining leverage. There Green's amendments "localized" the Teacher Corps by deleting "National" from its title, and by providing that local agencies, not the U.S. commissioner, would recruit, select, and enroll the volunteers. The day after the crucial House votes, Quie was heard to remark in the House lobby, by reporter John Herbers of the *New York Times*, that he could claim partial victory because of Green's successful "mini-Quie" amendments. Lounging nearby, veteran congressman Wayne Hayes replied, "If he won a victory, he was disguised as the lady from Oregon."[41]

The lady from Oregon was savaged in the liberal press,[42] and Cannon's bitter complaint about throwing Title III to the wolves was echoed by Dean Stephen Bailey of Syracuse University's Maxwell School, who wrote Doc Howe on letterhead stationery to deplore the Green amendment in particular and the typical arteriosclerosis of state education agencies in general.[43] Cater wrote Johnson that the "victory over Quie was a decisive one," and that "Mrs. Green's amendments are troublesome, but all of them can be ameliorated in the Senate."[44] On the same day Henry Hall Wilson wrote Johnson that the administration's eight major objectives on the education bill had all been achieved:

1. to defeat the Quie Amendment or any other amendment which would alter the basic concept of the program;
2. to fend off efforts of the southerners to reduce integration policy to "freedom of choice";
3. to avoid ripping open to the explosive point the church-state issue;
4. to preserve the Teacher Corps program;
5. to retain the flexibility of the Commissioner of Education in the administration of the basic piece of the program;
6. to position the Republicans with causing roll call votes against parochial schools and against civil rights groups;
7. to preserve without a position on the part of the Administration which was not involved with compromise on any of these points; and
8. to get a 1969 authorization out of the Congress this year so that all of these problems would not be a source of national criticism during an election year.

In my judgment all of these objectives have been achieved. It was very touch and go for awhile.[45]

Gaither wrote Califano of his dismay at the gutting of Title III, arguing plausibly that the modest $240 million would be spread so thinly across the fifty states as to have little or no impact, that the innovative raison d'être of Title III would be killed, and that the newly state-run Title III might turn into a Republican general-aid beachhead.[46] Gaither was right on the first two points, but Eidenberg and Morey have captured a central irony of Green's triumph.

> The irony of the 1967 education fight was that Edith Green was more instrumental in preserving the basic form of the education act than both the President and the House Democratic leadership combined. For the past two-and-a-half years the congressional Democrats and the President have accused Mrs. Green of being the most troublesome "wrecker" of education legislation, but without her amendments on the 1967 education bill, the southern Democrats might well have shifted their support to the Republicans on the Quie amendment and thus changed the whole nature of the act.[47]

THE POLITICAL ORIGINS OF BILINGUAL EDUCATION

Overshadowed in 1967 by the epic battle over the Quie substitute, and then over Edith Green's successful mini-Quie compromise, was a drive for a bilingual education bill led by Senator Ralph Yarborough of Texas. A maverick liberal Democrat in a state long dominated by conservative Democrats, Yarborough had been elected to the Senate in a special election in 1957, where he won only a plurality in a confused field of twenty-two candidates (there was no run-off provision). He was handily re-elected in the Johnson-versus-Goldwater landslide of 1964, but in 1970 he knew he would face stiff and well-heeled opposition in the primary from the dominant conservative Democrats. Attracting Hispanic support was crucial to cementing Yarborough's fragile New Deal coalition of poor whites, blacks, and Mexican-Americans.[48] So in 1967 Yarborough got himself appointed chairman of a special subcommittee on bilingual education of the Senate Committee on Labor and Public Welfare, and from that podium he launched a blitz of hearings that included a veritable road show from California to Texas to New York State. Those three huge states contained a quarter of the nation's population and, more important, most of its Hispanic population. Yarborough convinced all five senators to cosponsor with him the nation's first bilingual education bill (Yarborough was joined by Republicans John Tower of Texas, Thomas Kuchel and George Murphy of California, Jacob Javits of New York, and Republican Paul Fannon of Arizona, plus Democrats Jennings Randolph of West Virginia and Robert Kennedy of New York. The bipartisan political combination was formidable indeed.

Yarborough began his hearings normally enough in Washington on 18 and 19 May, where fellow senators and cosponsors could occasionally join him to hear an avalanche of testimony in favor of his bill, S. 428. Most of the testimony was by ethnic political lobbyists supporting the bill, rather than by educational experts in pedagogical and linguistic theory. Then Yarborough took his one-senator committee strategically on the road, hearing testimony in the Nueces County Courthouse in Corpus Christi (26 May), the Hidalgo County Courthouse in Edinburg, Texas (29 May, where his Senate committee was joined by Congressman Eligio de la Garza), San Antonio on 31 May, and Los Angeles on 24 June. The summer bilingual blitz culminated at P.S. 155 in East Harlem in late July, where Senator Kennedy and Bronx Borough president Herman Badillo expressed outrage that no Puerto Rican was a school principal and that so few were teachers in New York City.[49] By then the Yarborough effort was clear: it was for students whose "mother tongue is Spanish," and it would "pay for programs to impart a knowledge of and pride in ancestral culture and language" and for "efforts to attract and retain as teachers promising individuals of Mexican or Puerto Rican descent."[50]

Nowhere in all of Califano's comprehensive task forcing of 1966–67, nowhere in Gaither's three-inch-thick idea books for the president, nowhere on the Friday task force agenda, was there a recommendation resembling the Yarborough bill for bilingual education. This was not because the academic specialists and the White House staff had not thought of it. Rather, it was because they knew that the laws on the books (NDEA, ESEA, HEA, and, soon, EPDA) already provided ample authority for initiating experimental and demonstration projects in a linguistic field that was new and controversial. The acute social problem was demonstrable enough, as Commissioner Howe agreed in testimony before both the Yarborough committee and its House counterpart, chaired by Pucinski: the median years of schooling of Spanish-speaking Americans was only 7.1 years, as opposed to 12.2 years for Anglos.[51] The notion of instructing a small child in a language he could not understand seemed inherently unfair. Howe told Pucinski's subcommittee that experimental bilingual projects were being mounted under virtually every major ESEA title, especially I and III, that he had just appointed Armando Rodriguez as USOE's officer for Mexican-American program affairs, that new legislation was *not* needed, and that indeed there was danger in the "spotlight" approach to special legislation for every group. Howe agreed that the $7 million being spent under Title I in experimental and demonstration programs was modest (Pucinski called the concept of bilingual programs an "orphan" of Title I). But Howe also argued that the proposed $10 million first-year expenditure for a separate bilingual program amounted to only $6 per Spanish-speaking child, that USOE was already spending $13 million on bilingual programs under ESEA titles I and III in fiscal 1967, that the educational needs of Puerto Rican children in New York and Cubans in Florida and Mexicans in California were different and should not be shackled to a common program, and that the needs of Korean or Chinese students were ignored in a bill that emphasized the Spanish language. But Senator Yarborough was not primarily interested in the bloc vote of Korean Texans.

So Commissioner Howe argued largely in vain, for the political odds were too formidable. Howe knew that the Yarborough bill at bottom translated into Hispanic votes for the senator (and his cosponsors) in return for a special, separate, ethnically earmarked "Hispanic community action program" to provide teaching jobs for Puerto Ricans and Mexicans—"their hunk of the action." [52] Worse, Howe was caught in a special dilemma. When opposing the Quie and Green proposals that would curtail his authority, the commissioner had to emphasize the permissive and flexible range of his federal reach, with maximum deference to local preferences. But his opposition to the Yarborough bill suggested that he could *demand* bilingual programs from local districts under Titles I and III, which Howe was unwilling to do, and this played into the hands of Quie and Green. William Cannon told Cater that the Bureau of the Budget stoutly opposed such a special Hispanic program, and that ESEA Titles I and III already contained sufficient authority, but Cannon conceded that such ESEA titles depended heavily on local initiative and that California and Texas had a history of legislatively forbidding bilingual programs. [53] Gaither agreed but conceded to Califano the political dilemma that "it would be politically inappropriate to try to get local school districts to use Title III for this purpose when we are fighting to preserve the Commissioner's approval authority in the Congress."[54]

With Howe thus severely hobbled in his opposition to the Yarborough bill, Secretary Gardner appealed by letter directly to Lister Hill, arguing that existing titles and appropriations already provided not only more flexible authority but also more money than S. 428; that intensive instruction in English as a second language was a promising approach, which would be excluded by S. 428's requirement for instruction in Spanish; and that S. 428 was straying into the dangerous ground of ethnic entitlements.

> We firmly believe that the language of the legislation should avoid any restrictions to persons of particular ancestry or ethnic origin. S. 428 presents several difficulties in this respect.
>
> Programs assisted under S. 428 would be limited to students whose mother tongue is Spanish. Among the activities specified in the legislation are "efforts to attract and retain as teachers promising individuals of Mexican or Puerto Rican descent." The allotment formula is based on the number of persons of Mexican or Puerto Rican descent or who have Spanish surnames.
>
> Legislation should be directed to persons from non-English-speaking backgrounds because that factor—the language problem—has educational significance and that is the justification for legislation in the field of bilingual education. We believe it is an important principle that the statute should not provide that determinations be based upon consideration of ethnic or national origin (or surname) per se.[55]

But political arguments on the Hill are customarily more persuasive than educational arguments, and in early August Ralph Huitt reported to Cater and Barefoot Sanders that "there is considerable unhappiness on the Committee that the Administration is not supporting the Bilingual Education Bill."[56]

THE ELEMENTS OF THE COMING CRISIS

The upshot of all of this is that the administration compromised by supporting S. 428, and Congress compromised by removing the bill's most glaring ethnic entitlements.[57] Yarborough eventually lost his reelection bid (he lost the 1970 Democratic primary to Houston millionaire Lloyd Bentsen), but the militant Hispanic lobby basically won. Despite White House, DHEW, and BOB opposition to the Hispanic job corps implications of Yarborough's original bill, President Johnson had set a sympathetic tone when he told the graduates of Howard University on 4 June 1965 that "we seek not just legal equity but human ability, not just equality as a right but equality as a fact and as a result."[58] Given such political rhetoric to appeal to one group, Yarborough could scarcely be faulted for designing legislative entitlements to specifically benefit another. H.R. 7819 was delayed during the fall by Senate disputes over busing and DHEW fund cutoff procedures in the civil rights guidelines. So the conference report was delayed until 15 December, and in it the conferees split the difference between the House's one-year and the Senate's three-year authorizations, thereby authorizing expenditures through fiscal year 1970, which had the dual advantage of giving school officials more reasonable lead time for planning and ensuring that another Holy War over ESEA would be avoided in the election year of 1968. Otherwise, the conferees accepted most of the additional new programs in the heavily freighted Senate bill, including authorization for handicapped children, rural areas, school dropouts, school bus safety, and bilingual education. There was much here that the administration never asked for and did not want, but Johnson had won on the most crucial educational battle of 1967, the one over the Quie block-grant amendment; so on 2 January 1968, he signed H.R. 7819 into law (P.L. 90-247) as the best he could get.

But by the fall of 1967 the whipsaw effect of the contending forces was becoming increasingly noticeable. The expanding Vietnam War drove the president to attempt to hold down the domestic budget, but his commitment to rounding out the Great Society led him to seek start-up funding for new programs, often at the expense of the old. Also, the president's devotion to task forcing and to short-circuiting the bureaucracy (Charles Zwick, Johnson's last budget director, said that President Johnson "always had this feeling that you had to raise hell with the bureaucracy"[59]), led him to continue to encourage Califano's growing team to pursue its task forcing. On top of this Congress kept adding its own favorite programs, often mandating new program offices and thereby further fragmenting the line agencies. In response, and not surprisingly, morale in such massive shops as DHEW began to deteriorate, and even the loyalists at the Bureau of the Budget began to resent their growing exclusion from the White House program planning operation. The crisis was becoming acute by the fall of 1967, and the interaction between Califano's staff, William Friday's major outside task force, and Gardner's interagency task force illustrated its dimensions all too painfully.

7 / PLANNING FOR THE FINAL ROUND 1967–1968

CAMPUS VISITS, VIETNAM, AND GHETTO RIOTS, 1967

At the LBJ Ranch in late December 1966, President Johnson had asked Califano, McPherson, and Cater to make more college trips in 1967 in order to keep up the administration's contacts with the academic community.[1] But early congressional battles (especially those in the House) over such major controversies as the Quie amendment, foreign aid, and the role of the poor in running local community action agencies so consumed White House energies that, beyond occasional individual speech-making forays, the organized campus dinners could not be launched until late spring, which resulted in several unfortunate consequences.

The agenda for a late spring planning session for the university trips contained a preamble on the purpose of the trips, explaining that the White House staff was crisis oriented and hence needed to talk to "people who have time to think, to analyze what we are doing and to see problems which we are missing."[2] It gave as the prime example of the benefits of the 1966 trips the suggestions that led to the productive Hunt task force on child development, and it suggested three issues for campus discussion. The first was bureaucratic and organizational, centering on the complicated and often confused federal-state-local relationship, as had been recently pointed up by the Quie amendment and the Heller Plan for federal revenue sharing with the states.[3] The second suggested topic for discussion with the academicians was the alienation of three groups in American society: Youth—"Is the Nation in danger of losing a generation of Americans" [?]; the lower-middle class—"their disenchantment endangers our social programs and social progress"; and segments of racial minorities. The third topic was foreign aid and trade, or, more precisely, the rapidly diminishing public and congressional support of foreign aid.[4]

The topics were apt and serious enough, but they reflected a peculiarly Washington-centered and White House-based sense of the most pressing problems, especially the first and third. The Quie amendment and the Heller Plan and foreign aid were scarcely at the forefront of campus concern in 1967. Alienation of groups of citizens, especially restive campus youths (who were mostly white) and rioting ghetto blacks, was claiming their attention. But at all eight academic dinners of June and July 1967, Califano unwisely elected to direct the focus of the question of alienation "particularly [on] the *lower-middle class* and the threat which this poses to our social programs and to social progress."[5] So the academic trips of 1967 were not off to a very promising start, and for several reasons that extended beyond the uneven mesh between pressing campus concerns and the White House agenda. Clearly, much of the bloom was off the rose for the Johnson administration by 1967, especially on the campuses. Moreover, the timing was poor and the format was flawed. University of Chicago provost Edward H. Levi wrote Califano to urge holding such discussions during the regular academic year rather than during the summer, when so many of the best faculty were gone. To this frequent campus complaint Levi added another: with so little lead time, preparation, or structure, the group discussions tended to be unfocused and amorphous—often "in fact trivial or wrong."[6] Finally, the trips coincided with the massive burst of ghetto rioting in 67 cities from June through August, the worst being in Newark during 12–17 July and in Detroit from 23–28 July, so the latter campus discussions tended to be consumed by the urban riot problem.

Despite this unpromising beginning, Califano notified the president on 7 June of his schedule, explaining that he and Gaither would be accompanied by two other White House aides from a rotating pool, that they would travel to and from Washington by military aircraft in order to be at work the next morning, and that Gaither would take notes and prepare summary reports.[7] The schedule is outlined in table 3. Gaither's five-page summary of the kick-off Los Angeles dinner not surprisingly reflects a rather wandering, disjointed discussion, one summed up by Stanford Law School dean Bayless Manning who observed, Gaither re-

TABLE 3: Schedule for Academic Dinners, 1967

Date	Location	Host	Participants[1]	White House Aides[2]
14 June	Los Angeles, Calif.	Warren Christopher	21	Cater, Hamilton
20 June	Princeton, N.J.	Dean Marver Bernstein	14	Bohen
26 June	Chapel Hill, N.C.	President William Friday	14	Cater, Roche
29 June	New Haven, Conn.	President Kingman Brewster	15	McPherson, Hamilton
11 July	Austin, Tex.	Chancellor Harry Ransom	16	Roche, Sanders
13 July	Cambridge, Mass.	Richard Neustadt	13	Cater, Hamilton
18 July	Chicago, Ill.	Provost Edward Levi	16	Duggan, Levinson
20 July	New York City	McGeorge Bundy	10	Levinson, McPherson

1. Excludes White House contingent.
2. Excludes Califano and Gaither.

ported, that because so few new ideas had surfaced, that must mean that "(*1*) *everyone feels that we're on the right track and* (*2*) *that the problems are those of communication and implementation.*"[8] Gaither devoted considerable space to alienation of youth, especially as discussed by Stanford's dean of students, Joel T. Smith, but Gaither's summary alluded to Vietnam only once, and this did not quite square with the assessment of Stanford Law School professor Thomas Ehrlich, who subsequently wrote Califano that "most important, the pall of Viet Nam obviously hung over our meeting," and that "those in the universities—students and faculty—find no-one in the Administration who speaks *to* them." Ehrlich recalled a recent appearance at Stanford by Vice-President Humphrey, whose prepared speech never even mentioned Vietnam, although the war was "obviously the overwhelming concern of all present." When questioned about Vietnam from the audience, Humphrey responded "as though the audience was the Rotary Club International." "In short," Ehrlich concluded, "to an audience that continually agonizes about the problem of Viet Nam, would it not be better to reveal the Administration's own agony than to frame the matter in black and white?"[9]

And so it went. At Princeton, fourteen Princeton academics (eleven of them from the Woodrow Wilson School) sharply disagreed with each other over the wisdom of discouraging automobiles or lowering the minimum wage for youth, but even Gaither's summary recorded the consensus that "no intellectual in academic life and no bright student fails to have misgivings about Vietnam." John Roche, who was not there, would doubtless disagree; he attended subsequent meetings at the somewhat more hawkish southern campuses at the University of North Carolina at Chapel Hill and the University of Texas at Austin, where the considerably more hawkish Roche felt more at home. In North Carolina, the discussion hewed more closely to the Califano agenda, largely because the host and university president, William Friday, was currently chairing the administration's major outside education task force, but there was also insistence that "*the most disturbing thing about Vietnam was the inequitable draft system and the shelter of the university.*"[10] The Yale group was much more critical of the ham-handed federal bureaucracy and its restrictive categorical grants, especially in health, housing, and university research. This common university concern for more basic research funds, less red tape, more student aid (which would allow the schools to raise tuitions), and perhaps direct institutional aid as well, seemed, together with Vietnam, to be almost the only consensual elements in a sea of random notions and complaints. But they could scarcely be called exciting new ideas. By 20 July, when the last meeting was held in New York City, the urban riots dominated all discussion—although beyond deploring them, there was little consensus on how best to respond to them.[11] But clearly spending more and more billions on a dubious war in Vietnam while the American cities burned was a searing paradox that crippled Califano's efforts in the troubled summer of 1967. As provost (and economist) William Bowen of Princeton wrote Califano, "I am not a supporter of the Administration's policies in Vietnam. Viewed simply from the perspective of resource allocation, it seems to be tragic to be making the investment in Southeast Asia which we are making at this time, when the need for effective action by the Federal Government at home is so apparent."[12]

There was little that Califano and his domestic staff could do about Vietnam (Moyers had tried, failed, and left), and clearly President Johnson's credibility problem and reputation for cynical manipulation were rubbing off on Califano and his White House entourage. In his friendly "Dear Joe" letter, Stanford's Ehrlich had written, "I suspect that such meetings are held at least as much to demonstrate the President's interest in the academic community's judgments as actually to determine those judgments."[13] In August, the general counsel of DOT privately reported to Califano a subsequent conversation in Chicago with an unnamed participant in the academic dinner there.

1. He [the guest] characterized it as a public relations effort by the President for the benefit of the academics.
2. He doubted whether any of the participants prepared for the meeting, stating that none of them felt they had much incentive if they were going to be allowed only five or ten minutes to present their issues.
3. This man felt that the reaction of those present was that the White House was not seriously looking to these people for program ideas. . . .
4. He said the format was so abbreviated that it was doubtful whether leading academicians could be induced to contribute a real effort.[14]

Such evidence is derivative and impressionistic, as are Gaither's summaries. But it seems reasonable to conclude that even in the absence of particular problems of timing and war and riots, the unstructured nature and time limitations of the format for such idea-gathering academic trips was not conducive to systematic, focused, and sustained analysis of the strengths and weaknesses of alternative policy choices.

Nevertheless, on 7 August the indefatigable Califano reported to Johnson on the eight meetings with 115 of the Nation's leading experts covering virtually every field. He had written all 115 participants to solicit more detail on their ideas, and additionally he had scoured the president's staff, each department and agency head, the CEA, BOB, OST, and "bright young staff people" in general around the government, and from all this would be compiled yet another massive "idea book." "When this is completed, I will have a list of ideas and problem areas for your consideration to be focused on next year. After that we can put together groups from within or without the Government to address the problems. As we did last year, we will use White House staff people on each of the groups."[15]

Yet the twenty-three pages of new ideas (one per page, broken down by proposal, problem, and source) in the education section of Gaither's idea book for 1967 confirm a judgment that running about the campuses with an intellectual butterfly net was a poor approach to legislative agenda formulation. Most of the selected "ideas" fell into the scarcely novel why-not-do-more-of-this category, for example, *more* model schools, experimental schools, ghetto lab schools associated with urban universities, federal funds for school construction, comprehensive educational parks geographically situated to maximize racial and class integration, teacher training and instructional materials centers for handicapped students. There was much merit in all this, but it covered ground that was already being heavily worked by the professionals at DHEW as well as by previous and current task forces. A second cluster of recommendations reflected special university concerns or complaints, such as deploring grant restrictions and red tape, the irrationality of the federal distinction between college and university formal denominations (Was Dartmouth College less worthy of research support than Bob Jones University?), the lack of a national *social* science foundation, the need for a more direct involvement of universities with the various AID programs. Yale's president Kingman Brewster called for a federally supported loan program available to *all* college students with payback over life based on the amount of income earned. Paying for the college boom of the 1960s was of course a growing nationwide concern, but it was already being heavily debated by the Friday task force.

The closest the White House's entire academic visit enterprise of 1967 got to identifying one salient new idea to pursue, comparable to the intense concern over early childhood of the previous year, was the suggestion of Chancellor Harry Ransom of the University of Texas at Austin that so much attention was being concentrated on disadvantaged children that gifted children were being largely ignored. Ransom pointed to his own campus's Jagged Profile Program, which identified and admitted applicants who were not well rounded enough to qualify normally, but whose talents and interests seemed so intensely focused in one area—to the detriment of most others—that they held promise of genius. This concern for the overlooked gifted ultimately led to the appointment of an outside task force in the fall of 1967 under the chairmanship of Champion Ward, a Ford Foundation vice-president for educational programs.[16]

But because of the savage urban rioting that summer, Califano and his colleagues were more interested in using university expertise to solve urban problems, and this proposed new linkage most often took the form of a call to extend the land-grant college concept to the cities. This was a fuzzy concept that had been much in vogue since at least the early 1960s, and President Johnson had himself promoted it in his speech at Irvine in the summer of 1964. But on 11 September Califano enthusiastically recommended to the president that a new outside task force be appointed to explore the concept and report in 1968.[17]

Nevertheless, far more stale chaff than fresh wheat was reaped from the academic visits of 1967. A cynical view would hold that the idea-gathering function was ancillary to the public-relations and recruitment functions of the campus trips of 1967—besides, it was a nice excuse for an overworked and exhausted White House staff to get out of Washington in the summer. In his memoir, McPherson expressed a mild version of this cynical view: "The ostensible purpose [of the 1967 academic trips] was to gather ideas for the following year's legislative program. I was equally concerned about the erosion of good feelings between the university community and the Administration. I hoped that the visits would prove we were open to academic opinions; I was even willing to say we were dependent upon them." McPherson's assessment of the visits is revealing.

At Harvard, the conversation was good and the comments were knowledgeable and relevant. Most of the men around the table spent almost as much time in Washington, advising departments and Budget Bureau committees, as they did in Cambridge. They knew what was politically feasible and did not waste time proposing utopian measures. They told us about recent research in education, in the nature of effective community action, the delivery of health services, and so on. They put this in context with current programs and recommended improvements.

Visits to Yale and the Bay area in California, where professors traveled nearly as often to Washington as did the Harvard men, were also productive. Elsewhere the take was disappointing. For many distinguished scholars, the country's chief problems had to do with insufficient federal money for research in their fields, or unnecessary requirements for fellowship grants. The cities were burning down, the poor were still going without money, good schools, and medical care, the air and water stank; but what really concerned them was that HEW contracted for research with individual professors, and not with the department heads, or the other way around. For several other scholars there was only one problem—Vietnam. All else flowed from it or could not be remedied because of it.[18]

No evidence suggests attributing a cynical view to Califano and his immediate young staff, whose energy and zeal and indeed idealism seemed unflagging. But their peripatetic idea gathering could serve at best only as a prelude to the more focused, systematic, and sustained analysis of the major task forces, which were themselves preludes to executive branch and ultimately presidential decisions on the following year's legislative agenda. And in 1967 for educational policy, that meant William Friday's task force, which in the caliber of its membership and the scope and gravity of its charge easily matched the distinguished Gardner task force of 1964.

THE FRIDAY TASK FORCE

When in September of 1966, Califano asked President Johnson to approve a second outside task force force on education, he suggested a potential membership that had been recommended by Gardner, Cater, Cannon, and Shriver. Johnson approved with the scribbled admonition: "No press leaks—ask these men before you select them."[19] The appointed group (all were white males) remarkably resembled the recommended group, the major exceptions being that William Friday rather than Sidney Marland chaired the panel, and Harvard sociologist Thomas Pettigrew replaced David Reisman (see table 4).[20] The group first met in Washington on 22 November, where Commissioner Howe briefed them with a candid and critical analysis of the major problems affecting elementary-secondary and higher education and the continuing shortcomings of federal efforts. At that meeting the group decided to meet in Washington the second Friday and Saturday of the first six months of 1967, looking toward their 30 June reporting date. In December of 1966, Friday and Cannon, the executive secretary, received at their request a stream of letters from task force members suggesting major items and issues to be addressed, and in the next six months Cannon's office sent the members a massive amount of literature to digest, although major discussion centered on the Coleman Report and on the Civil Rights

Commission's more recent report, *Racial Isolation in the Public Schools*, plus USOE's report on future policy recommendations for federal aid to lower and higher education.[21]

As is the case with most such groups, the majority of the work was performed by a minority, and first among equals was Chairman Friday. But Friday was quick to acknowledge the crucial role of Cannon, among whose attributes were the combination of extensive experience and knowledge, a strong will and quick mind, a similar role on the Gardner task force, a discernible relish for the bureaucratic short-circuiting possibilities that were inherent in the task force device, and a strategic location in the Bureau of the Budget.[22] The task force naturally clustered into lower- and higher-education subgroups. Pittsburgh school superintendent Sidney Marland not surprisingly dominated discussion of elementary and secondary education, but he was joined by an unanticipated source of strength in Hugh Calkins, a lawyer and experienced school board member from Cleveland. At the task force's third meeting, on 10 and 11 February, an attempt was made to narrow priorities and force preliminary conclusions, primarily in the area of lower education (a subgroup was to report later on higher education). Marland took the lead in exploring ways to halt the exodus of able school executives and to recruit and train better teachers. The group agreed that the nation's teachers colleges were second-class institutions, but because taking them on frontally seemed so politically unpromising, it was thought better to encourage them to convert to liberal arts colleges with higher academic standards, leaving the teacher training to MAT programs at the major public universities and at superior private ones like Johns Hopkins University and Vanderbilt University. Major curriculum changes were needed as well to reach the lowest quartile of students who were simply not learning from their classroom experience. The task force agreed that "much if not all of what the Task Force wants can be accomplished under existing authorities in the Office of Education, National Science Foundation, and other agencies."[23] But clearly the growing problem of white exodus could not.

The question of the federal role in combating white flight raised all the explosive questions of federal control, social experimentation, busing for racial balance, and the like; and Harvard's Pettigrew led the arguments to use the federal leverage aggressively to maximize integration by race and class. Drawing heavily on *Racial Isolation in the Public*

TABLE 4: Outside Task Force on Education, 1966

Chairman	Vice-Chairman	Executive Secretary
William C. Friday President University of North Carolina	Sidney Marland Superintendent of Schools Pittsburgh, Pa.	William B. Cannon Chief Division of Education, Science, and Manpower BOB

Members

David Bell
Vice-President
Ford Foundation

Lee A. DuBridge
President
California Institute
   of Technology

John Fischer
President
Teachers College
Columbia University

Fred Harrington
President
University of Wisconsin

Edward H. Levi
Provost
University of Chicago

Thomas Pettigrew
Associate Professor
   of Social Educational
   Psychology
Harvard University

Hugh Calkins
Attorney
Cleveland, Ohio

J. W. Edgar
Superintendent of
   Public Instruction
State of Texas

John I. Goodlad
Director
University Elementary School
University of California
   at Los Angeles

Alexander Heard
Chancellor
Vanderbilt University

The Reverend Walter Ong
Department of English
New York University

Samuel M. Brownell
Professor
   of Urban Educational
   Administration
Yale University

Schools, as well as on his own research and writing, Pettigrew argued at the 17 March meeting that class appeared to be more important than race in determining educational achievement, but that both whites and blacks were harmed by segregated education; remedial or compensatory education was helpful but limited. What was crucial was true integration of race *and* class. This was best achieved when Negro enrollment in a school was more than 20 percent but less than 40 percent, and this goal was best achieved by constructing educational parks on a metropolitan basis that necessarily would involve the white suburbs, funded by massive federal aid as high as $50 million per complex.[24]

Cannon's minutes of the 17 March meeting merely summarized without comment Pettigrew's proposal for massive and highly conditional federal aid to lure suburbs into jointly constructing educational parks with the cities. Cannon also summarized with implicit disapproval the USOE proposals for the future pattern of federal aid:

> First, general aid to the States, on the basis of a State plan, consisting of a Federal supplementation grant and a replacement of State revenues. By 1970 the Federal Government would put up $12–13 billion for this program. Second, temporary categorical programs to take care of special poverty problems, stimulate innovation. This would cost something around $1 billion by 1970. Maximum devolution of responsibility and control to the States was the basic theme.[25]

Within the context of Commissioner Howe's proposal to devolve toward the states his Title III authority, this reminded the disgusted Cannon of the old leave-it-on-the-stump-and-run proposals of the Kennedy administration.[26] The task force itself was doubly divided over the question of general versus categorical aid. At the elementary-secondary level, general aid made sense because it involved an interconnected legal system with mandatory attendance, and it recognized the historic primacy of the states in public education. But categorical grants had the advantages of targeting specific populations, especially the disadvantaged; of conditional requirements that states change their financing formulas, which discriminated against cities; and that suburbs participate in educating inner-city children. In higher education the federal government dealt with discrete public and private institutions where attendance was voluntary and tuition was required, and categorical aid went to institutions rather than to constitutional-legal systems; and general aid looked increasingly attractive to the hard-pressed colleges and universities, because it was given not only to their students in the form of scholarships and loans, but also *directly to institutions.* The Friday-led subgroup on higher education, which included DuBridge (California Institution of Technology), Harrington (the University of Wisconsin), Heard (Vanderbilt University) and Levi (the University of Chicago), generally reflected the perspective of the prestigious American Association of Universities and favored not only expansion of HEA Title III aid to weak colleges (they talked exclusively about "Negro Colleges," although these always represented a minority of "developing institutions"), but especially of general institutional aid to the nation's *best* universities, especially the *private* ones.

By late April the task force had reached agreement to: *oppose* general aid to elementary-secondary education, including block grants of the Quie variety; *support* school construction grants to promote suburban/inner-city and race/class integration; *avoid* stress on minorities and discussion of racial balance; and support general institutional aid for universities.[27] By mid-May, consensus was reached on the main recommendations. For lower education, these were: radically increased funds for ESEA Title I, incentives to states to change their allocation formulas, a curricular "moon shot" effort to improve the instruction of poor children, and "A *metropolitan school* program involving grants to enable cities to join with suburbs in constructing *public* schools in a manner and a place which would attract a reasonable mix of classes and races."[28]

The Friday task force met its goal of turning in the final report by 30 June. This impressive, comprehensive and secret 149-page document boldly called for new and expanded federal programs to:

1. Double ESEA Title I appropriations over the next two fiscal years.
2. Induce states to favor cities in their allocation formulas.
3. Undertake a massive "moon shot" effort in curriculum and instruction to avoid the "national calamity" that a quarter of our children pass through school without learning the 3 Rs.
4. Appropriate $1¼ billion to construct city-suburb schools integrated by race and class in the fifty largest metropolitan areas.

5. Radically increase all present programs of aid to higher education, and add an *un*conditional program of *general* aid to *every* college and university equal to 10 percent of instructional costs plus $100 for each student.
6. Establish a National Social Science Foundation.
7. Experiment with a free freshman year.
8. Offer college compensatory and remedial services to minority students.
9. Upgrade Negro colleges by pairing them with *nearby* white universities (on an intraregional rather than the older North-South/white-black model of Michigan-Tuskegee).[29]

This brief summary of the report's most prominent and controversial highlights does not begin to do justice to its scope and detail. But it does suggest the unbreachably wide gulf between the Friday report's moonshot ambitions—which the president a year before had exhorted them to embrace—and the grim budgetary and political realities of 1967.

On 20 May, the members of the Friday task force met with President Johnson at the White House, together with Cater, Cannon, Howe, and Gaither. Friday's recollection of that meeting is vivid and painfully revealing: "We talked about the report for maybe five minutes, and then he spent the next forty-five minutes talking about Vietnam."[30]

SWAN SONG

So the powerful Friday Report, unlike the exquisitely timed Gardner Report, fell upon hard times and resistant ears. It did not die on the day of its nativity—the elaborately constructed task force machinery made sure that it would not—in fact, it enjoyed an unusual swan song that was rare in the task force annals and involved the president's careful violation of his own iron rule of secrecy. The circumstances were political, not surprisingly, and centered in general on the battle over the Quie amendment and the Republican block-grant strategy, and specifically on the midsummer report of the Educational Policies Commission of the normally Democratic NEA, which featured a proposal to abandon categorical aid for state block grants. Seeking to head off this alarming defection, Cater persuaded Johnson to approve a leak to the press, and Cannon persuaded Friday and his colleagues to agree.[31] Accordingly, on 21 August the *New York Times* reporter Marjorie Hunter correctly reported that the Friday task force had rejected general aid or block grants at this time. She also correctly listed all the task force members, and even quoted accurately from the text of a report that she was told (*in*correctly) was still incomplete: "We have concluded that *we do not favor general Federal aid to elementary and secondary education* (as distinguished from higher education) *at this time. . . .* Although . . . we favor it as an ultimately desirable—indeed, necessary—objective."[32] Hunter went on to explain that "The President approved leaking this story, since it underlines his position on categorical versus general aid."[33]

THE POLITICAL EDITORIAL OF COMMISSIONER HOWE

Meanwhile Califano was cranking up the task force machinery again to a summer's fever pitch. He first appointed eleven new outside task forces, most of which were scheduled to report well into 1968. Presumably this major effort was directed toward constructing a legislative agenda for President Johnson's reelection in 1968 and the subsequent Ninety-first Congress, and it included Champion Ward's task force on the education of gifted persons and Paul Miller's on urban educational opportunities. But the second session of the Ninetieth Congress in 1968 was a more immediate, known quantity, and toward this end Califano appointed twenty-four interagency task forces. Witness Califano's list of appointments for the last two weeks in August (see table 5). Gardner promptly bucked his education task force down to Howe, with an agenda that consisted of the ambitious Friday recommendations. Late in October Howe sent Califano an interagency task force report in response to an outside task force report that was remarkably candid in reflecting the collective frustration, disappointment, anger, and sinking morale of a federal bureaucracy in charge of the Great Society's educational cornerstone. The preamble to the report was a six-page political indictment of the recent proliferation of fragmented, underfunded, overpromised, categorical programs (with well over seventy legislative authorizations and more than 100 separate programs in USOE alone, not to mention the fifteen other federal departments and agencies running major and usually uncoordinated educational programs). The Gardner/Howe preamble of political analysis ticked off the major sources of their agency's and constituency's deep malaise.

TABLE 5: Califano Task Force Assignments, August 14–31, 1967

Date	Interagency Task Force	Chairman
14 August	Summer Programs	Sargent Shriver
17 August	Nutrition & Adequate Diets	Charles Schultze
18 August	Administration of Academic Science	Charles Schultze
21 August	New Towns for 1968	Charles Haar
21 August	Health	John Gardner
21 August	Quality of the Environment	Stewart Udall
25 August	Housing & Urban Development	Robert Weaver
28 August	Education	John Gardner
28 August	Manpower	Willard Wirtz
30 August	Civil Rights	Ramsey Clark
31 August	Child Development	William Gorham

1. Some of this organizational and programmatic abundance may be counter-productive of efficient educational outcomes; in any case, it generates a large measure of controversy and bureaucratic struggle, some of it a direct liability for the President. . . .

2. Because many of these programs came into being at a time of increasing budgetary stringencies, very few Federal programs are funded on a scale commensurate with what the Congress authorized or the Administration contemplated when the programs were first being developed.

3. Because of these generally restricted levels, a large share of recent appropriations has flowed into the administrative superstructure (primarily in the case of elementary and secondary education) at the State and local levels, rather than into actual field operations where their impact on the classroom and community would be more visible and where they would be more widely appreciated by the beneficiaries.[34]

As a consequence, there was little demand on the part of most educators for additional new legislation, apart from a residual support for general aid to institutions with no strings attached that had fueled much of the recent conflict over the Quie amendment. Criticism was mounting over overlapping and duplicating programs and "bureaucratic excesses" that siphoned off funds for teaching and research. "The result is a confluence of increasingly embittered and frustrated educational interests which view all new legislative proposals as competitive 'gimmicks' at best or even as 'political frauds.' 'Bold, new legislative programs' with negligible first-year budgets are no longer taken seriously, either on the Hill or in American education at-large."[35]

So on 23 October Howe wrote Califano that the far-reaching Friday proposals would be "enormously expensive. The integration proposals would be highly controversial and probably not politically viable."[36] Howe dutifully reported that a majority of his interagency task force also rejected for much the same reasons the Friday proposal for a new program of unrestricted grants to all colleges and universities, so they proposed instead that a commission be formed under Secretary Gardner to study the complex question of general aid to higher education. But Howe cheated a little bit and added, in his cover memo to Califano, his strong minority view that the president *should* present Congress in 1968 with a "bold, new" proposal for general aid to higher education. Califano was intrigued by the notion, and on 1 November he called in Cater, Gaither, Gardner, and Howe to discuss the worsening financial crisis in higher education. He then wrote Johnson that "this is the major problem in education today and probably the only major educational problem which cannot be solved by legislation you have already proposed and had enacted." Califano added, "I believe that this will produce the capstone for your remarkable record of support for education in this country. . . . If we can devise an imaginative program of basic aid to higher education, your record of support for education will be complete and unparalleled in human history."[37] Johnson approved a directive that Gardner and Howe explore the alternatives for legislative program recommendations in December.

A BUREAUCRATIC WAR

That started a bureaucratic war. The Office of Education was full of staffers whose categorical programs were limping along on withered appropriations, and to them the prospect of a potentially bottomless well of general aid to more than two thousand colleges and universities was appalling. On 8 November, DHEW's assistant secretary for planning and evaluation, William Gorham, attended a wrap-up meeting of the interagency task force on education called by Califano, where it was apparent to Gorham that "Joe Califano wants the Congress offered a proposal for a new Federal program of general stringless institutional support for higher education." Gorham promptly wrote Secretary Gardner that he and Wilbur Cohen agreed that this would be a "serious error" because most of the institutional aid would go to middle- and upper-income groups, such institutional entitlements were indiscriminate, rewarding both Podunk and Yale, and the alleged financial crisis in higher education had never been convincingly documented. "In my judgment," Gorham concluded, "the clear needs of our most disadvantaged citizens and their children should take precedent over the oddly inarticulated financial difficulties of our colleges and universities."[38] The financial difficulties were real enough, given the baby boom coming of college age, the consequential construction boom, the wartime inflation, and the eternal shortfall from tuitions; but if they were "oddly inarticulated," it was because the higher-education community was so disaggregated—by size, quality, race, sex, religion, region, wealth, and public-versus-private sponsorship. The Friday task force had been torn by the DuBridge-Harrington dispute, but they had been able to compromise down the middle (with somewhat dissembling logic) on a Solomonesque formula that provided for both per capita, flat-rate aid and a percentage of cost of instruction as well. But an institutional holding company like the ACE was inevitably paralyzed by such cross-cutting disputes. Gardner sensed this lack of consensus and persisted in opposing general aid to higher education. But Califano and Howe leaned the other way. So in mid-December a series of White House conferences was held to try to hammer out a policy consensus on financing higher education, and the core of this group consisted of Califano, Cater, and Gaither from the White House staff; Gardner, Cohen, Howe, and Peter Muirhead from DHEW; and from the Bureau of the Budget, Director Schultze and William Carey, who usually kept notes.[39] Other participants included, from time to time, Shriver, Donald Hornig, Huitt and Gorham, plus Wilfred Rommel from BOB. Occasionally attention was focused on vocational education, with an apparent consensus that vocational education was extremely expensive; virtually every evaluation showed that graduates of vocational schools performed poorly in comparison with standard high school graduates; and vocational programs were nevertheless extremely popular with the powerful American Vocational Association, which had strong alliances in Congress.

There was relatively little discussion at the December conferences of the broad range of issues in elementary-secondary education. This was partly because most of them had been thought through and fought through during the first session of the Ninetieth Congress, and the second session, in 1968, was clearly going to feature higher-education issues. The Friday "moon-shot" recommendations seemed to be too ambitious and expensive to consider seriously, and the Friday school integration proposals were both budget busting and political anathema. In August, Califano had impaneled an interagency task force chaired by William Gorham to assess child development in light of the Hunt Report. For an interagency task force, Gorham's group was unusually large and peppered with outsiders. Its twenty members included such weighty public servants as Gorham, Cater, Gaither, Alice Rivlin, Lisle Carter, plus Alexander Greene and Richard Carlson from BOB; also participating were Urie Bronfenbrenner of Cornell University and Nicholas Hobbes of Vanderbilt University—both former members of the Hunt task force. Gorham's impressive group met thrice in October and on 7 November sent Califano a thirty-four-page report that summed up the prevailing mood very nicely in the first paragraph: "In a stringent budget year, this Task Force devoted most of its attention to requirements for research and development, to suggestions on modest expansion or redirection of operating (service) programs, and to opportunities to learn more from our operating programs."[40]

The key was the phrase *"stringent budget year"*—Vietnam was devouring the Great Society's budget. Califano's December review could find no consensus on an LBJ "capstone" program of general aid to higher education. There wasn't going to be a "bold, new" capstone program for higher education in 1968, partly because of budget stringency, but also because there didn't need to be. By 1968, virtually all of the accumulated higher education laws were up for renewal and extension: the NDEA of 1958, the Higher Education Facilities Act of 1963, the HEA of 1965, with all their myriad titles and categorical programs and their growing, triangular linkages of subcommittee, agency, and constituency. By 1968 the massive momentum of the Great Society machine was politically unstoppable. President Johnson could propose a bare-bones budget, but with all those cherished Great Society laws on the books and up for renewal, Congress would instinctively inflate the authorizations (this excludes the uncherished ones, like much of the antipoverty war). Then Johnson would denounce irresponsible budget-busting committees in Congress. But it was a hypocritical rage, because Johnson had so mastered the camel's nose technique that the Great Society's vast network of "iron tri-angles" was fundamentally predicated upon. Charles Zwick, Johnson's last budget director, recalls the president's legislative strategy of minimally funding a program to get its foot in the door, then relying upon the constituency-agency-subcommittee triangle to jack up future budgets.

> The legislative technicians, and I include in there the President and Califano and Wilbur Cohen, were of the school that you take what you can get and run. Then they would come back and say, "Oh, just start it with five million or ten million, a foot in the door." And if you look at the HEW program, it's just loaded with little bitty programs. Some of them we haven't funded, but most of them we put a little bit in and then they come back and start working. . . . Wilbur Cohen, if he were here would say, "It's the only way you can get things done. You grab it and run when you can. You worry later about getting it funded, at a low level initially, and once you get the foot in the door you start."[41]

In 1968, Johnson was to be hoist with his own petard, not only because of Vietnam, but, paradoxically, because of the political foundations of the Great Society as well.

8 / THE PARADOX OF 1968

 President Johnson's firm commitment to construct an extremely tight budget for fiscal year 1969, a decision that foredoomed the major Friday proposals and Califano's hope for a capstone program of no-strings institutional aid for higher education, was rooted in his Vietnam escalation of 1965. The annual rise of consumer prices, which had averaged only 1.3 percent during the extraordinary expansion of 1961–65, had soared to 4.2 percent by 1967–68. The continued strong growth of the gross national product was sufficient to sustain a Johnsonian policy of "guns *and* butter," but not without a tax increase. Prior to 1967 Johnson had declined to propose one, apparently because although he believed that it was needed, he felt that it could not be passed. A major consequence of this inability or refusal to use fiscal policy to restrain the economy was that a disproportionate share of the burden fell to monetary policy, which, by restricting the money supply, drove interest rates up and created a crisis in the money markets and hence especially in the housing industry as early as 1966. A resultant "minirecession" temporarily relieved the overexpansion in the cold months of 1966–67. But by the summer of 1967, the dangerously overheating economy prompted the Troika (at this time consisting of Gardner Ackley of the CEA; Secretary of the Treasury Henry Fowler, and the director of the Bureau of the Budget, Charles Schultze) in June to urge Johnson to ask Congress for a prompt tax increase. Ackley recalls Johnson's dilemma in his oral history.

Clearly Johnson wanted to have both guns and butter; and he felt that it was wrong, not only in 1966, but also in 1967 and early 1968, to say that simply because you were having to spend more for guns that it would have to come out of programs for the poor, and out of education, and all the Great Society programs. This just really hurt. This was one of the reasons, I guess, why he eventually came around to the idea of a tax increase, so he could have them both. But he was having to cut the budget well below what he wanted to do; there had to be a certain amount of window dressing in the budget about preserving the Great Society programs and keeping them expanding at least on paper.[1]

In August Johnson formally asked Congress for a 10 percent surcharge on corporate and personal income taxes.

One consequence of this is that Congress fought the president bitterly over the politically explosive issue of tax increase versus expenditure reduction and did not get around to passing the highly unpopular tax increase until 28 June 1968 (it was the first such general tax increase since 1951). This was too late to dampen effectively the overheated economy, but it was close enough to the fall elections to inflict maximum pain upon the members of Congress. A more immediate consequence is that Johnson was thrown into intensive and painful negotiations, beginning in the fall of 1967, with the barons of the Hill's major financial committees (Wilbur Mills of the House Ways and Means Committee, George Mahon of the House Appropriations Committee, and Russell Long of the Senate Finance Committee) bargaining a tight budget for fiscal year 1969 in order to get his tax increase. During that same fall, while Congress was stalling the tax increase in committee and stalling the administration's open housing bill as well, the president was also taking a severe congressional beating on his proposals for foreign aid, model cities, and rent supplements for the poor. True, the administration's popular elementary and secondary education programs had been treated very generously in 1967, with Congress funding $3.9 billion for USOE to spend in fiscal 1968 and authorizing a $9.3 billion extension through 1970, even *without* the administration's request; but under the stringent new fiscal circumstances, the fate of the higher education programs in the administration's new budget was bound to be grim.

THE TIGHT EXECUTIVE BUDGET FOR FISCAL YEAR 1969

An indicator of higher education's lean prospects for fiscal year 1969 is Califano's eleventh-hour appeal to the president, by cablegram to the LBJ Ranch on 3 January, begging Johnson to reconsider his Christmastide disapproval of a modest $99 million increase in college student aid, to which "Schultze, HEW and I gave high priority." Saying, "I am not sure I made clear precisely what is at stake," Califano explained their main reason for appeal: "To avoid reducing below fiscal 1968 the number of entering freshmen who would receive Equal Opportunity Grants, while continuing aid for students now receiving it. This is the 4th year of student aid programs. Thus, to keep the number of entering freshmen receiving grants unchanged, it is necessary to increase the program. This will not be necessary after this year."[2] Johnson's blunt reply was, "Disapprove any increase," which meant that Great Society support for equal-opportunity grants to freshmen would drop from 105,000 in fiscal year 1968 to 63,000 in fiscal year 1969 even though enrollment pressures were still growing.

The president's annual Budget Message, sent to Congress on 29 January, called for a $3 billion increase for Vietnam and a hold-the-line approach to domestic programs.[3] Spending on education would rise to $4.7 billion, a modest $200 million increase over 1968 levels, but Johnson's appropriations requests ran generally *half* below what Congress had authorized the previous fall. Student-aid funds would increase $53 million to total $574.8 million. But the price of this was a drastic slash in college facilities construction from $817 million to $300 million. Johnson heavily larded the education section of his Budget Message with impressive figures demonstrating growth in expenditures and programs since 1964, but the real lean message for the immediate future was clear to veteran congressmen, lobbyists, and journalists.

When the president fleshed out his education program in the special message of 5 February, he couched it in the bold Rooseveltian rhetoric of declaring a fifth freedom: freedom from ignorance (to add to Roosevelt's freedoms of speech, of worship, from want, and from fear). Johnson called for small increases in such existing programs as Head Start and Upward Bound (both OEO programs), Follow Through, adult education, the Teacher Corps, and a "streamlining" of vocational education. He also proposed start-up seed money for seven small *new* programs, including bilingual education and the Corporation for Public Broadcasting (both authorized but not funded in 1967), stay-in-school dropout prevention, facilities sharing, and strengthening graduate education. Several of his proposals coincided with recommendations of the Friday task force, most notably the facilities-sharing Networks for Knowledge, pursuit of excellence in graduate education, Partnership for Learning and Earning in vocational education, and greater efforts in planning and evaluation. As Roy Reed reported in the *New York Times* the same day, the president seemed to be "searching for programs of initial low cost but with a potential for growth." Also in the *Times*, Fred Hechinger acknowledged Johnson's early admission that "to meet our urgent needs within a stringent overall budget, several programs must be reduced or deferred." But then Hechinger added: "Then he quickly tried to counter the economizing unpleasantness by issuing a call for changes or reforms which either will require only a little start-up money or no money at all, and another call for some blue-printing of entirely new actions which will be expensive at some unspecified time in the future, but cost nothing now. This second call concerned primarily higher education."[4] It was vintage Johnson. Wilbur Cohen, the old salami-slicer and master incrementalist, must have been proud of those new little "budget wedge" items tucked into even this bare bones domestic budget—for example, Networks for Knowledge, a small pilot program to provide financial incentives to colleges and universities to pool resources by sharing faculties, facilities, equipment, and library and educational services. (During the December program and budget review sessions, Schultze had attacked Networks for Knowledge as typical of the excessively proliferated, fragmented, and small categorical programs in DHEW, and especially in USOE.) Appropriately, Cohen was soon to preside over the whole salami-sliced, categorical DHEW empire.

THE CONGRESSIONAL AGENDA

Clearly the main educational agenda for Congress in 1968 was no less than the renewal, extension, and amendment of the three giant higher education acts of the past prolific decade: Eisenhower's NDEA of 1958; Kennedy's (posthumous) Higher Education Facilities Act (HEFA) of 1963; and Johnson's HEA of 1965, including the National Foundation for

Arts and Humanities Act. The trail-blazing NDEA alone had eleven complex titles, most of which in 1958 had been concentrated somewhat narrowly on the security-related fields of science, mathematics, and foreign languages. Renewals in 1962 and 1964 had, through the classic American process of pluralistic bargaining, extended NDEA's coverage to virtually all areas of education, private as well as public, on the politically appealing but intellectually suspect assumption that virtually all academic disciplines are ultimately related to defense. Add to that the four titles of Kennedy's HEFA of 1963 and the eight titles of Johnson's HEA of 1965, plus *their* subsequent extensions by amendments, and the educational agenda for Congress in 1968, despite President Johnson's tightly constrained budget, was *enormous* in its potential for renewal and expansion.

But Johnson had at least somewhat limited the higher-education agenda by avoiding any radical new departures in the pattern of federal aid to higher education, such as the Friday proposal for relatively no-strings institutional grants based on a combination of enrollment and instructional costs. This was important not because the Friday recommendations were wrongheaded; in fact, like most recommendations of the Friday report, they were reasonably well researched, balanced with compromise, and looked toward the future. Rather, it was because no consensus existed within the administration *or* within Congress on how best to assist higher education, and that in turn reflected the lack of consensus in the higher-education community itself. The Friday task force compromise, remaining secret in Johnson's jealously guarded task force closet (except, to paraphrase the Vicar of Bray, when leaks of loyalty no harm meant), did not reflect a broad constituency debate. Opinion within DHEW, USOE, the NSF, the Bureau of the Budget, and the White House staff was as deeply divided as was opinion within the academic community itself. Clark Kerr, who chaired the Carnegie Commission on Higher Education, was known to oppose general aid to higher education, whether in the form of block grants to the states or tuition tax credits. But the Kerr Commission's report was not due until July. Finally, in April of 1967, Secretary Gardner had appointed an Advisory Committee on Higher Education, chaired by Chancellor W. Clarke Wescoe of the University of Kansas. It was charged with examining the relationship between the federal government and institutions of higher education and recommending ways to improve that relationship. But the Wescoe committee was also not due to report until July of 1968. So under the conditions of severe budget constriction, the disarray of academic and constituency opinion, and the future reporting dates of major recommending bodies, President Johnson chose the prudent path, in his special message on education, of asking the secretary of health, education, and welfare to prepare a long-range plan on federal support for higher education in America.

THE COLLAPSE OF MORALE

But who was the secretary of health, education, and welfare? No one knew, because John Gardner had resigned on 25 January 1968. Late in December, Gardner had delivered an address at the annual meeting of the American Statistical Association (trained as a psychologist, Gardner had formerly taught statistics), where he had hinted at his profound misgivings about the course of American society and the inadequacies of the Great Society: "It does not seem to me that either the Congress or the public is fully aware of the alarming character of our domestic crisis. We are in deep trouble as a people. And history is not going to deal kindly with a rich nation that will not tax itself to cure its miseries."[5] Early in January Gardner told President Johnson that he was determined to resign, and Johnson probed him for half an hour to find out why. Gardner's own account of this painful meeting holds that he stressed the message that the country was falling apart and that Johnson could not hold it together. Gardner recalls that the president responded with a "cool self-evaluation and a melancholy realism" that belied his public image as the charging cowboy fullback.[6] Also in January, the director of the Bureau of the Budget, Charles Schultze, resigned. He recalls his general disgust at the disarray of Johnson's policy of guns-and-Great Society: "Looked at from the straight economic and immediate effectiveness standpoint, it was a sloppy, chaotic, underfunded set of operations. . . . You get annoyed and mad and frustrated and disgusted at how chaotic and sloppy some of it was, precisely because you're laying Vietnam on top of it and trying to nickel-and-dime these programs."[7] By then, morale in the executive branch, and especially in DHEW and USOE, which had accrued so much of the Great Society's programmatic legacy, was generally miserable. The Gardner/Howe interagency task force on education of 1967 had vented this frustration eloquently, and the follow-on Cohen/

Howe interagency task force of 1968 bitterly echoed the theme that there was already an overdose of underfunded legislation on the books. Samuel Halperin recalls the fatigue and malaise.

> I had the impression, particularly in 1967, 68, of great haste, great superficiality. And political naivete of the highest order[,] . . . the staff work of Gaither and Califano doesn't begin to compare, for example, to the sophistication of the staff work that Mr. Cater engaged in, let's say, in '64–'65. I have to say that by '67–'68 perhaps all of us were doing sloppier work. We were overextended, overtired, and our morale left a lot to be desired.[8]

Part of this growing agency resentment was clearly directed at Califano and his aggressive staff of "whiz kids." Witness Halperin, again:

> I think Mr. Califano gave the impression from afar that he would deal with Secretaries of Departments or with God Almighty —and then only grudgingly. Califano went to great lengths to make decisions. I don't believe he checked with the President on many key issues. With as few people around who knew the details of what was going on as possible, many of the decisions were made by him with a person such as Secretary Gardner who did not really know the substance and the detail of many of the proposals and couldn't be expected to. I found that Mr. Califano was arrogant, uninformed, bright but exceedingly thin because he was spread over such a broad area.[9]

Part of it stemmed, also, from the Johnson administration's increasing resort to the bureaucratic short-circuiting possibilities of the secret, White House-centered, task force device.[10] Recall the scorn even of the Bureau of the Budget's Harold Seidman, who had been White House liaison for Donald Price's 1964 outside task force on government reorganization, but who complained about the abuse of task forcing as early as 1966: "Task forceitis ran rampant. At least forty-five task forces were organized in the fall of 1966. Papers were circulated on an 'eyes only' basis and when agency people were included on the task forces they were reluctant to tell even their bosses about what they were doing. The task force operation bred a miasma of suspicion and distrust without producing very much that was useable."[11]

But the most morale-shattering bombshell of all burst on 31 March, when President Johnson announced that he would not accept renomination. Although Johnson claims in his memoirs that he and Lady Bird had decided this as early as 1964, and that he had told virtually all of his close associates,[12] both the press and his own White House staff had long assumed that such talk represented only a ventilation of normal presidential frustrations, and that Johnson would surely run for reelection. After all, he always had. As early as May of 1967 Califano had been gearing up for the 1968 campaign with Johnson's full knowledge and approval, detailing Fred Panzer to compile an accomplishment file, Fred Bohen to work up expenditure data on domestic programs and federal aid by congressional district, Gardner Ackley to collect economic data, and Alexander Trowbridge (as commerce secretary, he controlled the Bureau of the Census) to provide population data. But how should the considerable time and effort required to pay for gathering and organizing these massive data be paid for? Califano complained to President Johnson that "the government (at least on the domestic side) is clearly not geared to get the type of information we should have for campaigning and for program planning in a Presidential election year"; but he exclaimed that "it would be a shame not to use the incredible advantage we have in terms of information through the use of the Federal Government."[13] Califano's solution was disingenuous, though probably not novel: "Budget has a management survey fund and since this is management information which Budget legitimately needs, I think they can pick up the tab. This should be in no way be related to campaigning because its need and use are much more lasting. . . . In this way, we can serve two purposes—both political purposes vis-a-vis 1968 campaigning and program purposes at the same time."[14]

By late March of 1968, Califano had assembled a core of campaign planners,[15] and he had assigned to Robert Hardesty the task of constructing two books designed to assassinate the political character of Johnson's two most likely challengers for the nomination: Senator Eugene McCarthy ("a lazy, careless attitude; conservative stands; long-time supporter of special interest groups; Betrayer of youth"), and Robert Kennedy ("the hatchet man; protege of Joe McCarthy and his ruthless disrespect for civil liberties; a man emotionally and temperamentally unfit for the Presidency; a Johnny come-lately on Civil Rights").[16] As late as 25 March, Johnson approved borrowing John Robson from DOT to replace Gaither on campaign planning (Gaither was leaving to practice law in San Francisco), and on 28 March Robson reported to Califano on a meeting on LBJ's campaign posture that worried over the negative quality of the president's strengths ("more trustworthy than RFK; less disliked than RFK; a steady, if unimaginative, hand on the tiller") and over the vulnerabilities that were inherent in his image ("LBJ's personal war, and he's stubborn and inflexible about it; a belligerent President; inability to communicate with youth").[17] Then, just three days later, Johnson rendered it all irrelevant, except for Vice-President Humphrey, who inherited all the planning along with a politically disastrous legacy.

A VAST CONTRADICTION

By the spring of 1968, then, the discredited Johnson administration appeared to be in a state of exhaustion and collapse, with the country dissolved in ghetto and campus riots and massive demonstrations against the war in Vietnam. The Kerner Commission turned its guns on the embittered Johnson, at least implicitly; the campuses erupted in violence; and when Martin Luther King was murdered, the ghettos exploded again, especially in Washington and nearby Baltimore, where the majority of the population was black.[18]

In April, Johnson launched Califano and his staff on an intensive mission to explore how best to establish his school of public affairs, to be set next to his presidential library on the campus of the University of Texas at Austin.[19] In May, Johnson kindly turned down an offer to become Distinguished Professor of Government at his alma mater, Southwest Texas State College in San Marcos, and he accepted instead an offer to join the University of Texas as Distinguished Lecturer in Public Affairs.[20] Such exhaustion, loss of focus, and general disarray fits comfortably with our modern understanding of the flow and ebb of presidential power, and especially of recent lame-duck administrations.[21] As President Johnson told Harry McPherson, "You've got to give it all you can, that first year. Doesn't matter what kind of majority you come in with. You've got just one year when they treat you right, and before they start worrying about themselves. The third year, you lose votes. . . . The fourth year is all politics. You can't put anything through when half the Congress is thinking how to beat you."[22] But instead of lame-duck collapse, Johnson's Great Society agenda, especially in education, roared through Congress like a flood in 1968. How can we account for so vast a contradiction? The explanation lies paradoxically in a combination of two forces that are themselves ostensibly contradictory. One force represented the great momentum established by the Great Society's legislation machinery, which centered on the task force device but was deeply rooted in the modern presidential initiative in forming legislative agendas that began with Franklin Roosevelt. The second force represented the reassertion of congressional initiative, which predated President Nixon's problems with Watergate and the saucy freshman Democratic "Class of 1974." The reassertion of congressional authority surged in the spring of 1968, when powerful congressional conservatives bled Johnson for his tax increase and successfully extracted as its price a $6 billion reduction in fiscal year 1969 spending and a cutback of 245,000 in civilian employees in the executive branch. This was a protracted and brutal fight, and although Johnson treats it as a great victory in his memoirs, in fact he was badly bloodied by the resurgent Congress.[23]

IRON TRIANGLES

So why did we not get political paralysis in 1968, instead of the massive harvest of renewed Great Society legislation, especially in education? The major reason is that the overlapping educational constituencies had by the late 1960s formed their iron-triangle relationships with the congressional subcommittees and the executive agencies and, lacking any fundamental divisions in political issues (that is, Johnson's higher education amendments proposed mostly a little more of the same across the board, avoiding the big battle over aid to institutions or to students that raged during the early Nixon administration), the administration's 1968 proposals for renewals and amendments and minor modifications and a few tiny "budget-wedge" new programs went crunching through the congressional machinery with only diversionary congressional battles over drafting graduate students and withdrawing federal financial support from rioting students. The congressional season featured the customary conflicts between Oregon's interpersonally hostile but politically stalwart Democratic friends of federal aid to education, Edith Green and Wayne Morse (Mike Manatos wrote Barefoot Sanders on 27 April that "Morse will never do anything which gives the impression he will take direction from '*that woman*'").[24] Morse raged that in 1967 Congress had authorized $6.489 billion for education in 1968, but that the Johnson administration had requested only $3.791 billion under the same legislation for fiscal 1969, and that in the big push for higher education, the administration had retreated from the $1 billion commitment of 1968 to a mere $700 million for 1969. Most cuttingly, he asked how the Bureau of the Budget measured "the value of the life of one American Boy against the lives of a number of Viet Cong, the education of the boys and girls of this country against the present regime in South Vietnam, and the future of the lives of our boys and girls against national prestige."[25]

After lengthy spring hearings, the House passed the Higher Education Amendments of 1968 (H.R. 15067) on 25 July by a thundering roll-call vote of 389 to 15. It included *new* authorizations of $905,270,-000, and its total authorization was $2,458,270,000 for fiscal 1969 and $2,788,730,000 for fiscal 1970. President Johnson's fiscal 1969 budget request had been only $995.8 million for the same programs.[26] By the 25 September Senate-House conference, Congress had agreed to approve and fund and extend and renew and expand a cornucopia of education programs that included school breakfasts, the Indian Bill of Rights, bilingual-bicultural education, stay-in-school drop out prevention, Networks for Knowledge, facilities sharing, college remedial tutoring, increased student loans and scholarships, Talent Search, college housing, Education for the Public Service, international education, the Teacher Corps, law school clinical experience, the Arts and Humanities Foundation—the list rattles on. There were no *major* new programs, but the venerable NDEA, HEFA, and HEA were renewed and expanded, and seven new small programs were authorized. On 16 October, Lyndon Johnson signed the Higher Education Amendments and the Vocational Education Amendments of 1968—the fifty-ninth and sixtieth education laws of the Johnson administration.

Clearly, Lyndon Johnson instinctively understood the coalescence of "iron triangles" linking constituency group, agency, and subcommittee in a symbiotic embrace.[27] Indeed, Douglass Cater had written one of the major books on the alliance-formation process, whereby clientele groups forged enduring bonds of mutual interest with congressional subcommittees who authorized programs affecting their interests, and with agency officials who ran them.[28] The classical examples of iron triangles have been the agricultural extension network and the Army Corps of Engineers, and Harvard's Hugh Heclo is right to remind us that the United States Office of Education is not the Army Corps of Engineers.[29] But what the iron triangles did to Lyndon Johnson's austerity budget in education in 1968 is best summed up by the director of the budget, Charles Zwick.

> I was talking with one of the senior civil servants in the Budget Bureau two days ago, it was the day after that education vote in the House, and he said, "My God, Charlie, they talk about the military-industrial complex, you should have seen those educators there. They were hanging from the rafters, and they really do have muscle." . . . I've always said that if there was ever a "seventh day in May" after the military took over there'd probably be a counter revolution by the librarians, who would probably capture and run the country for the next hundred years. The librarian lobby is terribly powerful. They've got all the book publishers, the libraries and the universities and everybody else pushing here.[30]

An acknowledged master of the legislative process and the levers of power, Johnson was also a master raconteur (if an earthy one) who cherished a revealing metaphor about the momentum of legislative interest groups. Cater recalls Johnson's fondness for the yarn about the country boy who on first seeing a locomotive, doubted that they would ever get it going. But when he saw it build up steam and roar down the tracks, he said, "They'll never stop her."[31] By 1968, neither Johnson's bare-bones budget nor the Vietnam War nor the Revenue and Expenditure Control Act could stop her. Nor could President Richard Nixon, whose efforts to repeal the Great Society in education ultimately and ironically led to the breakthrough decision in higher education aid that Johnson had avoided in 1968.[32] Charles Lee left Morse's staff and during the 1970s used his intimate familiarity with the educational constituencies and the ways of the Hill to ramrod the Committee for Full Funding of Educational Programs, an exceedingly effective lobby with an unusually frank title.[33]

But by as early as the spring of 1968, the Johnson administration's Great Society had evolved from the unique steamroller of 1964–65 into an essentially modern form of embattled presidency that predated President Nixon and Watergate, with whom we customarily associate its attributes. These feature an economy characterized by inflation, high interest rates, and a worsening balance of payments. The president tries to hold down the domestic budget, and he battles a resurgent Congress, where iron triangles and entitlement programs threaten growing budget deficits; and presidential prerogatives in budgeting and expenditure are sharply challenged by such congressional initiatives as the Revenue and Expenditure Control Act of 1968 and the Congressional Budget and Impoundment Control Act of 1974. Of course, the emerging pattern of 1968 was only a faint image of what it was to become. It is ironical that the relative immaturity of iron triangles in education in the early 1960s provided the initial Great Society task forces, which through secrecy were considerably screened from the triangular base of agency-subcommittee-clientele group, with unusual room for innovative maneuver. But by the end of the Johnson administration, the very proliferation of Great Society categorical programs that task forcing had spurred in turn reinforced the growing triangular networks with a vested interest in maximizing their benefits by pressing willing congressional authorizing committees to exceed by large margins the president's budget requests, especially in education. By mid-1968, the vigorous campus-visit, task-forcing cycle would seem scarcely appropriate to the new circumstances. But by then the pattern was strongly ingrained.

LAME-DUCK CAMPUS VISITS

President Johnson's withdrawal from the presidential race on 31 March in fact did *not* fundamentally alter the White House's cyclical pattern of early summer academic visits and late summer-through-fall interagency task forces, although it did sensibly preclude the creation of new outside task forces to report to an unknown new president in 1969, and it did alter the agenda for the campus visits. Beginning in late May Califano and his colleagues held academic meetings in New York City, Stanford, Cambridge, Austin, Princeton, Washington, D.C., Chapel Hill, and New Orleans. Califano's agenda was limited to seeking advice on two topics: a study of the presidency that President Johnson thought should be made, and possible valedictory presidential addresses late in 1968 covering the country's major domestic and foreign problems. Matthew Nimetz kept the minutes of the Cambridge meeting, and they reveal the kind of critical scrutiny that the president's two proposals deserved from Harvard's distinguished faculty. First came Dean Price on the proposed study of the presidency: "Don Price wondered about its basic purpose. He could see the value of the study for an incumbent President, or for an incoming President. But it is hard for an outgoing President to have real influence.

The Hoover Report is a bad example because Hoover prepared it believing that Thomas Dewey would be elected President. The real issue is whether the new President will want to follow the recommendations."[34] Everybody present agreed that if such a study were to be done, it would need a public blessing from the new president, yet it should be started well before the election. Price and Richard Neustadt agreed that the most effective model was the Brownlow Committee, a tightly controlled three-man committee with a small but excellent staff. The study should not be controlled by the president, although it might well be symbolically sponsored by the three living ex-presidents. But could you usefully study the presidency without also studying Congress? Would it not properly take several years to complete?

When a slightly different Harvard group reconvened for an evening meeting on the question of outgoing presidential speeches, Neustadt led off: "Neustadt began the evening meeting by noting that he had drafted President Truman's State of the Union Message of 1953. He remarked that nobody noticed it, and that this is usually the problem of the outgoing President. Everyone is interested in what the new President will say and not in the advice of the old President." Neustadt also observed that Johnson's role would differ according to whether he was succeeded by a Republican or a Democrat. "For example, President Truman was tempted by two strategies: to cut the budget so that the Republicans would have to raise it, or to send up a big budget out of which the Republicans would have to cut attractive items. Actually, he did neither of these. Neustadt said that if Humphrey is elected, he might want the President not to say very much because failure to act on LBJ's recommendations might be embarrassing."[35] The historian Ernest May asked about the purpose of these speeches. Was it to help the new president or to speak to history? Why not simply use the major formal addresses that are available—the State of the Union Message, the Economic Report, and the Budget Message? Toward the end of the campus visits, Califano occasionally added to the agenda a third question: What actions might the president take before leaving office? But this was rarely helpful, because a room full of professors (plus customarily a small scattering of businessmen, foundation executives, and church leaders) typically produced a cacophony of favorite themes, or such unlikely suggestions as, "Admit that Vietnam was a mistake and pull out," or "Fire J. Edgar Hoover and General Hershey."

But in general during the spring and early summer of 1968, when Johnson's White House turned to the best and most experienced political minds in the academic community, the president received sound advice: he should not associate himself too closely with the new LBJ School of Public Affairs; nor should he associate himself too closely with any study of the presidency that his unknown successor would inherit; and also that the proposed series of valedictory addresses was fraught with pitfalls. Clearly Lyndon Johnson was struggling with a very large and wounded ego; it is to his credit that ultimately he avoided inflicting these potential wounds upon himself, upon his new school of public affairs, or upon his successor's administration.

LAME-DUCK TASK FORCING

In the fall of 1967, the tireless Califano had appointed two final outside task forces on education that were to make their report in the summer of 1968. On 30 June F. Champion Ward, who was vice-president for education and research for the Ford Foundation, sent President Johnson the report of the task force on the education of gifted persons.[36] It was a handsome, forty-three-page, typeset report that convincingly demonstrated the costs to society of failing to identify and encourage the unusually gifted child. Most of its recommendations were directed toward the states, communities, and private institutions; the only recommendations for the federal government were that the president create a Center for the Development of Exceptionally Talented Persons in DHEW, appoint an advisory council, and convene a conference. But it was far too late for Lyndon Johnson's administration to respond even to such modest initiatives. On 6 January 1969, Califano, in tidying up his affairs, sent Johnson another copy of the Ward report, with a cover memo that summarized it in a supportive way but made no recommendations.

Also in July of 1968, Paul Miller submitted his seventy-two-page task force report on urban education opportunities.[37] Miller requested releasing the report to the public, and while the predictable presidential response was a resounding "*No*," it was just as well, for the talented task force had failed to articulate its understanding of the urban land-grant extension model. That is, it had been unable to explain how colleges and universities can or should play a major role in solving complex urban problems.[38] The Bureau of the Budget's analysis of the report was devastating, finding the task force's concepts to be "nebulous" and "elusive." On the report's first recommendation that funding be substantially increased for all federal education programs for the urban disadvantaged, the BOB analysis commented that "this recommendation appears to be more a pious hope than a firm proposal. No specific funding levels were suggested. No order of priorities was given." Second, the report's major new program recommendation was for an Urban Education Services Act that would have the secretary of health, education, and welfare give grants to an "urban education service agency," a local group consisting of one or more colleges or universities, state and/or local government agencies, representative community groups, and elementary and secondary governing bodies. These amorphous groups would somehow be convened and led by the higher-education institutions, with $5 million start-up grants in fifty or more major cities. But there was no clear suggestion of what these new agencies would actually *do*, other than to get together and collaborate. BOB's analysis noted that "the recommendation essentially proposes a *mechanism* rather than a *program*. There is no description of *what* specifically should be done in the cities. The task force assumes that out of the interaction of the various local groups, some good programs will be developed. We doubt that such 'interaction' under the leadership of academics will result in the solution of many urban problems." The Bureau of the Budget's analysis concluded with the observation that the DHEW budget submission for the 1969 legislative program contained none of the Miller recommendations, and for good reason.[39]

But if the outside task forces were petering out in the summer of 1968, the interagency task forces were being once again appointed by Califano at a substantial level that approached the level of the previous year. Having appointed twenty-four interagency task forces in 1967, the indefatigable Califano appointed *nineteen more* in late 1968 to cover topics as disparate as marine science, product test information, workman's disability income—and *two* more on education.

ACADEMIC SCIENCE AND THE RIVLIN REPORT

One interagency task force focused its attention exclusively on higher education, and it is listed in Nancy Kegan Smith's research guide at the LBJ Library as the Task Force on Higher Education and the Administration of Academic Science and Research Programs. But the documents indicate that the effort actually began in August 1967 when Califano appointed Schultze to head a study of scientific research only, and to report in time to recommend a program for the second session of the Ninetieth Congress. The campus visits had abundantly demonstrated that university research professors were dismayed by the cutbacks in research funding that had accompanied the corresponding growth of nonresearch funding for higher education as in a zero-sum game, and by generally increased delays, red tape, complex and contradictory administrative requirements, and short-notice funding. But the problem was too complicated for such a timetable, and Schultze was leaving BOB, so on 11 October Califano replaced Schultze with Ivan Bennett, deputy director (to Donald Hornig) of the Office of Science and Technology, and gave him until 1 June 1968 to report. But this still wasn't enough time. Bennett would not report until 22 October, by which time it was too late for useful program formulation, especially in view of the fact that a Republican administration was elected shortly thereafter.

The Bennett report conceded most of the charges leveled by academic researchers, but its only major recommendation of immediate significant impact was to call for more money for the NSF in the fiscal year 1970 budget (the highly regarded NSF accounted for only 15 percent of federal academic research funding, the lion's share coming from such large mission agencies as the Department of Defense and DHEW).[40] Bennett also called for three-year "indicative planning" to help relieve the unstable, short-range funding problem, and also for some possible reorganization to strengthen scientific research, primarily through an upgraded OST or even perhaps a new cabinet-level department of higher education and science. But at an 11 December White House meeting on academic science and higher education, it was decided to leave the Bennett report as a "transition item," especially in light of the anticipated efforts of the Nixon administration in government reorganization.[41] (Under the leadership of Litton Industries executive Roy Ash, the Nixon administration did substantially reorganize the executive office of the president, upgrading the program planning function of a heavily staffed Domestic Council, and downgrading the Bureau of the Budget to an Office of Management and Budget, which was assigned to administrative functions only.)[42]

The same 11 December meeting discussed the "Rivlin report" on a long-range strategy for federal financing of higher education, which was not submitted to Gaither until 4 December by Alice M. Rivlin, who was assistant secretary for planning and evaluation at DHEW. At the heart of the Rivlin report was a compromise formula, similar in spirit to the Friday report recommendation, that would combine a broader program of Equal Educational Grants to needy students with direct institutional aid in the form of a cost-of-education allowance.[43] The needy full-time students would receive grants ranging from $200 to $1,500, depending upon family income, and the cost-of-education institutional allowance would be 35 percent of all individual federal grants. Rivlin also proposed the National Student Loan Bank, a nonprofit private corporation to be established by the United States Government, which would replace the guaranteed student loan program. The NSLB would issue its own securities to raise capital for student loans at fixed rates, with interest paid by the federal government during enrollment. The Friday task force had recommended a similar measure. Such a program would be especially appealing to the middle class and to expensive private institutions. At the White House meeting on 11 December, there was general agreement on the artful balance of the Rivlin proposals. But they would be extremely expensive, and William Carey cautioned that there was still no resolution of the strong contentions within higher education, so the president should not be led to believe otherwise. It was decided that there would be some mention of the recommendations in either the Economic Report or the State of the Union Message, and that the Rivlin report would be publicly released as a further stimulant to national debate on the issue—which it was.

THE LAST GREAT SOCIETY TASK FORCE ON EDUCATION

Finally, when Cohen was asked to chair the 1968 interagency task force on education, he promptly bucked the chairmanship down to Howe, after the manner of Gardner. The dispirited group met only twice; and its rather perfunctory, ten-page report of 11 October suggested a generalized weariness and resentment.

> The Task Force did not consider the implications of increased funding of existing authorities on our Nation's schools. In addition, no attempt was made to balance the importance of such increased funding of certain programs (such as Title I of the Elementary and Secondary Education Act and the Education Profes-

sions Development Act) against suggested new programs or areas of interest. There is some feeling in the Task Force that Federal education programs now in place are adequate to meet most of the needs of the schools if they could be funded at higher levels. We have an overdose of underfunded legislation on the books.[44]

The Bureau of the Budget's analysis of the report regarded it as "a tidying up of the Federal Government's education affairs, program consolidation, and relatively minor amendment of existing programs. Costs would be low or deferred until 1971. Many of the recommendations could be accomplished administratively."[45] But it would be wrong to suggest a picture of total bureaucratic exhaustion and despair, for these were professional civil servants of a generally high caliber. They no longer paid much heed to the recommendations of outside task forces—indeed, by 1968 there wasn't much left to pay heed to—but their internal bureaucratic machinery nevertheless generated twenty-three program proposals in their report, and three of them were new programs of substantial import: an ambitious new Day Care and Child Development Act, with comprehensive care available to *all* children; school construction grants, with federal debt service payments; and extending adult basic education eligibility from the 21 million with less than an eighth-grade education to the 64 million who had not graduated from high school. None of these potentially very expensive programs got by the Bureau of the Budget or the White House in transition, but it shows that, despite the general malaise and dispiritedness of a defeated administration, neither the senior career civil servants nor the political appointees were moribund. Indeed, the Great Society's legislative machinery was formidable even in defeat and disarray. As Lyndon Johnson noted with pride in *The Vantage Point*, his grand total of 207 Great Society laws "kept coming right to the end."[46]

EXIT JANUARY 1969

On the day following Nixon's victory, Califano met with Zwick, Okun, McPherson, Levinson, Nimetz, and Gaither to "discuss the status of the task forces established earlier this year, the 1969 legislative program, and the Economic, Budget and State of the Union messages." Califano reported to the president their general agreement that with a new Republican administration coming in, it would be inappropriate to submit a detailed legislative program and to build into that program the budget as you have done in past years. The State of the Union Message should not be patterned along the lines of your previous messages which outlined in some depth your legislative recommendations. Rather it should be a more general and personal document, identifying practices and goals.

But then Califano added:

Nevertheless, we do have a large number of task force reports and studies which have either been completed or will be completed within the next few weeks (partial list attached). In addition, we have some very significant proposals submitted in prior years by task forces, such as the Heineman recommendations on government organization. From both of these, we have significant and specific recommendations as to new programs.

We believe that we should complete the development of programs suggested by these task forces, essentially as we have done in previous years. This would be useful in developing recommendations for the Economic and Budget messages.

Johnson replied, "I agree."[47]

During the transition, while the White House and executive office staff worked on the three January messages, Johnson avoided the embarrassment of valedictory speeches and confined himself, as had other outgoing presidents before him, to public remarks incidental to meeting with the president-elect and his new cabinet appointees; to greeting visiting (mostly minor) foreign dignitaries; to thanking his White House secretaries, telephone operators, and security personnel; to handing out medals and military unit citations; to holding a couple of press conferences; and to receiving groups who expressed their appreciation—certainly these included leading American educators. Johnson's cooperation in the transition was externally gracious, although his refusal to share his task force reports with the Nixon administration, despite Califano's repeated requests for him to do so, was consistently adamant.

In his sixth and last annual State of the Union Message, which was delivered in person before a joint session of Congress on 14 January, President Johnson challenged the Ninety-first Congress to honor the social commitments of their Democratic predecessors by increasing expenditures to expand eight major New Deal and Great Society initiatives.[48] But education, interestingly, was not among them. (The eight were, in order of their being mentioned, housing and model cities, urban renewal, social security, medical care for expectant mothers and infants, antipoverty, job training, civil rights, and crime prevention.) By then, education was politically safe; it did not need to be on the endangered list. President Johnson also courageously asked for licensing and registering firearms, reorganizing the postal service, raising judicial and congressional salaries, and a random military draft.

Johnson's Budget Message, however, which was sent to Congress the following day, was a detailed, thirty-two-page document in which he boasted (as he was to do in his Economic Report on 16 January) about the belated tax surcharge and tight budgeting that had enabled him to reduce a record $25 billion deficit in 1968 to a predicted $2.4 billion surplus when fiscal year 1969 ended the following 1 June. But it also contained a substantial section on education, *all* of which was devoted to cataloging the Great Society's dramatic achievements in education between 1964 and 1970. Johnson was including his 1970 budget proposals, which was cheating a bit, because the first session of the Ninety-first Congress was able to pass no major education bill at all in 1969, including even the bill (H.R. 73111) providing fiscal year 1970 funds for ongoing education programs. But Johnson's aggregate, six-year totals are close enough to the mark, and they reflect a monumental physical achievement.

1. We are now assisting in the education of 9 million children from low-income families under Title I of the Elementary and Secondary Education Act of 1965.
2. We are providing a Head Start for 716,000 preschool children . . . and Follow Through for 63,500 children to preserve their gains.
3. About 182,000 children who suffer mental or physical handicaps requiring special educational methods are now enrolled in classes with Federal support. None of these programs were [*sic*] available in 1964.
4. Under the budget proposals for 1970, college students will receive a total of 2 million grants, loans, and interest subsidies

for guaranteed loans compared with 247,000 in 1964. This assistance is reaching about 1 out of every 4 students.

5. Between 1965 and 1970, the Federal Government will have assisted in the construction of more than $9 billion worth of college classrooms, libraries, and other facilities . . . a level of construction almost double the previous five years.

6. About 500,000 students will receive support for education and training in 1970 under Veterans Administration programs—principally the GI Bill—compared with about 30,000 in 1964.

7. More than 4 million high school students and 845,000 technical students will be enrolled in federally supported vocational education programs in 1970, an increase of 200% in 5 years.

8. Creation of the Teacher Corps, which in 1970 will bring 2,400 talented and concerned young people into the most demanding classes in the Nation—those in our city slums and poor rural areas.

9. Improvement in the quality of teaching through graduate fellowships and short-term refresher training which will reach about one teacher out of 11 in 1970.

How well has this massive legacy of the Great Society worked, viewed from the perspective of the 1980s? That will be the burden of the next, and final, chapter. It will involve a shift in approach and method, a change from the analytical narrative based on primary documents to a more editorially reflective epilogue based on the secondary literature. This narrative has traced policy origins in the 1960s in considerable detail, but policy formulation and adoption should not be assessed independent of policy implementation and evaluation. Evaluating the social programs of the Great Society was both a built-in policy requirement and a matter of partisan and ideological inevitability. It nurtured a cottage industry that by the early 1970s had already generated a newly sobered mood ranging from disappointment to cynicism. Chapter Nine will trace the evolution of that abiding debate as it bears on education policy, and continues with even renewed vigor in the 1980s.

9 / EPILOGUE

POLICY IMPLEMENTATION AND THE POLITICAL
CONTEXT OF FEDERALISM

In the aftermath of the Great Society, as the unrealistic euphoria that surrounded the antipoverty war led to a rather cynical reaction against it, most of the lightning was attracted to such core antipoverty programs as Model Cities, and especially to the 850 local community-action organizations spawned by the Economic Opportunity Act of 1964. Direct federal aid to a whole new stratum of neighborhood groups, many of them determined to run around or over city hall, had provided a powerful incentive for entrenched Democratic urban organizations to combine with normally hostile suburban Republicans and conservative southerners to bridle the antipoverty war during the Nixon and Ford years. Disillusioned social science academics also turned somewhat cynical in disowning the overoptimistic social assumptions of the 1960s,[1] and popular writers like Tom Wolfe could turn their gonzo journalism on spineless federal bureaucrats and rip-off-minded local activist groups, regaling us with such entertaining outrages as *Radical Chic and Mau-Mauing the Flak Catchers.*

But the new federal education programs of the 1960s marched through Congress and toward implementation under the antipoverty banner also, especially the large and novel ESEA, with its dominant Title I. So although it was not surprising that such programs would inherit their share of the disillusioned reaction of the 1970s, there are two additional reasons why Title I was destined to receive intense scrutiny in the early years of its implementation.

The first reason concerns the unique political context within which federal education programs historically operated. Structurally, the federal programs have traditionally been obliged to reach out toward the rural and urban poverty concentrations in counties and cities by way of intervening state bureaucracies, which in education had never been highly regarded as possessing administrative imagination and skill. Edgar Fuller and his Council of State School Officers were nobody's favorites in the Johnson White House, and the literature of American political science is full of complaints against the conservative bias of state administrators and malapportioned legislatures.[2] Attitudinally, the devotees of the "religion of localism" were deeply suspicious of federal intentions. This meant that ESEA and especially Title I had to lean over backward to minimize the kind of federal strings that were normally attached to categorical grants. Also, in order to maximize the political attractiveness of Title I in Congress, the funding formula had to appear to qualify almost every school district in the country, thereby spreading the funds so thin that pockets of poverty did not initially receive the concentration of resources and effort that was necessary to make much of a dent in the problem. Title I's $13 billion price tag for its first ten years looks hefty, but it customarily represented only 8 percent of annual total public school expenditures, and that represents *very* modest leverage. Compensatory education seemed to work only if it was begun early enough and was sustained over a four-to-five year period. But this costs over 50 percent more than normal education, and the 8 percent federal increment represented at once a novel inducement but a very small beginning.

The upshot of all this is that when Title I was implemented, it produced not *a* Title I program, but something more like 30,000 separate and different Title I programs. There is a growing body of literature on implementation in policy analysis that holds that the traditional, rational, comprehensive model of decision making was wrong in concentrating so heavily on the formulation of policy objectives through legislation and minimizing the important, and indeed sometimes crucial implications of program administration. Instead, Eugene Bardach in *The Implementation Game* has emphasized a bargaining model in which policy emerges only as it is implemented, and the relative diversity and independence of the interacting elements of the program heavily determine the outcomes of policy.[3] A recent implementation study of the Voting Rights Act of 1965, for instance, registers the complaint that compliance was compromised because local voting and registration officials were too independent of the federal compliance officials.[4] Yet the Voting Rights Act of

1965 was a tough, even radical law that harks back to the spirit of the first Reconstruction. State and local education officials, however, had always been proudly independent of the federal reach, and the regulatory and enforcement provisions of ESEA were far weaker than that contained in most federal categorical programs. Federal categorical grant programs had proliferated by 1978 to total 492, and 101 of these were in education alone. Other major areas of such proliferation were pollution control, area and regional development, social services, health, public assistance, and ground transportation, where federal monies often dominated state contributions, and because of this federal officials could call the tune.[5] In Eisenhower's interstate highway program, 90 percent of the funds were federal dollars, and hence federal dominance was almost total.[6] But in education the reverse was often true, especially at the elementary-secondary level. As Milbrey McLaughlin observed in her authoritative RAND study of Title I: "In a federal system of government, and especially in education, the balance of power resides at the bottom, with special groups. Accordingly, the implementation of federal initiatives relies in large measure on the incentives and preferences of local authorities."[7] Jerome Murphy's penetrating essay on the politics of implementing Title I points out that in addition to being understaffed, shaken by reorganization, untrained for and unaccustomed to administering such large categorical grant programs, as well as being passively dependent on the states for information and self-monitoring, the USOE officials in the Division of Compensatory Education resented and rejected the role of monitor, regulator, or enforcer. Murphy quotes one such official anonymously: "Title I is a service-oriented program with predetermined amounts for the states. This sets the framework where the states are entitled to the money. Other than making sure states got their money and making sure it was spent, there was no role for the Office of Education. I don't know anyone around here who wants to monitor. The Office of Education is not investigation-oriented, never has been, and never will be."[8] So in a real sense Title I represented the worst of both worlds: as a categorical program, it denied ultimate victory to longtime proponents of relatively no-strings general aid to education, especially for construction and teacher salaries. But as a weak and vaguely defined categorical program, it represented a frail instrument for achieving the inflated hopes of the Great Society to educate the children of the poor.

THE GREAT SOCIETY'S BUILT-IN EVALUATION
REQUIREMENTS

The second reason why Title I was destined for especially intense public
scrutiny was because ESEA contained unprecedented requirements for
systematic evaluation of policy outcomes, for evaluating what works, or
what doesn't. Controversy over the evaluation of the ESEA type of social
programs that were designed to intervene in the poverty circle began
even before ESEA was passed. In response to Title IV of the Civil Rights
Act of 1964, which had mandated within two years a USOE report on the
availability of equal educational opportunity, the Office of Education appointed James Coleman of Johns Hopkins University to lead a mammoth
nationwide survey. The resulting Coleman Report created a storm of
controversy when it was released in the summer of 1966, primarily because Coleman's massive regression analysis suggested that, in comparison with family background and socioeconomic factors, "school factors"
accounted for only a small fraction of the depressed achievement of minority students.[9] In 1965, Commissioner Keppel encouraged Carnegie
and Ford funding for Ralph W. Tyler's Exploratory Committee on Assessing the Progress of Education. But when the White House Conference
on Education was held in July 1965, under the chairmanship of Carnegie Corporation president John Gardner, the Tyler committee's proposed national assessment attracted heated debate among the delegates,
with opponents stressing the dangers of monolithic federal control of
curriculum.[10] It was in this volatile climate that Senator Robert Kennedy,
who feared that school administrators would ignore the wishes and interests of poor parents in spending Title I funds, demanded there be included
in ESEA a unique provision for systematic evaluation of the program's
effectiveness in meeting the special educational needs of disadvantaged
children. This was done through John Brademas's friendly amendment
in the house, and Senator Kennedy "patted it on the fanny" as it sailed
without a comma change through the Senate and down to Stonewall,
Texas, for Lyndon Johnson's signature.

So, simultaneously launching a program that few of its architects and
proponents clearly understood, and being in the middle of a chaotic
reorganization, USOE was in for some early, frequent, and rather embarrassing evaluations. As early as 1968, Bailey and Mosher in *ESEA* concluded that although evaluations of the impact of ESEA to date were
"largely impressionistic and self-serving," the "limited, hard evidence

that does exist on attempts to improve the educational money and services is devastatingly pessimistic."[11] In 1972 Joel Berke and Michael Kirst published the report of the major 1968–69 Gardner study, funded by the National Urban Coalition (and hence heavily by the Ford Foundation) and sponsored by the Maxwell School at Syracuse University.[12] This evaluation was based on data from 575 school districts during ESEA's initial implementation period, 1965–69, and the results were depressing in the extreme to the champions of equity through federal aid. The new infusion of federal aid, Berke and Kirst concluded, was too small in relation to total educational expenditures to have any significant redistributionist impact, so school district wealth, not need, continued to determine per-pupil expenditures.[13] The affluent continued to dominate the overall school expenditure benefits, and the "religion of localism" still governed. Worse, the modest urban redistributionist effect of ESEA Title I was countered by the effects of ESEA Titles II (textbooks and libraries), III (supplementary service centers), NDEA Title III (instructional equipment), and vocational aid, all of which tended to flow disproportionately toward suburb and countryside. In brief, concluded the report, "the story in general is grossly disappointing."[14]

In 1975 Milbrey Wallin McLaughlin published her Rand educational policy study of the ESEA Title I evaluations from 1965 through 1972. She was testing the hopes of reformers like Kennedy, who viewed mandated evaluation as a means of achieving *political* accountability, and also the hopes of reformers like DHEW's William Gorham, who sought *management* accountability by applying PPBS cost-benefit principles, which had become a Washington fad associated most notably with Robert McNamara's "whiz kids" in the Pentagon. McLaughlin's major conclusion was that seven years and $52 million worth of evaluation efforts had produced dismal failure, an "empty ritual" that "may have done more harm than good." She found the dual roots of failure in the multiple and diverse goals of such broadly aimed social action programs, which are difficult to transform into measurable objectives, and in the federal system itself, whereby USOE did not really "run" Title I. Rather, 30,000 Local Educational Agencies (LEAs) ran it according to the preferences of entrenched local interests. They resisted federal efforts at data collection, which in turn functioned not to strengthen the educational system but "instead to undermine it, and to demoralize education personnel at all levels."[15]

Norman C. Thomas reached a similar gloomy conclusion in *Educa-*

tion in National Politics. A political scientist, Thomas agreed that implementation of policy was less exciting than its formulation and adoption, but he insisted that it was equally important, if not more so.

> Organized interests, especially education clientele groups and the bureaucrats, recognized this as did some members of Congress, most notably Edith Green, and the careerists in the Bureau of the Budget. But the failure of Congress to exercise more careful and exacting oversight, and the inability of the Presidency to mount effective monitoring of the bureaucracy, resulted in a considerable amount of slippage in the achievement of policy objectives once programs had been authorized and funded. Much of this slippage occurred because of the symbiotic relationship that existed within the policy triangles between the agencies, Congressional subcommittees, and clientele groups which [Theodore] Lowi has characterized as "interest group liberalism."[16]

The politics of pluralism was "highly elitist in composition and provided an inhospitable environment for substantial policy changes." It favored defenders of the status quo, or at best the cautious custodians of incremental change, especially because the required sequential approvals provided a multiplicity of access points for organized interests to thwart initiatives and frustrate action.

Finally, the emerging scholarly suspicion that after a decade of operation, Title I and its associated compensatory educational programs had largely failed—as, by the logic of extension, had the bulk of the Great Society's social programs—was reinforced in 1978 by the publication of Julie Roy Jeffrey's *Education for the Children of the Poor.*[17] Jeffrey's ambitious book, which did not receive the attention it deserved, began as a historical dissertation on the origins and implementation of ESEA, but it emerged as a broad-ranged and damaging assessment of the antipoverty war in general and particularly of education as an instrument of social reform and upward mobility—as, in Lyndon Johnson's words, "the only valid passport from poverty." Her bibliographical grasp is extensive (although it does not basically extend beyond 1972), and because her survey is both descriptive and critical (but from a political and historical perspective rather than from a technical one), it is a good source for tracing such important storms of controversy in the running educational debate as those that centered on the arguments of James Coleman, Charles Silberman, Arthur Jensen, Christopher Jencks, the Westinghouse and Rand reports on school effectiveness, and the like.[18]

ASSESSING COMPENSATORY EDUCATION

Throughout the extremely volatile debate over the effectiveness of compensatory education, Title I specifically and ESEA in general were not without their staunch defenders—nor were, of course, the dream of the Great Society and its programmatic legacy.[19] Chief among these was Samuel Halperin, who had left DHEW with the Nixon transition to head George Washington University's Institute for Educational Leadership. Admittedly a partial observer, Halperin used the occasion of ESEA's tenth anniversary to catalog its virtues in the *Phi Delta Kappan*.[20] He admitted that Title III's $1.4 billion for supplementary centers and services, which represented the boldly subversive design of Cannon and the Gardner task force to flank the local educational establishments and force innovation, had largely disappeared into the blur of the states' bureaucratic mediocrity after Edith Green's transfer of 1967–68. Halperin also conceded that "no truly persuasive evidence [exists] that they have sparked substantial changes in the schools or that they have catalyzed enduring partnerships between the schools and the vast untapped cultural and artistic resources of their respective communities."[21] Similarly, Halperin admitted that Title IV, which sought to create a dozen great education R&D laboratories, had fallen on hard times: "The eighteen federally funded labs and centers have no continuity of funding, no real resources to move their investments from product development into large-scale classroom practice. Indeed, educational research and development has become something of a pariah on the priority list of federal policy makers in eduation."[22] As for whether Johnny and Jane were learning to read, Halperin devoted a mere paragraph to the crucial and hotly debated question of Title I's effectiveness (he placed it near the end of his essay, just prior to the acknowledged failures). He claimed only that recent tentative evidence was beginning to suggest that if Title I programs could concentrate long and intensively (that is, expensively) enough upon disadvantaged children, then early gains could be sustained rather than lost.

But this was not primarily what Halperin had in mind, for his was a finely tuned political mind, having been a former chief legislative strategist at DHEW. To a man whose tenure went far enough back to remember the Holy Wars of the Kennedy years, with all their rancor, the ESEA, for all its frustrations and disappointments, represented a political quantum leap with multiple spinoffs. First, ESEA had broken the log jam on federal aid to education with a smashing House vote of 263 to 153 that permanently signaled the retirement of the old paralytic Holy Wars. Second, ESEA spotlighted the needs of children, and fueled a massive conceptual shift of the congressional and educational debate from such policy disputes as shortages of classrooms and teachers and teachers' salaries, to focus instead on the children of the poor. Third, ESEA fueled the equality movement, included both preschool and out-of-school children, and spawned spreading parallel state compensatory and bilingual programs and education programs that aided the handicapped. Fourth, ESEA promoted parental and community involvement in the schools, including public and nonpublic cooperation, and recruited good-quality personnel for service in education. ESEA also promoted the evaluation and accountability movement. Finally, ESEA strengthened the federal system, through Title V's addition of over 2,000 new staff members to state departments of education, and it also promoted the creation of state planning and evaluation units, educational data systems, and assessment and training programs.

But Halperin's best evidence for supportive arguments lay less in the field than on the Hill, where the permanent coalition for federal aid to education rallied to the ESEA despite repeatedly damaging evaluations of Title I and plummeting national SAT scores. In 1974, the House passed the strengthening ESEA amendments by a lopsided vote of 380 to 26. In 1978, Congress approved a $50 billion, five-year reauthorization of ESEA by a smashing vote of 86 to 7 in the Senate and 350 to 20 in the House.[23] Halperin did not, however, allude to iron triangles, the effective lobbying of Charles Lee's Committee for Full Funding, and the post-Watergate Democratic majorities in Congress.

In the *Phi Delta Kappan*'s decennial assessment of ESEA, the negative side of the op-ed format was argued by William W. Wayson of Ohio State University. He attacked ESEA from the left, celebrating its revolutionary breakthrough as more of a Bay of Pigs than a Yorktown, arguing that it was essentially a case study in "institutional intransmutability," and that it represented a "local and state victory over federal attempts to use education to improve the status of the poor."[24] Wayson's prime assumption was radical: that local educators have a "vested interest in practices that systematically harm disadvantaged children"—not because they wish to do so, but because school systems had historically perpetuated the existing distribution of goods and power in local districts. Federalism's three-tiered system of filters and barriers, he argued, was paralleled at the level of the school district by a bureaucratically locked-in, three-tiered system consisting of the superintendent's central office, the principal's school building, and the teacher's classroom.[25] Each level, Wayson claimed, was considerably more autonomous than was generally recognized, but all three resented the parallel thrust of Title I's remedial programs, which were not integrated into the "normal" instructional program, partly as a result of the sociology and politics of local education, and partly as a product of federal auditing requirements, which produced separate Title I teachers and classrooms. And the result of all this was more rather than less internal tracking, segregation, and disruption.[26]

Wayson's evidence was anecdotal, and his critique was curiously ambivalent about the role of principal and teacher, seeing them at once as both the agents of the jealous boundary maintenance and indifference of the status quo (or worse) to the needs of the children of the poor, and yet seeming to view them also as potential reformers who were surprisingly independent of the central office and higher authorities. He gives us no clue as to how the latter rather than the former role may be achieved and rewarded. But subsequent research has at least pointed to its possibility and has thereby revealed a major weakness of the era's dominant mode of social research, which was symbolized by the Coleman and Jencks and subsequent reports based on hypothesis testing through multiple statistical regression of ever more massive aggregations of data. Their strength was that they reminded us that it was naïve to expect the public schools alone to remedy the effects of shattered homes and pathological neighborhoods of poverty, much less to take on such defaulted responsibilities of the crumbling modern family as moral and religious and sex education. Their chief weaknesses were, first, that they were best at *disproving* hypotheses, at statistically indicating what didn't work. Second, such massive statistical aggregations inherently blurred fine distinctions. Lost in the mass of disappointment and failure were schools—indeed, *public* schools—that *did* teach Johnny and Jane to read and to count, despite James Conant's consolidated monster-schools, despite the brain-numbing fare on television, despite plummeting SAT scores and indifferent school bureaucracies, and even despite the truly Great Planning Disaster of chic "open" schools without walls in slums.[27] A handy and heartwarming guide to such possibilities is journalist Robert Benjamin's *Making Schools Work*, which profiles schools that work amidst a sea of gloom in such unlikely places as the South Bronx; Modesto, California; and Madison Heights, Michigan (and others).[28] Their secret to success is not arcane and centers not on innovative methods of equipment or compensatory "pullout" programs. Rather, it centers on old-fashioned leadership: a strong principal, tightly structured time-on-task, homework, dedicated teachers who are supported and protected and who are rewarded more for performance than longevity, discipline to sustain such an environment, and parental involvement. Nothing much is novel there, just old-time schoolmarm wisdom from the world we have lost (excluding the private schools, most of which of course have enjoyed the advantage of excluding our society's most damaged casualties).

But that editorial digression is not completely fair to Halperin and Wayson, who were debating the effectiveness of ESEA in 1975. On balance, Halperin had the edge. This is partly because however much truth there was in Wayson's indictment of local school bureaucracies and the failure of ESEA to enlist them as allies in its novel antipoverty premises, he did not offer us an alternative model, and Halperin was an expert in the political world of the possible, at least at the federal level. By 1975, the accumulative evaluation of ESEA's Title I was shattering in light of the misty hopes for early compensatory intervention in the midsixties. Title II had mostly pacified the Catholics, and Title V had mostly bought off Edgar Fuller's recalcitrant state superintendents and had somewhat improved and modernized their staffs. But Title III, the darling of Bill Cannon and the Gardner report, had been safely neutered by Edith Green, and Title IV's educational R&D labs were orphans without discernible impact. Yet in spite of this uneven and, in spots, rather dismal record, Congress kept renewing and refunding ESEA. Why?

Halperin's argument implicitly suggests that if the demonstrated effectiveness of the major ESEA programs was the major concern of the "permanent" education coalition in Congress, the coalition would have dissolved and rationally written off the commitments of 1965 as a well-intentioned flop. But the permanent coalition seemed to have three other major goals in mind that were not explicit, but which it regarded as still being served. One was to get the mule's attention, not with a two-by-four, but rather with a $16.7 billion carrot over ten years for all ESEA titles— to thereby induce local school districts to shift their attention from the median student to the bottom fifth of the pupils who seemed to be learning virtually nothing at all, or at least little that was socially useful. Another was an intention to use much of ESEA to redistribute income toward the poor, which it modestly did. Yet a third, more immediate, and practical congressional desire was to service and please the expanding universe of beneficiary groups who formed the clientele link with agency and subcommittee in that fascinating proliferation of iron triangles that culminated in the Carter administration and its new Department of Education, and that thereby inadvertently participated in creating a political environment characterized by inflationist fear, soaring federal deficits, and out-of-control entitlement programs that led to the Reagan counter-revolution of 1980.

One year into the Reagan administration, ESEA Title I became Chapter 1 of the 1981 Education Consolidation and Improvement Act (ECIA), which signaled the new Republican administration's commitment to a significantly reduced, block-grant approach to federal aid. In 1982 the astute Milbrey McLaughlin (with Lorraine McDonnell) completed another NIE-funded Rand study of the uneasy federal and state interaction in education policy, and the results and trends were not very encouraging.[29] Although public education accounted for roughly one-third of most state budgets and usually represented the largest single item, compensatory education for the disadvantaged remained a low political priority (except for the handicapped, where powerful new clientele groups were politically effective). Excluding the handicapped, state-level support for social equity goals remained quite low, and with federal support for the old ESEA Title I effort clearly receding, state education agencies (SEAs) were unlikely to take up the slack. Despite considerable administrative strengthening under ESEA's Title V, SEAs were generally incapable of long-range planning, were unable to predict potential problems and were organizationally fragmented by the very multiplicity of federal categorical grant programs that were the legacy of the 1960s. Because "the federal government has stressed administrative compliance, almost to the total exclusion of program content or quality," the states had done likewise.[30] Furthermore, as Jackie Kimbrough and Paul Hill demonstrated, the proliferation of federal categorical grant programs and their increasingly unfunded requirements had produced unintended interferences and cross-subsidy.[31] Interference was the main problem, and a major source was the interruption of core classroom instruction by frequent pullouts for Title I or bilingual programs (in heavily Hispanic districts, pullouts could reach six or seven daily, so that by grade five many Hispanic children had received *no* instruction in science or social studies). Categorical programs often replaced the core curriculum in reading and math, with pullout and auditing logistics dominating educational policy. The conflict of categorical and core programs also produced a clash of teaching methods, staff conflicts, segregated student groups, and it imposed heavy administrative burdens on teachers and principals.

Long depressed by and defensive about the sustained litany of damaging evaluations of Title I efforts, the proponents and defenders of compensatory education more recently have been cheered by studies supporting its increased effectiveness.[32] A prudent comment on this still open debate was offered by Carl Kaestle and Marshall Smith in the *Harvard Educational Review*.

> These gains, if real, are modest when contrasted with the original promise of Title I to overcome disparities in achievement between the children of the poor and the rich. Against the litany of earlier negative evaluations, the results are promising, but against national data showing that achievement scores of middle and high school students have declined steadily for years and that drop-out rates in the inner cities are increasing, the results seem insignificant.[33]

Kaestle and Smith echo Paul Hill's critique of the segregationist tendency of compensatory education:

> [T]he creation of the separate Title I administrative structure placed no pressure on the regular structure to improve and ensured that little of lasting importance would remain if federal dollars were withdrawn. In light of the growing evidence about the importance of the climate and coherence of school administrative structures and the collaboration and involvement of the staff in the development of effective schools, the Title I approach seems to have been doomed to produce mediocre results. By maintaining an independence from the core programs of the school, the

Title I effort insured that its influence and effects were marginal. After almost two decades of intervention the Title I program stands primarily as a symbol of national concern for the poor rather than as a viable response to their needs.[34]

As successor to Lyndon Johnson, President Nixon acknowledged that "we will all have to be education presidents now." His administration's substantial education legislation of 1972, and President Carter's of 1978, basically continued in the Kennedy-Johnson tradition, adding thirteen titles and more than 100 categorical programs to the statute books. These included major new commitments to women, the handicapped, the elderly, and to students whose primary language was not English. Yet Kaestle and Smith conclude of this legacy that

> except in the area of desegregation, however, federal programs operated on the margin of local school system programs. Supplemental activities for low-scoring students in poverty areas, special classes for bilingual youngsters, new procedures for handling handicapped children, equal levels of sports activities for girls and boys are all important issues, and they have taken much time and energy to work out. Yet they are not central to the workings of the regular school program. Taken together these activities assumed great weight because of their symbolic value; taken separately they were often seen as interfering with the real business of the schools.[35]

Then when the Reagan administration came in with its reduced block grants, McDonnell and McLaughlin concluded that "to weaken the federal partnership with states and local districts that has prevailed for the past fifteen years is to harm a largely powerless constituency."[36] This was certainly not Reagan's constituency, but it is not clear that the Kennedy-Johnson legacy, which had been sustained and enlarged during the 1970s, had been very effective in substantially improving the education of the children of the poor, who were the liberal wing of the Democratic Party's natural allies and clients. It wasn't for want of trying, or for the lack of good intentions. But the unique history of federal aid to local education, especially at the elementary level, made the "partnership" something of an odd couple—or, given the three-tiered liaison of local, state, and federal educational agencies, it became too often a troubled ménage à trois. And in some cases, where politics so clearly dominated substance, the new programs made matters much *worse*.

THE RACIAL AND ETHNIC POLITICS OF EDUCATION

Racial and ethnic political appeals have been a major source of electoral success for recent liberal Democratic regimes, but by the same token they have often been the Achilles' heel of sensible domestic policy. Budgetary set-asides for racial and ethnic groups have clashed with the principle of individual equality of citizenship upon which the republic was founded and have led to bizarre competition over ethnic entitlements. Since the Republican administrations of presidents Nixon and Ford never effectively mastered their Democratic Congresses, there is a strong line of domestic program continuity between the Kennedy victory of 1960 and the culminating administration of President Carter through 1980. During those two decades of dramatically expanding federal involvement in education, including the major Nixon expansion of 1972 of aid to college students rather than to institutions (a bill that Nixon claims he almost vetoed), the access of the disadvantaged to the fruits of education at all levels was greatly expanded. But the political fault lines also began to manifest themselves, mostly in the form of demands for overcompensation to benefit historically disadvantaged blacks, Hispanics, and American Indians. Such new and apparently permanent national commissions as the Commission on Civil Rights, the Equal Employment Opportunity Commission, and the offices of civil rights in such major domestic funding and enforcement agencies as DHEW and the departments of Labor and Justice, were early staffed and controlled by members of the "affected class" and their ideological allies. The prolonged and mutually frustrating efforts of these federal investigatory, lobbying, and enforcement agencies, together with even more important efforts by the federal courts, to achieve and maintain racial desegregation of the nation's schools, has produced a vast literature and is beyond the scope of this inquiry.[37] I will concentrate here on three less prominent areas of federal intervention in education, where racial and ethnic politics has tended to skew rational judgment and the allocation of increasingly scarce resources, because educational programs cannot realistically be considered in isolation from educational politics.

The first, and least offensive of the three, concerns HEA Title III for aid to "developing institutions." It is historically clear that what the Gardner task force had primarily in mind for Title III were the slightly more than a hundred historically black colleges that were generally characterized on the debit side by severe underfunding, faculty weakness, curricular backwardness, and racial hostility and condescension from the dominant white community. But when the Johnson administration tried to define the euphemism "developing institutions" into some reasonable and racially blind index of underdevelopment, there were more than twice as many white as black institutions included, and one could scarcely exclude the struggling white colleges from access to federal tax dollars because of genetic deficiencies in skin color. So what began as an awkward interracial fight over a tiny initial appropriation of $5 million for 1966 emerged in the 1980s as a tense battle over a $130 million program (the largest nonresearch program of federal *institutional* aid to colleges) that in the lean late 1970s had drawn in the numerous community colleges, thereby pitting black against white, two-year against four-year and private against public colleges.[38] The program remained politically popular in Congress, but officials of black colleges complained that hordes of newly eligible white colleges were horning in on their terrain, and Republicans grumbled that in any event the underdeveloped colleges never seemed to graduate from the program. A General Accounting Office report of 1979 cited waste and mismanagement that made the program "largely unworkable," and congressional hearings in 1980 and a series in the *Washington Post* in 1981 cited scandals in the Title III program that primarily involved hustling educational consulting firms and either naïve or complicit black college administrators, or both.[39] All of this, however, only mirrored the historic tension of racial politics and did not constitute a major horror show.[40] But the next development in too many ways did.

BILINGUAL EDUCATION IN THEORY AND PRACTICE

Congress first passed the Bilingual Education Act in 1968, as Title VII of the revised ESEA, and it was renewed in 1974, the same year in which the Supreme Court, in Lau v. Nichols, ruled that school districts serving substantial numbers of children with English language deficiencies must do something special for these pupils, although Lau did *not* specify bilingual education as the remedy, and it did not deal at all with bicultural education (nor, indeed, did the Bilingual Education Act of 1968). The following year the Voting Rights Act of 1965 was amended to equate linguistic disadvantage to racial discrimination. This made mandatory the provision of bilingual ballots in many jurisdictions and extended to certain linguistic groups such extraordinary federal protections as blacks enjoyed against at-large elections, district lines that might "dilute" their electoral power, and suburban annexations that would add white voters. Also in 1975, DHEW's Office of Civil Rights (OCR) began to threaten termination of all federal aid unless targeted school districts negotiated an agreement to adopt what OCR disingenuously called the "Lau remedies" of bilingual *and* bicultural education (the former meaning instruction in the child's ethnic language, and the latter meaning instruction in the history and culture of the pupil's ethnic group, or "affirmative ethnicity"). By 1978, OCR had signed on 518 bilingual-bicultural projects in sixty-eight languages and dialects, although 80 percent were in Spanish; and OCR had targeted 334 additional school districts on a hit list for withdrawal of federal funds unless bilingual-bicultural agreements were signed. In a parallel development, federal judges began to interpret Lau to mean that bilingual programs were *required*, and a federal judge in Texas even ordered the state's schools to run "transitional" bilingual programs through the *twelfth grade*! This was, of course, not bilingual transition toward English competency, but rather bicultural maintenance at taxpayer expense of an ethnic group that was federally certified for entitlement.

These developments were so extraordinary and so controversial that in 1977 Samuel Halperin's Institute for Educational Leadership invited Noel Epstein, the national education writer for the *Washington Post*, to join the institute for half a year as its journalist-in-residence to investigate the phenomenon. Epstein's resultant book, *Language, Ethnicity, and the Schools*, concluded that OCR had misinterpreted Lau and had required bilingual-bicultural programs for political reasons even though there was virtually *no* scientific evidence that the bilingual approach was effective or was in any way superior to an alternative policy of intensive immersion in English—a TESOL (teaching English as a second language) model in which the OCR was politically uninterested.[41] Epstein's language was a model of dispassionate inquiry into a controversial subject, but he questioned whether it was "a federal responsibility to finance and promote student attachments to their ethnic languages and cultures, jobs long left to families, religious groups, ethnic organizations, private schools, ethnic publications and others."[42]

What had clearly happened was that militant Hispanics had successfully exploited the Bilingual Education Act of 1968, and the Lau decision of 1974 (which had involved Chinese children in San Francisco) had thwarted any serious efforts in the alternative methods of intensive immersion in English as a second language (TESOL), had transformed bilingual into bicultural education, and in the process had transformed a transitional language program into a tax-supported subcultural maintenance program based upon claims for historical justice for groups that they alleged had been conquered and discriminated against in American society. The prime model was not pedagogic, it was Quebec Française. And given patterns of virtually uncontrolled immigration, its potential for political and social cleavage, for rending the social contract and the American consensus, was equally severe. It was both a spectacular political and an economic success for the Hispanic political activists, as tens of thousands of Spanish-speaking persons found teaching jobs. As Joseph Califano, a strong supporter of bilingual education and a secretary of DHEW under Carter, complained,

> Of most serious concern to me was that HEW's bilingual program had become captive of the professional Hispanic and other ethnic groups, with their understandably emotional but often exaggerated political rhetoric of biculturalism. As a result, too little attention was paid to teaching children English, and far too many children were kept in bilingual classes long after they acquired the necessary proficiency to be taught in English. Due in part to the misguided administration of bilingual programs, 40 percent of students whose first language is Spanish dropped out of school before earning a high school diploma.[43]

"Doc" Howe admitted that the bilingual education program had become a "mess," a "Hispanic job corps and community action program" that was of great benefit to Hispanic militants and Spanish-speaking teachers. The only losers were the Hispanic children and their parents.[44]

As Abigail Thernstrom has forcefully argued in her essay on language in the *Harvard Encyclopedia of American Ethnic Groups*, the bilingual/bicultural movement owed much of its momentum to the Black Power movement, and both had completely turned around the original if somewhat novel judicial logic of Chief Justice Earl Warren in the Brown decision, which had held that "to separate [children] from others of similar age and qualifications solely because of their race generates a feeling of inferiority as to their status in the community that may affect their hearts and minds in a way unlikely ever to be undone." Now, ironically, Black Power and Brown Power advocates were saying that to *assimilate* children into an "alien" culture creates such feelings of inferiority. But Thernstrom ably demonstrates that the political and cultural premises upon which Black and Brown Power were based were radically different, so the surface similarity of their logic was spurious. Once the Bilingual Education Act was passed, however, and a federal administrative staff was formed to enforce it, Thernstrom notes a familiar political phenomenon in Washington's bureaucratic life: "The staffing of the Division of Bilingual Education by ethnic militants followed an administrative tradition: government programs aimed at a particular group are often run by militant members of that group. Politically aggressive veterans administer veterans' programs; civil rights enthusiasts staff the Office of Civil Rights in the Department of Justice; and so forth."[45]

When the Bilingual Education Act was renewed in 1974, senators Kennedy and Cranston were able to transform it from a mere (and vague) bilingual program of 1968 into a bold commitment to biculturalism and affirmative ethnicity. But in 1978 a four-year study by the American Institutes for Research, sponsored by USOE, concluded that most of the Hispanic students involved did not need to learn English, that those who did were not in fact acquiring it, that most bilingual programs were aimed at linguistic and cultural maintenance rather than at learning English and being assimilated into American culture, and that the segregated Hispanic students who were already alienated from school simply remained so.[46] Only one third of the 11,500 Hispanic students studied were placed in the bilingual track because of their need for English instruction, and only 16 percent were monolingual in Spanish. Most of the placement was based on Hispanic surname, not language tests. The congressional hearings of 1978 produced a consensus that while "politically active ethnic leaders wanted [cultural] maintenance programs, most parents did not."[47] As a result, the 1978 renewal required a parental majority on mandatory advisory councils—an injection of democratic due process that the entrenched Hispanic political activists bitterly resented. But as the writer Richard Rodriguez explains in his moving autobiography

Hunger of Memory, for a Hispanic child growing up in a Spanish-speaking household in America (in his case Sacramento in the 1950s), growing up means necessarily and painfully growing away: learning English while not losing Spanish; becoming assimilated into the American middle class, which means assimilation not into a homogenized culture, but into a common public life in which English, as the language of 96 percent of the body politic, is the cultural cement of the extraordinary and yet precarious unity of our nation of immigrants.[48]

THE NADIR OF THE ETHNIC POLITICS OF EDUCATION

The Carter administration's most striking symbolic reward to the NEA for its vigorous campaign support in 1976 was the creation in 1979 of a cabinet-rank Department of Education. The new department was presided over by a former federal judge, Shirley Hufstedtler, who was quickly captured by the senior bureaucrats and who in 1979 was persuaded to issue the ukase that decreed the "Lau remedies" of bilingual/bicultural education with no alternatives permitted. But the nadir of ethnic politics to which that administration was so prone is symbolized by a bizarre two-year Indian college called Deganowidah-Quetzalcoatl University. In 1971, a handful of militant Indians occupied a deserted army base near Davis, California, and eventually persuaded the federal government to let them remain to establish a school to teach Indians their own history, culture, and religion. They leased the 643 acres of land at no cost and illegally sublet parts of it to local farmers and an engineering firm for $128,500 in profit. Their college was funded by the Department of Education to the annual tune of $489,000 in 1982, when federal auditors reported widespread mismanagement and fraud.[49] The school's chancellor, Dennis Banks, was wanted on a felony warrant from South Dakota, where he faced riot and assault charges stemming from the violent demonstrations he had led at Wounded Knee in 1973. But California's Democratic governor, Jerry Brown, blocked Banks's extradition. D-Q University had originally promised the government that the college would enroll at least 200 students. But because they never could attain such an enrollment, D-Q's federally paid administrators began signing one another up as both students and teachers in each other's classes. Chancellor Banks taught an independent study course to board chairman David Risling. Risling, in turn, taught governance and management procedures to Banks and several trustees. Dean of students Carlos Cordero also taught Banks. D-Q's controller taught six of this staff in fiscal management, and the registrar taught her assistant registrar about registration with taxpayers paying their salaries and tuitions. The federal auditors visited scheduled classes in a quest for real students, and although no students and no teachers showed up for "Introduction to Indigenous Counseling" or for a seminar in natural science, a course on "Native American Law" actually produced a teacher and four of the course's 19 registered students. In all, the auditors found 39 students in classes that had 133 registered. D-Q's president, Steven Baldy, denounced the audit as a "political document," and promptly sued the U.S. Government for discrimination.

But enough of horror stories. The point is that liberal Democratic regimes pay a severe penalty for their traditional solicitude for the nation's historically exploited groups, and that price has too often taken the form of political blackmail. Public resentment of this abuse of tax dollars played no small part in President Carter's rejection at the polls in 1980. It is still too soon to pass judgment on the education policies of the Reagan administration, although the early returns suggest a few tentative conclusions. One is that the Reaganite hostility to a strong federal role in education (beyond defense-related R&D) is not shared by a congressional majority that clings with surprising tenacity to the consensus forged during the Kennedy-Johnson years, which survived and even prospered under the Nixon and Ford administrations, and which was strongly reinforced under Carter. A second is that despite President Reagan's "safety net" rhetoric, his budgetary and programmatic insensitivity to the plight of the disadvantaged falls solidly in the midst of conservative Republican tradition and should surprise nobody. A third is that Reagan's budget slashes in college-student aid, especially loans, *are* surprising, for this affects a natural Republican constituency in the upwardly mobile middle class. But given his incredible tax cut of 1981 and the resultant record deficits of the early 1980s, perhaps the best explanation comes from Willie Sutton, who was asked why he robbed banks. He replied, "Because that's where the money is." And yet a fourth is that in the Reagan White House, consistent with its rhetoric, priority goes to the private sector, and especially to the archconservative constituencies represented by Protestant fundamentalist schools and colleges. All this, however, must await future historians.

THE AMBIGUOUS AND IRONICAL LEGACY OF THE
KENNEDY-JOHNSON YEARS

The federal government has historically been more effective at aiding higher education than elementary-secondary education. The 1960s represents the golden age of American higher education, but to stretch it to its full length, from 1955 to 1974, consider the magnitude of this spectacular transformation.[50] Presidents Eisenhower through Nixon, with their Democratic congresses, were centrally instrumental in this transformation, although the Kennedy-Johnson executive policies lie at its core:

1. From 1955 to 1974 the number of college students rose from 2.5 million to 8.8 million.
2. The percentage of young adults in the eighteen-to-twenty-four-year-old cohort attending college rose from 17.8 percent to 33.5 percent.
3. The number of blacks attending college rose from 95,000 to 814,000.
4. The percentage of women attending college rose from one-third to one-half.
5. In 1955, there were 400 community colleges, mostly vocational-technical, teaching 325,000 students (averaging 800 students each). By 1974, 973 community colleges were teaching 3.4 million students (averaging 3,700 students each).
6. The number of college faculty members rose from 266,000 to 633,000. Masters degrees rose from 58,000 to 278,000, and doctorates from 8,800 to 33,000.
7. From 1950 to 1981, United States professors won 93 of 173 Nobel Prizes.

Eisenhower sharply accelerated the transition with the NDEA in 1958, and by the time Neil Armstrong walked on the moon in 1969, 1.5 million men and women had gone to college on NDEA's student loan program, and 15,000 had completed doctoral degrees. The Kennedy breakthrough in 1963 accelerated college construction to such an extent that during one period in the late 1960s a new community college was opening every *week*. Johnson brought the major breakthrough on undergraduate and graduate scholarships in 1965, and also in research fellowships and grants outside the sciences. The National Endowments for the Arts and the Humanities have for the most part faithfully followed the crucial model of the civilian peer review panel pioneered by Vannevar Bush at the new National Science Foundation beginning in 1950, and the two endowments have vastly enriched the nation's cultural knowledge of its origins, its legacy, and its possible futures.

But the greatest irony of this extraordinary era of educational boom and commitment is that it coincided with a disastrous nineteen-year stretch of plummeting SAT scores, with American high schools graduating 300,000 functional illiterates a year. Part of this nosedive reflects a Great Society success, with more poorly prepared blacks and Hispanics taking the SAT and going to college. Part of it reflects the severe constraints on the effectiveness of the federal aid programs at the elementary and secondary level, as I have already discussed, with blame apportioned to all sides. But for most of it the federal role was largely irrelevant, for its cause lay in a vast tide of social change that flowed from the complex interplay of social, demographic, technological, and other forces over which the federal government had virtually no control (excluding to some degree the judiciary), no matter *what* their policies were in the 1960s.

It was the new age of television, and of the corresponding national decline of our children's ability to read (and hence to write), and perhaps, more important, of the decline of the *habit* of reading. It was an age of participatory democracy and relevance, with atrophied requirements for general education in the colleges, withering standards for math and science and language in the high schools, weakened elementary school three Rs, and trendy social studies electives. In the public schools, at least, homework tended to disappear, as too often did discipline and time-on-task. And a poignant smaller irony within the larger one involves the expansion of women's liberation, which by opening up professional and business opportunities to talented women who had been long trapped and underpaid in the classroom, thereby drained the public schools of the bedrock core of their strength. It was also an era of teacher unionization, with the NEA and the American Federation of Teachers competing successfully to organize the school districts. What resulted, in part, was accelerated pay raises, but also strikes against the public interest, a single pay scale that mocked economic reality and drove talented math and science teachers from the schools, and a resistance to teacher competency testing that combined with union protections to make it virtually impossible to dismiss incompetent teachers.[51] With the flight of the talented women and the underpaid math and science teachers, the quality of the public school teachers fell into steep decline. Teaching had never drawn the best students, but by 1979–80 the nation's college students planning to major in general education scored an appalling average of 339 on the verbal portion of the SAT test, which was 80 points below the already dismal national average.[52] Add to this the disruptions inherent in the massive busing schemes ordered by federal judges to achieve racial balance in large metropolitan school districts, and it is easy to understand why the brighter students whose parents could afford to fled the public schools for private ones, and why the students of middle ability who were left behind fell into precipitous academic decline.

In *The Troubled Crusade*, Diane Ravitch concluded that by 1980, "to an extraordinary degree, the consensus that had undergirded American education for most of its history seemed to be dissipating, and the emergence of rival claimants mirrored growing uncertainty about the purpose of education. . . . Outside intervention assumed that local officials were not to be trusted to do the right thing, and distrust is a corrosive sentiment, especially in an institution where parents entrust their children to the care of strangers."[53] For this dangerous unraveling of consensus, Ravitch apportioned to the federal interventions their share of the burden of blame: "The lesson of the federal categorical programs (such as bilingual education, compensatory education, and special education), federal directives, and court orders, it appeared, was that each interest group had to look out for itself, to get as much federal protection and as many public dollars as possible."[54] But in the wake of the critical commission reports of 1983, Ravitch indicted the sins of omission and commission of other institutions. Why not also blame the colleges and universities, whose lowered entrance requirements had undermined high school graduation requirements? "Why not blame them for accepting hordes of semiliterate students and establishing massive remedial programs, instead of complaining to the high schools that gave diplomas to the uneducated?" Why not blame businesses and employers, "who set up multi-million dollar programs to teach basic skills to their work force instead of telling the public, the school boards, and the legislatures that the schools were sending them uneducated people?" Why not blame state legislatures, "which quietly diluted or abolished high school graduation requirements? Why were they willing to pile on new requirements for nonacademic courses (drug education, family life education, consumer education, etc.) while cutting the ground away from science, math, history, and foreign languages?" Why not blame the press, "which has been indifferent to educational issues, interested only in fads, and unaware of the steady deterioration of academic standards until a national commission captured its attention?" And why not blame the courts, "which have whittled away the schools' ability to maintain safety and order."[55]

While presidents Kennedy and Johnson were trying in unprecedented ways to help the bottom fifth of the nation's school population, which indeed desperately needed help, the vast middle, the vital center of the public trust in its future, was beginning to collapse, and the top talent was fleeing to the private sector. Arrayed against such vast social forces, the federal efforts of the 1960s aimed at remedial rescue were occasionally heroic, often of limited effectiveness, and on rare occasions were even outrageous. But overall, the Kennedy-Johnson initiatives were vastly overwhelmed by the social tides that flowed around them. If the Kennedy-Johnson administrations cannot legitimately claim credit for successfully rescuing the children of the poor, then at least they gave it the first serious try; and neither can they fairly be asked to shoulder the major burden of blame for Johnny's and Jane's modern inability to read and count. So the federal interest in the quality of American education legitimately abides with us, even against the Reagan tide. We should learn from our history what the federal government does well, and maximize it in our future. We should also learn from a critical and candid scrutiny of our history where we seem consistently to have failed, to have fallen far short of our expectations, to have ensnarled ourselves unprofitably in the mesh of federalism's inherent dilemma over federal control. The programmatic legacy of the 1960s cautions us that policy is inseparable from politics, that the federal system is a delicate ecology wherein a price must be paid for sudden imbalance, and that the ostensible triumph of reform holds unintended consequences. Future historians will explore how well we have learned the lessons of the past.

Notes

INTRODUCTION

1. The National Commission on Excellence in Education, *A Nation at Risk: The Imperative for Educational Reform* (Washington, D.C.: Government Printing Office, 1983). The eighteen-member panel, which was appointed by Secretary of Education Terrell H. Bell in August 1981, was chaired by David P. Gardner, president of the University of Utah and president-elect of the University of California. Its members included A. Bartlett Giamatti, president of Yale; Albert H. Quie, former governor of Minnesota and ranking minority member of the House Committee on Education during the Johnson administration; and Glenn T. Seaborg, Nobel Laureate in chemistry at the University of California at Berkeley.

2. Robert Wood et al., *Report of the Twentieth Century Task Force on Federal Elementary and Secondary Education Policy* (New York: Twentieth Century Fund, 1983).

3. The panel also included Brewster Denny, Chester Finn, Patricia Graham, Charles V. Hamilton, Diane Ravitch, and Wilson Riles—few of them notable Reaganites.

4. The National Task Force on Education for Economic Growth was created by the Education Commission of the States. See the *Chronicle of Higher Education*, 11 May 1983.

5. For the troubled early history of the United States Office of Education, see Donald R. Warren, *To Enforce Education* (Detroit: Wayne State University Press, 1974). As Warren's title suggests, he is a partisan of a vigorous USOE, but his documentary research is superior to the largely descriptive journalism of Harry Kursh in *The United States Office of Education* (Philadelphia: Chilton, 1965).

6. A useful survey is Sidney W. Tiedt, *The Role of the Federal Government in Education* (New York: Oxford University Press, 1966). See also Homer D. Babbidge, Jr., and Robert M. Rosenweig, *The Federal Interest in Higher Education* (New York: McGraw-Hill, 1962); and *The Historic and Current Federal Role in Education* (Washington, D.C.: Government Printing Office, 1961), which is a report prepared by Charles A. Quattlebaum of the Legislative Reference Service of the Library of Congress at the request of Senator Wayne Morse, who chaired the subcommittee on education of the Senate Committee on Labor and Public Welfare.

7. An excellent analytical summary of the evolution of federal aid from the Lanham Act through the Elementary and Secondary Education Act (ESEA) of

1965 is Norman C. Thomas, *Education in National Politics* (New York: McKay, 1975), chapter 2. The Lanham formula for impacted aid in lieu of taxes, which in 1950 was extended through Public Law 81–815 for school construction and through Public Law 81–874 for operating expenses, became highly popular with Congress and public school beneficiaries because it imposed virtually no federal controls, it was easy and inexpensive to administer, and its aid was widely distributed.

8. Historic resistance to general federal aid is reflected in the defeat of the Hoar, Perce, and Burnside bills of the 1870s, the Blair bills of the 1880s, and the Smith-Towner bill of 1919. See Gordon C. Lee, *The Struggle for Federal Aid* (New York: Teachers College, Columbia University Bureau of Publications, 1949); and Anne Gibson Buis, "An Historical Study of the Federal Government in the Financial Support of Education" (Ph.D. diss., Ohio State University, 1953).

9. Robert Bendiner, *Obstacle Course on Capitol Hill* (New York: McGraw-Hill, 1964), 36–37. Bendiner's journalistic indictment of congressional obstructionism concentrates on the failed elementary and secondary school aid bills.

10. James L. Sundquist, *Politics and Policy: The Eisenhower, Kennedy, and Johnson Years* (Washington, D.C.: The Brookings Institution, 1968), 156.

11. This was not true for higher education, where the GI Bill and the NDEA provided ample precedent for direct federal aid to students, not institutions.

12. Frank J. Munger and Richard F. Fenno, *National Politics and Federal Aid to Education* (Syracuse: Syracuse University Press, 1962).

13. Ralph W. Tyler, "The Federal Role in Education," *The Public Interest*, Summer 1974, 164.

14. Hugh Davis Graham, "The Transformation of Federal Education Policy," in *Exploring the Johnson Years*, ed. Robert A. Divine (Austin: University of Texas Press, 1981).

15. Stephen K. Bailey and Edith Kern Mosher, *ESEA: The Office of Education Administers a Law* (Syracuse: Syracuse University Press, 1968); Eugene Eidenberg and Roy D. Morey, *An Act of Congress* (New York: W. W. Norton, 1969); and Thomas, *Education in National Politics*. See also Philip Meranto, *The Politics of Federal Aid to Education* (Syracuse: Syracuse University Press, 1967). Two doctoral dissertations, both from the University of Chicago, strikingly demonstrate the qualitative difference in perspective and insight between contemporary social science research and archival-based research (neither was written by a historian): compare Philip C. Kearney, "The 1964 Presidential Task Force on Education and the Elementary and Secondary Education Act of 1965" (Ph.D. diss., University of Chicago, 1967), with Robert E. Hawkinson, "Presidential Program Formulation in Education: Lyndon Johnson and the 89th Congress" (Ph.D. diss., University of Chicago, 1977).

16. Both presidential archives have been officially "open" since the early 1970s, and their education collections have generally been among the first to be processed. The Lyndon Baines Johnson Library and Museum, Austin, Texas (hereafter cited as LBJ Library), officially opened with a symposium on education in 1972, although no historian helped plan the symposium and no historian appeared on it (see Kenneth W. Tolo, ed., *Educating A Nation: The Changing American Commitment* [Austin: Lyndon B. Johnson School of Public Affairs, 1973]). The papers of the Nixon administration have remained closed in the National Archives in Washington until protracted litigation clarifies their status and ultimate location.

17. The text of eleven of the major Kennedy task force reports were published early in book form in *New Frontiers of the Kennedy Administration* (Washington, D.C.: Public Affairs Press, 1961). The twelfth and final chapter, "International Frontiers," is the text of Kennedy's inaugural address.

18. For a survey of the evolution of central clearance, see Richard E. Neustadt, "The Presidency and Legislation: The Growth of Central Clearance," *American Political Science Review* 48 (1954): 641–71.

19. William E. Leuchtenburg, "The Genesis of the Great Society," *The Reporter*, 21 April 1966, 36–39. See also Adam Yarmolinsky, "Ideas Into Programs," *The Public Interest*, Winter 1966, 70–79. Patrick Anderson in *The President's Men* (Garden City, N.Y.: Doubleday, 1968), 330–34, credits Richard Goodwin for pressing the task force ideas on Johnson, and Bill Moyers for organizational brilliance in launching them. For Johnson's retrospective assessment of the task forces, see *The Vantage Point: Perspectives of the Presidency 1963–69* (New York: Holt, Rinehart and Winston, 1971), 326–28.

20. An invaluable aid to research on the task forces is "Presidential Task Force Operation during the Johnson Administration," an eighteen-page mimeographed guide prepared by LBJ Library archivist Nancy Kegan Smith in June 1978. See also "Policy Formulation during the Johnson Administration," an unfinished nineteen-page speech drafted by aide James Gaither but never delivered by President Johnson, in the Gaither file, container 300, LBJ Library, Austin, Texas.

21. The leading student of the function of task forces in policy formulation is Norman C. Thomas. See Norman C. Thomas and Harold Wolman, "Policy Formulation in the Institutionalized Presidency: The Johnson Task Forces," in *The Presidential Advisory System*, ed. Thomas E. Cronin and Sanford I. Greenberg, (New York: Harper and Row, 1969); Thomas and Wolman, "The Presidency and Policy Formulation: The Task Force Device," *Public Administration Review* 29 (September/October, 1969): 459–70; Thomas, "Presidential Advice and Information: Policy and Program Formulation," *Law and Contemporary Problems* 35 (Summer 1970): 540–72; Cronin and Thomas, "Educational Policy Advisors and the Great Society," *Public Policy*, Fall 1970, 659–86; and Thomas, "Policy Formulation for Education: The Johnson Administration," *Educational Researcher* 2 (May 1973): 4–8; and Nathan Glazer, "On Task Forcing," *The Public Interest*, Spring 1969, 40–45. A superior analysis of Nixon's important planning groups in educational policy is Chester E. Finn, Jr., *Education and the Presidency* (Lexington, Mass.: Heath, 1977).

22. Two veterans of the Bureau of the Budget have expressed sympathy for the president's bureaucratic problem yet are critical of the task forces: William D. Carey, "Presidential Staffing in the Sixties and Seventies," *Public Administration Review* 29 (September/October 1969): 450–58; and Harold Seidman, *Politics, Position, and Power: The Dynamics of Federal Organization* (New York: Oxford University Press, 1970), 90–91. For a more recent assessment, see Hugh Davis Graham, "Short-Circuiting the Bureaucracy in the Great Society: Policy Origins in Education," *Presidential Studies Quarterly* (Summer 1982): 407–20.

23. Douglass Cater, "The Political Struggle for Equal Educational Opportunity," in *Toward New Human Rights: The Policies of the Kennedy and Johnson Administrations*, ed. David C. Warner (Austin: Lyndon B. Johnson School of Public Affairs, 1977), 325–40.

24. Chester E. Finn, Jr., *Education and the Presidency*, 103.

CHAPTER 1

1. Theodore C. Sorensen, *Kennedy* (New York: Harper & Row, 1965), 358.
2. Myer Feldman, interview with author, Washington, D.C., 7 May 1981.
3. William T. O'Hara, ed., *John F. Kennedy on Education* (New York: Teachers College Press, 1966), 6–7. Herbert Parmet's two-volume biography of Kennedy reflects scant concern with educational issues, other than for their political ramifications. See Herbert S. Parmet, *Jack: The Struggles of John F. Kennedy* (New York: Dial, 1980), and Parmet, *JFK: The Presidency of John F. Kennedy* (New York: Dial, 1983).
4. See generally Frank J. Munger and Richard F. Fenno, *National Politics and Federal Aid to Education* (Syracuse: Syracuse University Press, 1962), chapter 1, for a history of the legislative struggles from 1820 through 1961. On the Spellman-Barden-Roosevelt dispute, see Robert Bendiner, *Obstacle Course on Capitol Hill* (New York: McGraw-Hill, 1964), 90–97; and Diane Ravitch, *The Troubled Crusade: American Education 1945–1980* (New York: Basic Books, 1983), 33–42.
5. Kennedy cited the Supreme Court's cautious approval of the "child-benefit" theory in the Everson decision in 1947, whereby New Jersey's provision of public busing to parochial school pupils was held to benefit the child and not the church school (see Everson v. Board of Education, 330 U.S. 1 [1947].
6. James L. Sundquist, *Politics and Policy: The Eisenhower, Kennedy, and Johnson Years* (Washington, D.C.: The Brookings Institution, 1968), 156–73.
7. Beginning in 1956, the Powell Amendment was a perennial offering by the congressman from Harlem, Adam Clayton Powell, that would bar any proposed federal school aid to segregated schools. Although it was customarily denounced by the NEA, the AFL-CIO, most congressional supporters of federal aid, Adlai Stevenson, and Harry Truman, and it was even opposed by President Eisenhower and rejected by the House Education and Labor Committee on which Powell sat, it was usually adopted on the floor, only to sink when Republicans who had joined northern Democrats to adopt Powell's amendment then turned around and joined southern Democrats in voting against the amended bill. As such it represented a classic Brutus kiss and contributed to the bizarre political atmosphere that stymied federal aid until the midsixties. See Bendiner, *Obstacle Course*, 121–30.
8. *Congressional Record*, 17330, 17331. Senator Kennedy had not totally disengaged himself from federal aid efforts during the 1950s. In January 1958 he introduced S.3179, which provided for federal grants to states for school construction, but it died in committee. Kennedy supported the NDEA in 1958, and in 1959 he joined with Senator Joseph Clark (D., Pa.) and, in 1960, with Senator Jacob Javits (R., N.Y.) also, to strip the non-Communist affidavit from the NDEA student loan requirements. That effort, S.2929, passed the Senate in the summer of 1960 but died in the House. Kennedy was to redeem that commitment as president in 1962.
9. *Politics and Policy*, 174.
10. Democratic advantages during the 1958 elections included economic recession and the specter of *Sputnik*; Republican "right-to-work" drives in industrialized states like Ohio and California, which galvanized organized labor; Eisenhower's dispatch of paratroopers to Little Rock in 1957, which antagonized southern Democrats; and the Sherman Adams–Bernard Goldfine scandal.

11. Much of the pre-1958 stalemate was accounted for by close margins of 234 (D.) to 201 (R.) in the House and 49 (D.) to 47 (R.) in the Senate, in addition to the customary regional and ideological cross-pressures and the split partisan control of the presidency and Congress.

12. Sundquist, *Politics and Policy*, 180–87; Fenno and Munger, *Federal Aid*, 155–69; Bendiner, *Obstacle Course*, 160–71. Sundquist reports, but without direct evidence, the rumor that Lyndon Johnson persuaded Democratic senator J. Allen Frear, Jr., to vote for reconsideration even though Frear had voted against the amendment.

13. When asked about federal aid for teachers' salaries at a news conference, Eisenhower replied, "I do not believe the Federal Government ought to be in the business of paying a local official. If we're going into that, we'll have to find out every councilman and every teacher and every other person that's a public official of any kind . . . and try to figure out what his right salary is. . . . I can't imagine anything worse for the Federal Government to get into" (*Congress and the Nation 1945–1964* [Washington, D.C.: Congressional Quarterly Press, 1965], 1209). Eisenhower's counterproposal, which the controlling congressional Democrats ignored when it was submitted in 1959 (S.1016, H.R. 4268), called for a $2 billion federal commitment, stretched out over thirty to thirty-five years, to help local school districts service their long-term construction debts; teachers' salaries and direct grants to needy areas were omitted.

14. See the *New York Times*, 3 January 1960. The standard authority on the campaign of 1960, although biased toward Camelot, is Theodore H. White, *The Making of the President 1960* (New York: Atheneum, 1961). White is stronger on imagery, personality, and mood than he is on issues; and he misses the education issue almost entirely.

15. *The Joint Appearances of Senator John F. Kennedy and Vice President Richard M. Nixon, Presidential Campaign of 1960*, Senate Report 994, 87th Congress, I Session (1961), pt. 3:84–85. This is the first volume in a four-volume series entitled Freedom of Communications, which were published by the Senate Commerce Committee's subcommittee on communications.

16. *The Speeches, Remarks, Press Conferences, and Study Papers of Vice President Richard M. Nixon*, 1 August–7 November 1960, S. Rept. 994 (1961), pt. 2:279–86.

17. Ibid., 283.

18. *New York Herald-Tribune*, 25 September 1960.

19. Sidney Kraus, ed. *The Great Debates* (Bloomington: Indiana University Press, 1962), 360.

20. Ibid., 361.

21. Munger and Fenno, *Federal Aid*, 183. The NEA avoided formal presidential endorsements until its 1976 endorsement of Jimmy Carter.

22. *The Speeches of Senator John F. Kennedy*, S. Report 994, pt. 1:1235.

23. On the 1960 task forces, see Sorensen, *Kennedy*, 234–40.

24. The only exception to the policy of not announcing the task forces until they delivered their reports to the president in early January was Senator Paul Douglas's task force on area redevelopment, which promptly began holding public hearings in West Virginia to redeem an early Kennedy campaign pledge.

25. Sorensen notes that only the reports on tax reform and Cuba were deemed too sensitive to be released. Of the earlier committees that had been appointed in

the summer, only Adlai Stevenson's on foreign policy was judged too sensitive to permit either identification of the members or release of the report.

26. Task force members who subsequently joined the administration included Adolph Berle, Mortimer Caplin, Wilbur Cohen, Henry Fowler, Lincoln Gordon, Walter Heller, Donald Hornig, Francis Keppel, James Tobin, and Champion Ward. Paul Samuelson, however, resisted Kennedy's plea to join the administration.

27. The mutually acknowledged "very smooth transition" between the senior Kennedy aides, especially Sorensen and Feldman, and the senior BOB staff, with director-designate David Bell in the middle, is described from the BOB perspective by Phillip Hughes, who was head of the Division of Legislative Reference. See transcript, "Phillip S. Hughes, Oral History Interview," 24 April 1968, John Fitzgerald Kennedy Library, Boston, Massachusetts (hereafter cited as JFK Library). The enterprising staff of the BOB's Division of Legislative Reference had first compiled such a volume in 1953—the "Ikelopedia." See also "David Bell, Oral History Interview," 11 July 1964 and 2 January 1965, JFK Library (permission is restricted), which refers to "Sam" Hughes and BOB's Division of Legislative Reference as Sorensen's "right arm."

28. Transcript, "Myer Feldman Oral History Interview," 29 May 1966, JFK Library, 303. The Feldman oral history is an unedited series of fourteen interviews of approximately fifty pages each (permission restricted). On page 291 of the seventh interview, Feldman begins discussing the morning after the 1960 election.

29. Sorensen, *Kennedy*, 238.

30. For education policy, see transition memorandums of 9 December 1960 and 13 December 1960, container 376, Office of the Director, OMB Records Division, National Archives.

31. The secondary literature generally ignores the Hovde task force, with the exception of Hugh Douglas Price's excellent case study "Race, Religion, and the Rules Committee: The Kennedy Aid-to-Education Bills," in *The Uses of Power*, ed. Alan F. Westin (New York: Harcourt, Brace & World, 1962), 1–71. Price discusses the Hovde task force on pages 21–23 but then largely dismisses its impact.

32. John Gardner recalls that Governor Abraham Ribicoff of Connecticut, an early Kennedy supporter whose reward was to pick his cabinet portfolio (he turned down the post of attorney general and selected secretary of health, education, and welfare), was an unofficial member of the task force and often acted as de facto chairman (John Gardner, interview with author, Washington, D.C., 7 May 1981).

33. Price, "Race, Religion, and the Rules Committee," 21.

34. "Feldman Oral History Interview," 305.

35. Ibid., 305-6.

36. Transcript, "Francis Keppel Oral History Interview," 21 April 1969, LBJ Library, 2.

37. *New York Times*, 7 January 1961. Hovde had originally proposed a $1 billion annual program for college facility construction but had been persuaded by nervous Kennedy aides to reduce it by half.

38. "Feldman Oral History Interview," 310.

39. Ibid., 311. Wilbur Cohen, who chaired the Kennedy task force on health and social security, recalls that when he submitted his report, a week after Hovde, the president ripped off the last three pages containing expensive recommenda-

tions on increased unemployment insurance before releasing the report to the press: "As soon as I handed him a copy of the report, the President said the one thing he didn't want to repeat was the situation in connection with the education task force report submitted by Mr. Frederick Hovde, President of Purdue University, where the papers played up the enormous billion dollar cost of all their recommendations. I thought this was significant because the President didn't like these big cost figures. He didn't want the idea getting over that he was a man who was just interested in spending a lot of money" (Transcript, "Wilbur Cohen Oral History Interview," 11 November 1964, 27, JFK Library). Typical of the conservative attack on the Kennedy task forces, especially those chaired by Hovde, Douglas, and Samuelson, is the editorial in the *Wall Street Journal*, entitled "The Steps on a Distant Journey," on 11 January 1961.

40. *New York Times*, 18 January 1961.

41. See Larry Berman, *The Office of Management and Budget and the Presidency, 1921–1979* (Princeton: Princeton University Press, 1979), especially ch. 4.

42. Richard Neustadt, "Memorandum on Staffing the President-elect," 30 October 1960, 18 Transition File E2–24/60, Records of the Bureau of the Budget, OMB Records Division, National Archives.

43. Transcript, "Phillip Hughes Oral History Interview," 24 April 1968, JFK Library, 2–12. The Hughes interview suggests far more continuity with the Eisenhower administration, and I believe that Berman exaggerates the discontinuity. But Hughes's description of the Kennedy transition emphasizes the degree to which Kennedy's insistence on getting America moving again was most congenial to the bureau's mood. He gives Sorensen and Feldman high marks for being aggressive and tough-minded quick studies, who themselves had to make a major transition from the ad hoc, crisis-management atmosphere of Senate staffers to the presidency's and the BOB's long-range view of the budget process and legislative central clearance.

44. Memorandum, Labor and Welfare Division to the Director, 13 December 1960, Director file, container 375, OMB Records Division, National Archives.

45. Price, "Kennedy Aid-to-Education Bills," 22.

46. Memorandum, Labor and Welfare Division to the Director, 25 January 1961, Director file, container 376, OMB Records Division, National Archives.

47. Ibid.

48. These recommendations of the Division of Labor and Welfare staff were transmitted without endorsement by Director Bell to Sorensen and Feldman on 25 January 1961, with a copy to Secretary Ribicoff.

49. Price, "Kennedy Aid-to-Education Bills," 25.

50. Memorandum of transmission, Bell to Sorensen and Feldman, 24 January 1961, OMB Records Division, National Archives.

51. Memorandum of Conversation by Jack Forsythe, Wilbur Cohen, and Myer Feldman, 13 February 1961, Feldman file, container 27, JFK Library. S.8 authorized $1.8 billion in federal grants for school construction and teachers' salaries, based on a flat rate of $20-per-child, and with an equalization formula that appealed to legislators from poor southern states. Senator Lister Hill and Congressman Carl Elliott were Democratic New Dealers from Alabama who had long championed federal aid to education, but who feared federal sanctions in school desegregation.

52. *Public Papers of the Presidents of the United States: John F. Kennedy, 1961* (Washington, D.C.: Government Printing Office, 1962), 107–11.

53. In 1960, the federal budget for elementary-secondary programs totaled $2.32 billion and included $263 million for aid to impacted areas, $304 million for school lunch/milk (including surplus commodities), and $225 million for military and Indian education and certain NDEA titles.

54. *Public Papers: Kennedy, 1961*, 154–55.

55. Memorandum, Sorensen to President Kennedy, 12 April 1961, "Education and Religion" folder, Sorensen file, container 33, JFK Library.

56. *New York Times*, 20 June 1961.

57. *New York Times*, 3 July 1961.

58. Wilbur Cohen to author, 20 April 1981.

59. *Public Papers: Kennedy, 1961*, 516.

60. Memorandum, Ribicoff to President Kennedy, 20 July 1961; memorandum, Cohen to Sorenson [*sic*], 7 August 1961 and 9 August 1961, Sorensen file, container 32, JFK Library.

61. Memorandum, Sorensen to President Kennedy, 9 August 1961, Sorensen file, container 32, JFK Library.

62. Memorandum, Sorensen to President Kennedy, 14 August 1961, Sorensen file, container 32, JFK Library.

63. Price, "Kennedy Aid-to-Education Bills," 66. Price covered essentially the same ground two years later in "Schools, Scholarships, and Congressmen," in *The Centers of Power*, ed. Alan F. Westin (New York: Harcourt, Brace & World, 1964), 53–105.

64. Price, "Kennedy Aid-to-Education Bills," 67.

65. *New York Times*, 6 September 1961.

66. *New York Times*, 4 October 1961.

67. *Public Papers: Kennedy, 1961*, 574. Sorensen's year-end summary of Kennedy's record in domestic affairs concluded that the administration's biggest disappointment was education and claimed that "no other piece of domestic legislation received as much Administration effort, leadership, contracts, etc." See Sorensen's draft of 29 December 1961, "The Kennedy Record in Domestic Affairs, 1961," Sorensen files, JFK Library.

CHAPTER 2

1. Memorandum, Ribicoff to President Kennedy, 6 October 1961, Sorensen file, container 34, JFK Library. Ribicoff sent copies to Sorensen, O'Brien, and David Bell.

2. Ibid.

3. *Public Papers of the Presidents of the United States, John F. Kennedy, 1962* (Washington, D.C.: 1963), 9.

4. Ibid., 110–17.

5. Staff memorandum of M. S. March, "Analysis of HEW's proposals for 1962 education legislation," Director file, container 410, OMB Records Division, National Archives. The memo conceded with considerable understatement that the Bureau of the Budget's recommended approach "might not be enthusiastically received by the NEA which has favored a seniority basis for pay scales and wants a general teachers' subsidy bill."

6. *Public Papers: Kennedy, 1962*, 114 (emphasis added).

7. Ibid.

8. *New York Times*, 11 February 1962.

9. *New York Times*, 8 February 1962.

10. *Public Papers: Kennedy, 1962*, 121.

11. *Congressional Quarterly Almanac: 1962* (Washington, D.C.: Congressional Quarterly Press, 1963), 235.

12. The organizations were the American Council on Education, the Association of American Universities, the American Association of Junior Colleges, the Association of American Colleges, the American Association of State Colleges and Universities, and the National Association of State Universities and Land-Grant Colleges.

13. The five organizations were the American Association of School Administrators, the American Vocational Association, the Council of Chief State School Officers, the National Congress of Parents and Teachers, and the National School Boards Association. All had been closely associated with the NEA.

14. *Congressional Quarterly Almanac: 1962*, 240.

15. See Carl M. Brauer, *John F. Kennedy and the Second Reconstruction* (New York: Columbia University Press, 1977), 144–51. By January 1963, the Department of Justice had filed four more such suits in Alabama, Mississippi, and Louisiana.

16. The standard study is Stephen Hess, *Organizing the Presidency* (Washington, D.C.: The Brookings Institution, 1976), 78–92; but see also Patrick Anderson's superior journalistic insight in *The President's Men* (Garden City, N.Y.: Doubleday, 1968), 195–298; R. Gordon Hoxie, *The White House: Organization and Operations* (New York: Center for the Study of the Presidency, 1971); Richard Tanner Johnson, *Managing the White House* (New York: Harper & Row, 1974), especially ch. 5; Lewis W. Koenig, *The Chief Executive* (New York: Harcourt-Brace-Jovanovich, 1975); Thomas E. Cronin, *The State of the Presidency* (Boston: Little, Brown, 1975); Stephen J. Wayne, *The Legislative Presidency* (New York: Harper & Row, 1978); and Bradley D. Nash, *Organizing and Staffing the Presidency* (New York: Center for the Study of the Presidency, 1980), especially ch. 2.

17. Transcript, "Wilbur Cohen Oral History Interview," 24 May 1971, JFK Library, 69 (permission restricted).

18. Ibid.

19. Ibid., 68.

20. Transcript, "Francis Keppel Oral History Interview," 21 April 1969, LBJ Library, 1–2.

21. Memorandum, Daly to O'Brien, 20 July 1962, Sorensen file, container 33, JFK Library.

22. Ibid.

23. Memorandum, Manatos to O'Brien, 21 July 1962, Sorensen file, container 33, JFK Library.

24. Memorandum, Sorensen to President Kennedy, 24 July 1962, Sorensen file, container 33, JFK Library.

25. Memorandum, Cohen to Sorensen, 3 August 1962, Sorensen file, container 33, JFK Library.

26. Ibid. The memo included no definition for "good cause shown."

27. Ibid.

28. See the *Congressional Quarterly Almanac: 1962*, 235–38, and House Report 2435. The conference committee compromise passed by a vote of 7 to 2, with the dissenters being, interestingly, two veteran senators: the New Dealer Lister Hill of Alabama, and the anti–New Dealer Barry Goldwater of Arizona.

29. Transcript, "Keppel Oral History Interview," LBJ Library, 3.

30. See generally the *Congressional Quarterly Almanac: 1962*, 230–40.

31. *New York Times*, 4 September 1962.

32. Ibid.

33. *Public Papers: Kennedy, 1962*, 573.

34. Staff memorandum, "A New Federal Program in Education," 30 October 1962, container 410, OMB Records Division, National Archives. This was an early draft; the polished and official version was dated 7 November.

35. Ibid.

36. George J. Hecht to President Kennedy, 9 November 1962, White House Central Files (hereafter cited as WHCF), JFK Library.

37. *New York Times*, 23 November 1962.

38. Memorandum, Sorensen to President Kennedy, 25 November 1962, Sorensen files, container 36, JFK Library.

39. Staff memorandum, "Suggested Approach for Administration Education Proposals," 5 December 1962, container 410, OMB Records Division, National Archives.

40. Ibid.

41. Transcript, "Keppel Oral History Interview," 21 April 1969, LBJ Library, 4.

42. Transcript, "Cohen Oral History Interview," 24 May 1971, LBJ Library, 70–72. Prior to 1935, the Public Health Service had relied solely on its own employees rather than on project grants; from 1935 to 1946, the PHS had turned increasingly to grants, but only to state and local public health agencies and individual researchers. The Hospital Survey and Construction Act of 1946, sponsored by Senator Lister Hill (D., Ala.) and Congressman Harold H. Burton (R., Ohio) and designed to modernize national health resources, which had grown obsolete since the Depression and World War II, authorized project grant expenditures of $75 million a year for five years to public *and private nonprofit* groups and institutions as well as to the states. In 1946, the religious issue did not seriously arise, and the popular program had been regularly extended in time and expanded in scope since 1946.

43. Transcript, "Keppel Oral History Interview," 21 April 1969, LBJ Library, 5.

44. Ibid.

45. *Public Papers: Kennedy, 1963*, 107–8.

46. *New York Times*, 1 February 1963.

47. *New York Times*, 6 February 1963.

48. Transcript, "Keppel Oral History Interview," 21 April 1969, LBJ Library, 6.

49. Sundquist, *Politics and Policy: The Eisenhower, Kennedy, and Johnson Years* (The Brookings Institution, 1968), 205–10. The detailed chronology of Douglas E. Kliener in *The Vocational Education Act of 1963* (Washington: American Vocational Association, 1965), centers on vocational education but covers all education legislation enacted in 1963.

50. *New York Times*, 28 May 1963.

51. H.R. 6143 authorized the $1,195,000,000 for only the first three years of

the construction and rehabilitation program, on a one-third federal matching basis, as follows: (1) $690 million in matching grants for undergraduate academic facilities, with 22 percent reserved for public and private junior colleges and technical institutes; (2) $145 million in matching grants for graduate facilities; and (3) $360 million in loans for all higher education institutions, repayable at low interest rates within fifty years.

52. Edgar Fuller to Editor, *St. Louis Post-Dispatch*, 26 June 1962, Sorensen file, container 33, JFK Library. The five organizations are identified in n. 13.

53. Ibid.

54. Massachusetts v. Mellon, 262 U.S. 27 (1923).

55. Frothingham v. Mellon, 262 U.S. 447 (1923). Mrs. Frothingham had sued the District of Columbia to enjoin enforcement of the Sheppard-Towner Act, but Justice Sutherland held that, while individual citizens possessed standing to sue municipal corporations, the relationship between their federal tax payments and national expenditures was so remote that they could not show sufficient injury to claim standing to sue. The modern federal grant-in-aid program originated with the Weeks Act of 1911, which encouraged state participation in fire-prevention programs and included such major new programs as the Smith-Lever Act of 1914 for agricultural extension, the Federal Road Act of 1916, and the Smith-Hughes Act of 1917 for vocational education. The Court began to decide and approve the merits of such programs in the late 1930s, when it belatedly began to approve the major New Deal measures. In 1968 the Supreme Court vastly expanded the standing of individual taxpayers to sue in Flast v. Cohen, 392 U.S. 83 (1968).

56. Edith Green had included a similar amendment in her original subcommittee bill, but it was rejected by the full Education and Labor Committee, after which she had promised her colleague James Delaney, a Catholic and member of the Rules Committee, that she would not re-offer the amendment.

57. *Public Papers: Kennedy, 1963*, 878.

58. Transcript, "Keppel Oral History Interview," 21 April 1969, LBJ Library, 6. See also Eugene Eidenberg and Roy Morey, *An Act of Congress* (New York: W. W. Norton, 1969), ch. 4.

59. The major exception was H.R. 4879, which would extend and expand the Library Services Act of 1956 by providing new funds to construct as well as operate libraries and extend the program to cities as well as rural areas. But similar versions of the bill had passed the Senate and were well along in the House by the end of the 1963 session, and the noncontroversial bill was passed in 1964. See Lawrence W. Pettit, "The Policy Process in Congress: Passing the Higher Education Facilities Act of 1963" (Ph.D. diss., University of Wisconsin, 1965).

60. Brauer, *Kennedy and the Second Reconstruction*, 311–20.

61. Press release, "Remarks of the President upon Signing H.R. 6143: The Higher Education Facilities Act of 1963," 16 December 1963, Sorensen file, container 33, JFK Library.

62. Ibid. Kennedy was almost as far off the historical mark when he told the NEA in mid-November that "it is my strong belief that when this Congress goes home it will have done more in the field of education than any Congress in the last 100 years—really, I suppose, since the Morrill Act which established the land grant colleges."

63. Ibid.

CHAPTER 3

1. Quoted in Mark I. Gelfand, "The War on Poverty," in *Exploring the Johnson Years*, ed. Robert A. Divine (Austin: University of Texas Press, 1981), 128. On the origins of the antipoverty war, see Carl M. Brauer, "Kennedy, Johnson, and the War on Poverty," *The Journal of American History* 69 (June 1982): 98–119; and James T. Patterson, *America's Struggle against Poverty, 1900–1980* (Cambridge: Harvard University Press, 1981), 99–154.

2. The role of education in the early war on poverty is explored in Julie Roy Jeffrey, *Education for the Children of the Poor* (Columbus: Ohio State University Press, 1976), ch. 2. See also Philip Meranto's discussion of the development of an antipoverty rationale for federal aid to education in *The Politics of Federal Aid to Education in 1965* (Syracuse: Syracuse University Press, 1967), ch. 2.

3. Memorandum [Sutton], Labor and Welfare Division to the Director, 8 January 1964, EX LE/FA 2, WHCF, LBJ Library.

4. The three-year extension of NDEA added the academic subjects of history, civics, geography, English, and reading as categories qualifying for equipment and teacher-training institutes. The revised NDEA also extended to private-school teachers the original act's 50 percent loan forgiveness feature and eligibility for federal stipends while attending teacher-training institutes. The aid-to-impacted-areas program was extended to include for the first time the District of Columbia in 1964. A separate Library Services and Construction Act was passed in 1964 also. Probably the most consequential education legislation of 1964, however, was contained in Titles IV and VI of the Civil Rights Act, which provided for bringing federal desegregation suits and for cutting off federal funds to segregated school systems. See Gary Orfield, *The Reconstruction of Southern Education: The Schools and the 1964 Civil Rights Act* (New York: Wiley-Interscience, 1969), and "David Seeley Oral History Interview," 25 July 1968, LBJ Library.

5. Others involved in coordinating the initial task forces were Gardner Ackley, Francis Bator, Douglass Cater, Myer Feldman, Donald Hornig, Charles Schultze, Elmer Staats, and Lee White. An essential aid for researching the task force operation is "Presidential Task Force Operation During the Johnson Administration," an eighteen-page guide prepared by LBJ Library archivist Nancy Kegan Smith in June 1978. See also "Policy Formulation During the Johnson Administration," an unfinished nineteen-page speech that was drafted by aide James Gaither but never delivered by President Johnson.

6. *Public Papers of the President of the United States: Lyndon Johnson, 1963–64* (Washington: Government Printing Office, 1965), 1:705.

7. Memorandum, Kermit Gordon and Walter Heller to Bill Moyers, 30 May 1964, EX LE 2, WHCF, LBJ Library. The eleven remaining task force suggestions on the Gordon-Heller list were: (4) agriculture, (5) transportation policy, (6) reorganization and economy, (7) foreign economic policy, (8) defense reconversion, (9) income maintenance, (10) poverty, (11) area and regional development, (12) power and water, (13) federal fiscal support for state-local governments, and (14) anti-recession policy.

8. Memorandum, Bill Moyers to Gardner Ackley et al., 6 July 1964, EX FG 600, container 361, WHCF, LBJ Library.

9. Ibid. The original task force model developed for Johnson by Moyers and his senior associates combined predominant outsider participation with secret, White

House-level policy planning at considerable risk, and was possible only because the Great Society blueprint was predicated upon a set of optimistic assumptions about the economy, the efficacy of federal intervention, and the future that was widely shared by the liberal Democratic constituency that dominated the outside task forces, especially on the nation's campuses and in the major foundations. Chester Finn has perceptively analyzed the contrasting Nixon model of 1969–70, which featured secretive working groups of loyalist insiders who enjoyed a monopoly of presidential information, were screened from cabinet and agency interference, and assumed a hostile Congress. See Chester E. Finn, Jr., *Education and the Presidency* (Lexington, Mass.: Heath, 1977).

10. Memorandum, Moyers to Ackley et al., 6 July 1964, EX FG 600, container 361, WHCF, LBJ Library.

11. Moyers's official list of 22 July shows a slightly different configuration. The task force on civil rights never materialized, presumably because the Civil Rights Act of 1964 was passed on 2 July. But two more task forces were added, one on environmental pollution and one on programs to improve the world-wide competitive effectiveness of American business, to bring the total to fifteen task forces planning in 1964 for the 1965 legislative agenda.

12. "Task Forces on the 1965 Legislative Program: Issue Papers," 17 June 1964, Moyers file, container 94, LBJ Library. Staff of the Council of Economic Advisors also assisted in preparing the issue papers.

13. Ibid.

14. Ibid.

15. Ibid.

16. Ibid.

17. President Johnson noted and resented the elitist skew in 1964 against the South (two members) and the Midwest (five members), and subsequent outside task forces were consciously broadened. William Friday's outside task force on education in 1966, for instance, was more evenly balanced, with one university representative each from Harvard University and Yale University, the University of Chicago and the University of Wisconsin, the University of California at Los Angeles, California Institute of Technology, the University of North Carolina and Vanderbilt University—plus the superintendent of public instruction for Texas.

18. Memorandum, William B. Cannon to David Mathiasen, 9 September 1964, container 411, OMB Records Division, National Archives.

19. Keppel to Gardner, 17 September 1964, container 412, OMB Records Division, National Archives. Keppel, interview with author, Cambridge, Mass., 1 April 1981.

20. Transcript, "Francis Keppel, Oral History Interview," 21 April 1969, LBJ Library, 13. Keppel also wanted to avoid antagonizing the highly organized Washington lobby of the state commissioners of education, the Council of Chief State School Officers, and many of his like-minded "old guard" senior administrators at USOE. See Robert E. Hawkinson, "Presidential Program Formulation on Education" (Ph.D. diss., University of Chicago, 1977), ch. 3; and Stephen K. Bailey and Edith K. Mosher, *ESEA: The Office of Education Administers a Law* (Syracuse: Syracuse University Press, 1968), ch. 3.

21. Cannon, interview with author, Washington, D.C., 15 September 1981.

22. Memorandum, Cannon to the Director, 16 October 1964, container 412, OMB Records Division, National Archives.

23. Memorandum, Gardner to Education Task Force Members, 24 September 1964, container 411, OMB Records Division, National Archives.

24. *Report of the President's Task Force on Education*, 14 November 1964, Task Force file, container 1, LBJ Library. A surprisingly candid assessment of the contribution of the Gardner task force may be found in the DHEW Administrative History, vol. I, part 3, 42–64, LBJ Library.

25. *Public Papers: LBJ, 1963–64*, vol. 1. See also Hawkinson, "Presidential Program Formulation," 130–40.

26. *Report of the President's Task Force on Education*, 27.

27. See Morton Sosna, "The National Endowment for the Humanities," in *Government Agencies*, ed. Donald R. Whitnah, Greenwood Encyclopedia of American Institutions (Westport, Conn.: Greenwood Press, 1982).

28. *Public Papers: Johnson, 1963–64*, 28 September 1964, 2:1141.

29. Memorandum, Goodwin to President Johnson, 20 July 1964, EX ED/ PR8-1, WHCF, LBJ Library.

30. Theodore White, *The Making of the President 1964* (New York: Atheneum, 1964), 352.

31. Walter Heller sent Bill Moyers a detailed campaign memorandum on 1 October providing "*pointed ammunition to attack the Goldwater (and Republican platform) proposals for tax credits for educational expenses.*" See memorandum, Heller to Moyers, 1 October 1964, Moyers file, container 6, LBJ Library. Heller included attacks on the tuition tax credits proposal by the University of Wisconsin president Fred Harrington, the Association of State Universities and Land-Grant Colleges, and Vice-President Allan Cartter of the American Council on Education. The Gardner task force report also rejected tuition tax credits, as did the Bureau of the Budget and the Treasury Department.

32. Memorandum, Cater to President Johnson, 14 July 1964, EX FG 600, WHCF, LBJ Library; memorandum, Moyers to All Task Force Liaison Officers, 21 July 1964, EX FG 600, WHCF, LBJ Library.

33. The Michel-White-Cater correspondence is found in EX FG 600, container 363, LBJ Library.

34. Memorandum, Cater to President Johnson, 3 November 1964, EX FG 600, container 361, LBJ Library.

35. Bailey and Mosher, *ESEA*, 41.

36. Memorandum, Celebrezze to Moyers, 1 December 1964, William Moyers file, container 99, LBJ Library. Keppel's memo proposed three bills, the first dealing with lower education, the second to aid urban university extension and calling for a "Domestic Fulbright" program to assist "developing colleges," and the third to expand college-student aid through work-study jobs and federally guaranteed student loans by commercial lenders. But his political emphasis was overwhelmingly on the problem of aid to lower education.

37. Ibid.

38. Ibid.

39. Ibid.

40. Memorandum, Cater to President Johnson, 19 December 1964, EX FG165-4, WHCF, LBJ Library. Cater identified the monsignors as Hurley and Hochwald [*sic*, the correct spelling is Hochwalt] (Washington), McManus (Chicago), McDowell (Pittsburgh), Hughes (Philadelphia), Foudy (San Francisco), Stuardie (Mobile), Applegate (Columbus), Donahue (Baltimore), Lyons (Wash-

ington), Ulrich (Omaha), Curtin (Saint Louis), Behrens (Des Moines), and the attorney William Consedine for the NCWC. Keppel estimated that private schools would receive as much as 10.1 percent to 13.5 percent of the ESEA funds; parochial schools had approximately 15 percent of total school enrollments.

41. Bailey and Mosher, *ESEA*, 41.

42. Eugene Eidenberg and Roy Morey, *An Act of Congress* (New York: W. W. Norton, 1969), 81.

43. Hawkinson, "Presidential Program Formulation," 107. Robert Hunter reported to Cater on 9 December 1964 that a poll taken by Benton & Bowles that autumn revealed that for the first time the primary concern of the American electorate was education, not defense. Memorandum, Cater to Valenti, 26 May 1965, EX ED, WHCF, container 1, LBJ Library.

44. It is difficult to judge how to assess the Edith Green "problem." The rationale for the bad reputation that she had earned from the Democratic administrations of the 1960s was that she was a frustrated Oveta Culp Hobby who wanted to be secretary of DHEW and, failing that, sought vengeance by seeking Republican and boll-weevil (southern conservative) Democratic allies. Yet she also fought mightily for education programs and was generally regarded as a member of Congress with a formidable ability to torpedo the administration's program. The archival evidence suggests deep male resentment against a powerful and assertive woman. The archival evidence also captures O'Brien aide Charles Daly denouncing Congresswoman Green as a "psychotic female" and being overheard by a female Green staffer who told on Daly to her boss. Daly executed the required mea culpa, and Green was gracious. Keppel's base allusion to Edith Green's perennial "changes of life" suggests a generalized male resentment of female power in a man's game—although it is clear that Mrs. Green could be both abrasive and erratic.

45. Leuchtenburg, "Genesis of the Great Society," 39. Hawkinson's account in "Presidential Program Formulation" is highly useful for this crucial period of decision, especially 114–19. See Moyers's briefing memorandums to President Johnson, "Legislative Program for Education," ND, EX LE/FA 2, WHCF, and Moyers file, containers 100–101, LBJ Library.

46. Memorandum, Cater to Moyers, 23 December 1964, Cater file, container 5, LBJ Library. Keppel had the support of James B. Conant, and of course of the Council of Chief State School Officers, but the White House rated it a low priority.

47. Amendments to reform the aid-to-impacted-areas program had been introduced in Congress, and DHEW was conducting a study of their economic impact. The question that Moyers's brief posed for Johnson was "whether to delay reforms until DHEW's study of this legislation, now in progress, is completed early next summer." Johnson's answer was "Yes." The popular bills regarding impacted areas had proven to be excellent vehicles for passing education bills—most recently the Vocational Education Act of 1963 and the NDEA Amendments of 1964.

48. Transcript, "Keppel Oral History Interview," 21 April 1969, LBJ Library, 7. Wilbur Cohen recalled the distinctive Johnsonian exhortations at the same meeting: "So I want you guys to get off your asses and do everything possible to get everything in my program passed as soon as possible, before the aura and the halo that surround me disappear. Don't waste a second. Get going *right now*. Larry, Wilbur—just remember I want this program fast, and by fast I mean six

months, not a year" (quoted in Merle Miller, *Lyndon: An Oral Biography* [New York; G. P. Putnam's Sons, 1980], 409). Cater wrote the president on 16 February that "all the chief education lobbyists are now lined up behind the bill" and added that "even Edgar Fuller of the State School Officers has gotten into line on the bill" (Cater to President Johnson, 16 February 1965, EX LE/FA 2, WHCF, LBJ Library).

49. *Act of Congress*, 75–95.

50. Transcript, "Keppel Oral History Interview," 21 April 1969, LBJ Library, 8.

51. Transcript, "Wilbur Cohen Oral History Interview," 10 May 1969, LBJ Library, Tape no. 4, 14–15.

52. Eidenberg and Morey, *An Act of Congress*, 90.

53. Charles Lee, interview with author, Washington, D.C., 30 June 1981. Lee recalled that Cohen objected to Morse's original and rather complicated multiple-variable formula for identifying poor children, in part because DHEW would be forced to depend on the Department of Labor for the data. DHEW and Labor were constantly embroiled in turf disputes during the 1960s, partly because of an inherent overlapping of jurisdiction concerning education and manpower training, and partly because the secretary of labor, Willard Wirtz, was the most notoriously turf-minded bureaucrat in the cabinet.

54. *Act of Congress*, 96–168; Bailey and Mosher, *ESEA*, 37–71; Jeffrey, *Education for the Children of the Poor*, 59–95.

55. Eric F. Goldman, *The Tragedy of Lyndon Johnson* (New York: Knopf, 1969), 307. In a reversal of his Medicare strategy, which was solicitous of Wilbur Mills and flexible toward House bargaining, Johnson was determined to ram ESEA through Congress with force-draft speed.

56. Transcript, "Keppel Oral History Interview," 21 April 1969, LBJ Library, 9–10. Frustrating White House problems with both Chairman Powell and subcommittee chairman Green are nicely suggested by O'Brien's ten-page memorandum of 8 March reporting to Johnson on the crucial House hearings. O'Brien praised Johnson's shrewd choice of Phil Landrum of Georgia to ramrod the bill, applauded the steady loyalty of Carl Perkins, related that he was successful in browbeating Powell into line by threatening to take the Education and Labor Committee away from him, and reported on Mrs. Green's continuing "industry" (that is, sabotage). "(1) She argued passionately on Monday in caucus and Tuesday in committee for a delay of several weeks in reporting out the Education bill; (2) She negotiated with the Republicans to work out a substitute proposal. (3) She began agitations to stir up the religious issue which culminated Friday in her calling Protestant leaders into her office to tell them this bill will put Catholic priests in the public schools."

Jack Valenti reported to the president on 24 March that O'Brien was "fighting against Mrs. Green and judicial review," and that "Mrs. Green is trying to pick off the Jewish vote." On 30 March, Cater reported to the president that "Adam Clayton Powell is burning mad over Edith Green's behavior on the Education Bill. He has threatened three reprisals: (1) Remove vocational rehabilitation from her Subcommittee jurisdiction. (2) Fire her sister from the Committee staff. (3) Entrust John Brademas with the sponsorship of the Higher Education Bill." President Johnson wrote in reply, "O.K. All 3." The March memorandums are contained in EX LE/FA 2, container 38, LBJ Library. See also Eidenberg and Morey, *Act of Congress*, 96–172.

57. José Chavez, "Presidential Influence on the Politics of Higher Education: The Higher Education Act of 1965 (Ph.D. diss., University of Texas at Austin, 1975). Chavez was able to explore the newly opened LBJ Library; appendix B contains a transcript of his interviews with Cater, Keppel, Peter Muirhead, and Samuel Halperin in 1974.

58. Memorandum, O'Brien to President Johnson, 6 August 1965, EX LE/FA 2, WHCF, LBJ Library.

59. Memorandum, Cater to President Johnson, 25 August 1965, EX LE/FA 2, WHCF, LBJ Library.

60. Philip Reed Rulon, *The Compassionate Samaritan: The Life of Lyndon Baines Johnson* (Chicago: Nelson-Hall, 1981), is a biography of Johnson that centers on his role as champion of education.

CHAPTER 4

1. Bill Moyers, quoted in Hugh Sidey, "The White House Staff vs. the Cabinet: Hugh Sidey Interviews Bill Moyers," *The Washington Monthly*, February 1969, 9.

2. Charles Aikin and Louis Koenig, "The Hoover Commission: a Symposium," *American Political Science Review* 43 (October 1949): 933.

3. See Otis Graham, Jr., *Toward a Planned Society: From Roosevelt to Nixon* (New York: Oxford University Press, 1976). I am heavily indebted in this section to my brother's analysis of the difference between planning and Planning, and the formidable obstacles to achieving success in either.

4. Neil MacNeil and Harold W. Metz, *The Hoover Report, 1953–55* (New York: Macmillan, 1956), 299.

5. Eisenhower appointed three secretaries of health, education, and welfare: Oveta Culp Hobby (1953–55), Marion B. Folsom (1955–58), and Arthur S. Flemming (1958–61).

6. The other professors were Rowland A. Egger of Princeton University, Ferrel Heady of the University of Michigan, and Robert W. Tafts of Oberlin College. The other federal officials were Solis Horwitz from the Department of Defense, James M. Frey from the Department of State, and Eugene P. Foley from the Small Business Administration.

7. "Organization of Federal Education Activities," 2 October 1964, container 409, OMB Records Division, National Archives.

8. "Report, Task Force on Government Reorganization," 6 November 1964, container 1, Task Forces file, LBJ Library.

9. *Organizing the Executive Branch: The Johnson Presidency* (Chicago: University of Chicago Press, 1981), 189.

10. Director of the Bureau of the Budget to Mr. Chairman, 5 April 1965, container 409, OMB Records Division, National Archives.

11. "Reorganization of the Government's Educational Activities," n.d., container 409, OMB Records Division, National Archives.

12. Ibid.

13. Ibid.

14. Memorandum, Science and Education Branch to Hirst Sutton, 23 September 1964, container 412, OMB Records Division, National Archives.

15. Memorandum, Emerson J. Elliott to Howard V. Stone, 1 December 1964, container 412, OMB Records Division, National Archives.

16. Memorandum, Cannon to Staff, 9 December 1964, container 412, OMB Records Division, National Archives.

17. Memorandum, Labor and Welfare Division to Harold Seidman, 30 November 1964, container 409, OMB Records Division, National Archives.

18. Ibid. See also Clifford Berg to Seidman, 3 December 1964, and Berg and Hazel Guffey to Seidman, 4 December 1964, container 409, OMB Records Division, National Archives.

19. Memorandum, Sutton to Staats, 5 March 1965, container 409, OMB Records Division, National Archives.

20. Memorandum, Cater to President Johnson, 1 July 1965, EX LE/Fa 2, WHCF, LBJ Library. Cater's next four choices were Clark Kerr, Kermit Gordon, Carl Elliott, and Boisfeuillet Jones.

21. Transcript, "Henry Loomis Oral History," 15 August 1968, LBJ Library, 5. Bailey and Mosher have a sprightly account of the USOE reorganization, with more attention to structural and administrative detail, in Stephen K. Bailey and Edith K. Mosher, *ESEA: The Office of Education Administers a Law* (Syracuse: Syracuse University Press, 1968), ch. 3.

22. Transcript, "Douglass Cater Oral History Interview," 29 April 1969, LBJ Library, tape no. 1, 23–24.

23. Transcript, "Francis Keppel Oral History Interview," 21 April 1969, LBJ Library, 22. See also Richard A. Dershimer, *The Federal Government and Educational R&D* (Lexington, Mass.: Heath, 1976), 70–73, which reflects some of the manuscript and oral history sources in the Johnson Library.

24. Francis Keppel, interview with author, Cambridge, Mass., 1 April 1981. Thereafter, all new supergrade appointments for USOE had to be cleared through Johnson loyalist Marvin Watson in the White House, which further hampered the recruitment of senior staff during the reorganization. The oral history of Lucille Anderson, who was secretary to five commissioners of education, beginning with John Studebaker in 1936 and ending with her retiring under Harold Howe II in 1966, reflects the USOE loyalist resentment at the political impingement of the Johnson White House, with its outside task forces, its radical reorganization and its attendant displacement of specialists with generalists. See transcript, "Lucille Anderson Oral History Interview," 15 July 1968, LBJ Library.

25. Notes of Executive Group Meeting, 2 April 1965–27 June 1966, Kathryn Heath Collection, National Institute of Education Library. The biweekly notes were marked "Administrative Confidential" beginning 22 April 1965. In his oral history interview, Walter Mylecraine denies the charge of brutality, but he clearly also shared Loomis's contempt for the clientele-oriented "educationists" and their fear of federal control (see transcript, "Walter Mylecraine Oral History Interview," 12 July 1968, LBJ Library).

26. Memorandums, Cater to President Johnson, 12 and 14 April 1965; Cater to Celebrezze, 15 April 1965, EX FG 165-4, WHCF, LBJ Library. In his oral history, Loomis claims that the Ink task force was a response to *his* demand for White House support, because "when you had violated every sacred cow in the pasture . . . it was going to cause a hell of a stink on the Hill." Furthermore, he claims that he sent Mylecraine rummaging through the USOE staff to see if he could find anyone useful, and that Mylecraine had found in Russell Wood an atypically smart young lawyer ("no educator") who together with his colleague, John

Hughes, joined Loomis and Mylecraine in constructing a "shadow organization" that became 90 percent of the Ink report (Transcript, "Loomis Oral History Interview," 15 August 1968, LBJ Library). Given the tendency of Washington egos to claim credit for inventing the wheel (in his oral history Secretary Celebrezze even claims that *he* discovered the formula that led to the breakthrough for ESEA!), it is difficult to sort out the credit lines.

27. Memorandums, Cater to President Johnson, 12 and 14 April 1965; Cater to Celebrezze, 15 April 1965, EX FG 165–4, WHCF, LBJ Library.

28. Memorandum, McMurrin to Ribicoff, "Proposal for Reorganization of the Office of Education," 16 January 1962, container 409, OMB Records Division, National Archives. See Bailey and Mosher's more extensive discussion in *ESEA*, ch. 3. Wayne Reed's oral history recalls that when he joined USOE in 1951, Commissioner Earl McGrath had reorganized the office according to level. In 1962 McMurrin leaned back toward function, and in 1965 the Ink/Keppel/Loomis reorganization reverted to the organizational primacy of level. Reed also acknowledged that the reorganization was widely understood throughout USOE as a structural prelude to achieving cabinet department status (see "Wayne O. Reed Oral History Interview," 8 July 1968, LBJ Library).

29. "Recommendations of the White House Task Force on Education," 14 June 1965, Task Forces file, container 10, LBJ Library.

30. *ESEA*, 86. The Ink report also provided for six offices outside the bureaus (disadvantaged and handicapped, equal educational opportunities, legislation, planning and evaluation, administration, and public relations), and two centers (statistics and contracts), plus the strengthening of the field offices in the nine DHEW regions.

31. *ESEA*, 88–89. Loomis defensively observed, "We didn't fire anybody"; but many of the educational academics were unhappy with their new managerial job descriptions and especially unhappy over the elimination of consulting in Hawaii, so early retirements, transfers, and resignations followed quickly thereafter.

32. Transcript, "Henry Loomis Oral History," 15 August 1968, LBJ Library, 30.

33. Despite his braggadocio, in his oral history Loomis has kind words for the displaced Wayne Reed, who welcomed the threatening Loomis and was "absolutely superb" in his cooperation. To Loomis, the very qualities that made Reed, an "educator" from Nebraska, a poor deputy, also made him a "beautiful help" as liaison to the nervous old guard. Not surprisingly, Loomis gave highest marks to fellow Harvard alumnus Frank Keppel—they were, he said, "Mr. Inside and Mr. Outside." Loomis was to return to public service as deputy director of the United States Information Agency in the Nixon administration.

34. Transcript, "Dwight Ink Oral History Interview," 5 February 1969, LBJ Library, 10. A generally dim assessment of the efficacy of the reorganization of USOE is shared to varying degrees by Bailey and Mosher in *ESEA*; moreso by William Cannon and William D. Carey of the Bureau of the Budget (both in OMB Records Division memorandums and in interviews with author in Washington, D.C., Cannon on 15 September 1981, and Carey on 8 May 1981); and even in the Administrative History of HEW, especially chapter 1, "Bureau of Elementary and Secondary Education." See also the oral history interview with Nolan Estes, the BESE's first associate commissioner, 23 July 1968, LBJ Library. Wayne Reed's oral history decries the excessive speed and ruthlessness of the decimation

of the old specialists, which "left painful scars" and was called by the specialists "the year of the locusts" ("Wayne O. Reed Oral History Interview," 8 July 1968, LBJ Library).

35. See Gary Orfield, *Reconstruction of Southern Education: The Schools and the 1964 Civil Rights Act* (New York: Wiley Interscience, 1969), ch. 4. Wilbur Cohen was dispatched to Chicago to work out a compromise, which he successfully accomplished. Cater's oral history faults Keppel's judgment in this celebrated incident, as does Orfield's account. But for a defense of Keppel, see David Seeley's letter of 22 March 1972 to the LBJ Library, which is included in Keppel's oral history file (LBJ Library). Seeley's own oral history, however, is basically critical of the "bungling" in his agency, which produced a "disaster" (Transcript, "David Seeley Oral History Interview," 25 July 1968, LBJ Library, 39–44).

36. Memorandum, Cater to President Johnson, 2 April 1965, Cater file, container 13, LBJ Library.

37. Memorandum, O'Neill to Cater, 31 March 1965, Cater file, container 13, LBJ Library. A balanced discussion of the evolution and structure of DHEW from an insider's viewpoint is Rufus E. Miles, Jr., *The Department of Health, Education, and Welfare* (New York: Praeger, 1974).

38. Ibid.

39. Ibid.

40. "Task Force Report on Intergovernmental Program Coordination," December 1965, container 412, OMB Records Division, National Archives. The other task force members were William G. Colman, Herbert Kaufman, James L. Sundquist, Stephen B. Sweeney, and Robert C. Wood.

41. "The Bureau's Role in the Improvement of Government Organization and Management," part 4 of the Bureau of the Budget's Administrative History, LBJ Library, 1:124–51.

42. Letter, Schultze to Muskie, 15 November 1966, Documentary Supplement to BOB Administrative History, vol. 2, LBJ Library.

43. Ibid.

44. For a more extended discussion, see Redford and Blissett, *Organizing the Executive Branch*, especially chapters 5–9. Congress created the Department of Commerce and Labor in 1903, but labor unhappiness led to its division into the Department of Commerce and the Department of Labor in 1913.

45. "Ben W. Heineman Oral History Interview," 14 April 1970, LBJ Library.

46. See Redford and Blissett, *Organizing the Executive Branch*, 195–215. A logical participant was Harold Seidman, director of the BOB's division of Management and Organization. But Seidman had grown bitter as the growth of Califano's domestic staff increasingly preempted the Bureau of the Budget in policy planning. Seidman's participation was rejected by the task force, and he in turn vetoed participation by a top member of his staff—this was brought out in an interview between Seidman and Redford and Blissett.

47. "A Final Report by the President's Task Force on Government Organization," 15 June 1967, Task Forces file, container 4, LBJ Library.

48. Ibid.

49. Heineman, McNamara, and Schultze preferred to locate the OPC within a completely reorganized and reoriented Bureau of the Budget, but they agreed with the task force majority that the creation of OPC was far more important than its precise location within the executive office. Heineman also argued strongly for

the creation of a director of the executive office of the president, a kind of domestic czar for program coordination and resolution of interagency conflict resolution, but the majority of his task force colleagues opposed such a post, as had the Price task force.

50. In a six-page report submitted on 15 September 1967, the task force suggested that a supercabinet might contain the following departments: Social Services, Natural Resources and Development, Economic Affairs, Science and Environmental Preservation, Foreign Affairs, and National Security Affairs—with Justice probably remaining. See Redford and Blissett, *Organizing the Executive Branch*, 103–4.

51. Heineman Report, 10.

52. Memorandum, Charles S. Murphy to President Johnson, 22 November 1968, EX FG 11–18, WHCF, LBJ Library.

53. Ibid.

54. Transcript, "Heineman Oral History Interview," 16 April 1970, LBJ Library, 26.

55. *Organizing the Executive Branch*, 214–15. The major Nixon departure from the Heineman design was in establishing the Domestic Council embodying the conciliar idea earlier advanced by Shriver and Muskie, rather than coordination and program development through institutional (executive office) staff.

CHAPTER 5

1. Moyers, interview with Hugh Sidey, *Washington Monthly*, February 1969, 79.

2. Ibid., 79–80.

3. Transcript, "Harry McPherson Oral History Interview," 19 December 1968, LBJ Library, tape no. 3, 37.

4. See Patrick Anderson, *The Presidents' Men* (Garden City, N.Y.: Doubleday, 1968), ch. 6, especially 252–71. With the Vietnam War and inflation heating up, the Watts riot erupting, and, *more* important in the summer of 1965, the president's honeymoon with the public and the news media quickly dissipating, Johnson ditched the exhausted George Reedy and appointed Moyers, which, according to Anderson, "came as a shock to him and almost everyone else in Washington."

5. Joseph Califano, quoted in Anderson, *The Presidents' Men*, 366.

6. Wood's 1964 outside task force, half of which was made up of academics, was followed in 1965 by a nationally heavyweight group with clear White House priority, one containing only two professors (Wood and Harvard Law School's Charles Haar), but star-studded with such strategically placed luminaries as Edgar Kaiser, Walter Reuther, Whitney Young, Kermit Gordon, Ben Heineman, and Abraham Ribicoff. On the Wood task forces, see Emmette S. Redford and Marlan Blissett, *Organizing the Executive Branch: The Johnson Presidency* (Chicago: University of Chicago Press, 1981), especially 34–36 and 127–29.

7. The college and university presidents were Harvie Branscomb of Vanderbilt University, Margaret Clapp of Wellesley College, John Fischer of Columbia Teachers College, Charles Odegaard of the University of Washington, and Harry Ransom of the University of Texas. The only mere professor was the historian John Hope Franklin of the University of Chicago, but academic associations were

shared by Harold Howe II, who was executive director of the University of North Carolina's Learning Institute, and Pauline Tompkins, general director of the American Association of University Women. Also serving were Mrs. Arthur Goldberg, James Linen III of *Time*, President Herman Wells of the Indiana University Foundation, and William Marvel of Education and World Affairs. For Frankel's account, see Charles Frankel, *High on Foggy Bottom: An Outsider's Inside View of the Government* (New York: Harper and Row, 1968), 63–77.

8. President Johnson emphasized his strong commitment to the international studies program in major addresses at the Smithsonian Institution on 16 September 1965, in his 12 January State of the Union Message for 1966, and in a 2 February message on world health and education. The Bureau of the Budget's International Division regarded Frankel's program design as "quasi-heroic" in "packaging" a grand "Johnson Doctrine" to take the Great Society beyond our shores, but as essentially barren of new ideas. It would stand on education alone, thereby excluding "health, personal security, social justice: all the other instruments for the international war on poverty, disease, ignorance, prejudice." Worse, it would establish "OE beachheads abroad" through a network of Educational Attaches to help Frankel's cultural affairs officers run "the local U.S. alumni office." Worst of all, it ignored the major federal organization problems, dismissing them with the naïve assertion that "if the basic premises and purposes of such a program can be clearly defined, the problem of parcelling out operational responsibility for it to various agencies *should settle itself*" (Memorandum, International Division to Cannon, 1 September 1965, container 412, OMB Records Division, National Archives).

9. The others were Wilbur Cohen on health, Alan Boyd on maritime problems, Cohen on welfare, Stanley Surrey on tax reform, and Boyd on transportation. Califano's status report of 11 August included task forces headed by McPherson on population and family planning, Ackley on income maintenance, and, by mid-September, John Doar on civil rights. But these do not appear in LBJ Library archivist Nancy Kegan Smith's compilation of 1978 and presumably were dropped—like the original civil rights task force of 1964.

10. Memorandum, Califano to Celebrezze, 28 July 1965, EX FA 600/T, WHCF, LBJ Library.

11. Memorandum, Keppel to Califano, 10 August 1965, EX ED FG 600/T, WHCF, LBJ Library.

12. Joseph A. Califano, Jr., *A Presidential Nation* (New York: Norton, 1975), 47.

13. Memorandum, Cannon to the Director, 30 August 1965, container 412, OMB Records Division, National Archives. In September Commissioner Keppel became assistant secretary of health, education, and welfare for education.

14. Memorandum, Keppel to Califano, 8 October 1965, EX FG 600/T, WHCF, LBJ Library. A more detailed examination of the Keppel task force of 1965 can be found in Hawkinson, "Presidential Program Formulation in Education: Lyndon Johnson and the 89th Congress" (Ph.D. diss., University of Chicago, 1977), ch. 5.

15. Memorandum, Califano to Task Forces, 9 September 1965, EX FA/600-T, WHCF, LBJ Library.

16. Louis Fisher, *President and Congress: Power and Policy* (New York: Free Press, 1972), especially ch. 4.

17. See Lawrence C. Dodd and Richard L. Schott, *Congress and the Administrative State* (New York: Wiley, 1979).

18. Richard F. Fenno, Jr., *Congressmen in Committees* (Boston: Little, Brown, 1973), studies six equivalent sets of committees in both chambers from the Eighty-fourth Congress to the Eighty-ninth Congress (1955 to 1966), the education committees being one of the sets.

19. Ibid., 130–32.

20. Memorandum, Wilson to President Johnson, 13 July 1966, EX LE/FA 2, WHCF, LBJ Library.

21. *New York Times*, 13 January 1966 and 25 January 1966. The president proposed a budget for Great Society social programs of $14 billion for fiscal year 1967 (spending for fiscal year 1966 was set at $10.8 billion), but the actual net government outlays were closer to $12.9 billion, owing primarily to new methods of financing and accounting. Clearly the new funding levels were considerably reduced by the expanding demands of the Vietnam War (*Congressional Quarterly Almanac, 1966* [Washington, D.C.: Congressional Quarterly Press, 1967], 286–87).

22. James Tobin, "The Political Economy of the 1960s," in *Toward New Human Rights*, ed. David C. Warner (Austin: Lyndon B. Johnson School of Public Affairs, 1977), 50.

23. *Congress and the Nation, 1965–1968* (Washington, D.C.: Congressional Quarterly, 1969), 128. Johnson's original total budget estimate for fiscal year 1967, $112.8 billion, fell short of actual expenditures by approximately $12 billion.

24. Dean M. Kelley and George R. LaNoue, "The Church-State Settlement in the Federal Aid to Education Act: A Legislative History," in *Religion and the Public Order: An Annual Review of Church and State and of Religion, Law, and Society, 1965*, ed. Donald A. Giannella (Villanova, 1966), 110–60.

25. *Hearings before the General Subcommittee on Education of the House Committee on Education and Labor on the Elementary and Secondary Education Amendments of 1966*, 89th Cong., 2d sess., pt. 2 at 814, 18 March 1966.

26. Memorandum, Halperin to Cohen and Keppel, 21 March 1966, EX LE/FA 2, WHCF, LBJ Library.

27. Howe to Gardner, 14 July 1966, EX LE/FA 2, WHCF; and Cohen to Morse, 15 July 66, EX LE/FA 2, WHCF, LBJ Library.

28. Memorandum, Huitt to Cater and Wilson, 18 February 1966, EX FA 2, WHCF, LBJ Library.

29. Memorandum, Huitt to Schultze, Cannon, Cater, and Wilson, 27 April 1966, EX LE FA 2, WHCF, LBJ Library.

30. Memorandum, Huitt to Cater and Wilson, 29 March 1966, EX LE/FA 2, WHCF, LBJ Library.

31. Memorandum, Halperin to Huitt, 22 March 1966, EX LE/FA 2, WHCF, LBJ Library.

32. Memorandum, Cater to President Johnson, 22 June 1966, Cater file, container 15, LBJ Library.

33. Ibid. Johnson approved a meeting with Hill and added, "Also talk to Mansfield, Dirksen, et al."

34. Memorandum, Wilson to President Johnson, 13 July 1966, Cater file, container 15, LBJ Library.

35. Memorandum, Cater to President Johnson, 14 July 1966, Cater file, container 15, LBJ Library.

36. Memorandum, Cater to President Johnson, 16 July 1966, Cater file, container 15, LBJ Library.

37. *New York Times*, 4 November 1966. The major bills included $1.3 billion for the Model Cities Program, $3.6 billion over three years for higher education, $6.1 billion over two years for lower education, $3.5 billion over five years to combat water pollution, bills to advance "truth-in-packaging" and to control hazardous substances, and expanded programs in public health and medical manpower.

38. *Congressional Quarterly Almanac, 1966*, 286–316; Eugene Eidenberg and Roy D. Morey, *An Act of Congress* (New York: Norton, 1969), 175–206. Congress also extended and expanded the Library Services and Construction Act and extended G.I. Bill of Rights education benefits to peacetime "Cold War" veterans, that is, servicemen who became veterans after 31 January 1955, when the "Korean G.I. Bill of Rights" expired.

39. Larry Berman, *Planning a Tragedy: The Americanization of the War in Vietnam* (New York: Norton, 1982), xx.

CHAPTER 6

1. On Califano's role in forming DOT, see Emmette S. Redford and Marlan Blissett, *Organizing the Executive Branch* (Chicago: University of Chicago Press, 1981), ch. 3; and Patrick Anderson, *The Presidents' Men* (Garden City: Doubleday, 1968), 352–64.

2. Califano, interview with Robert Hawkinson (on tape), 11 June 1973, LBJ Library. Califano regarded the original task force reports of 1964–65 as "very general in their conclusions, even superficial," especially in their lack of cost estimates.

3. The Gaither file is the chief repository for the task force operations; see Nancy Kegan Smith, "Johnson Task Force Operation," mimeographed guide, LBJ Library.

4. Transcript, "Harry McPherson Oral History Interview," 19 December 1968, LBJ Library, tape no. 3, 15; 16–17. McPherson's 285-page transcript from nine tapes represents the class of the LBJ Library's rich oral history collection; the perceptive and candid quality of his reflections also characterizes his memoir, *A Political Education* (Boston: Little, Brown, 1972).

5. Larry Berman, "Johnson and the White House Staff," in *Exploring the Johnson Years*, ed. Robert A. Divine (Austin: University of Texas Press, 1981), 195. Although neither Anderson nor Redford and Blissett mention the marginal Kintner, Berman concentrates on him, apparently because he left so many memorandums in the Johnson archives. This illustrates a potential danger of archival research, because it is not clear whether the memorandums were of much consequence. Joseph Laitin, a veteran bureaucratic survivor, recalls that Kintner cranked out so many self-important memorandums because he had little else of substance to do (Laitin, interview with author, Washington, D.C., 26 April 1981).

6. Memorandum, Kintner to President Johnson, 9 May 1966, EX ED PR 18, WHCF, LBJ Library.

7. Memorandum, Rostow to President Johnson, 11 May 1966, EX ED CO1–1, WHCF, LBJ Library.

8. Memorandum, Califano to President Johnson, 9 August 1966, Califano file,

container 63, LBJ Library. In his oral history interview, Gaither reports that in addition to the campus visits, Califano solicited ideas from all the members of the White House staff, all agency and department heads, and such key political appointees as Robert Wood and Charles Haar (recruited from previous task forces). Gaither hit the ground running: "I began really the day I got here, which was July 27, 1966, with the representatives from CEA, Budget, OST, to collect ideas from virtually every source imaginable . . . Sid Brown, who was formerly a special assistant to Charles Schultze who was Director of the Budget; Bill Hooper from OST; and Wilford Lewis from CEA. We collected ideas from virtually every budget examiner and every top official on the Budget Bureau, all of the so-called idea men in government—people like Herb Holliman (?) who was Under Secretary of Commerce and was always full of ideas; Wilbur Cohen; members of the Council of Economic Advisors; Charlie Zwick who was Assistant Director of the Budget; Bill Cannon, who was division chief of the Education and Science Division in the Budget Bureau—bright young people in the government like Les Brown of the Department of Agriculture for one. And we had a series of meetings with bright young people in the government who had been identified by John Macy" (Transcript, "James Gaither Oral History Interview," 19 November 1968, LBJ Library, tape no. 1, 5).

9. Rostow's memorandum to Johnson of 11 May 1966 mentions outside groups working in the international area that are not reflected in Nancy Smith's list of 26 June 1978, which in turn drew heavily on the Gaither file on domestic task force operations. Clearly the Smith master list largely excludes task forcing in foreign affairs, which in any event likely would have remained small, elite, mainly in-house, and highly confidential. Johnson and his foreign policy advisors would surely never have dreamed of commissioning an outside task force dominated by university professors and charged with determining what best to do about Vietnam or the Dominican Republic.

10. Memorandums, Elliott to the director, 21 October 1966; Cannon to the Director, 3 December 1966, container 412; Cannon to the director, 6 December 1966, container 414, OMB Records Division, National Archives.

11. Memorandum, Schultze to President Johnson, 7 November 1966, EX FI 4, WHCF, LBJ Library. The remarkable speed with which the fiscal and budgetary window on opportunity of 1965 disappeared is illustrated by two memorandums to the president from CEA chairman Gardner Ackley. On 2 June 1965, Ackley wrote Johnson that the CEA had met with eight of its senior academic consultants and all agreed that in light of a slowing growth rate, "*they would like to see more fiscal stimulus in early 1966.* In any case, they *urged a strongly expansionary budget for fiscal 1967.*" On this note the budgetarily huge and fiscally redistributionist ESEA and HEA went roaring through. But by December of 1965, Ackley was calling for "*a significant tax increase . . .* to prevent an intolerable degree of inflationary pressure" (Memorandums, Ackley to President Johnson, 2 June 1965, EX FG 11-0; and 17 December 1965, EX F 14, WHCF, LBJ Library).

12. Ibid.

13. Transcript, "Gaither Oral History Interview," 19 November 1968, LBJ Library, tape no. 3, 2.

14. Bureau of the Budget Administrative History, part III, "The Bureau's Contributions to Program Develpment," 1 : 101–2, LBJ Library (emphasis added).

15. Transcript, "Gaither Oral History Interview," tape no. 1, 20.

16. Memorandums, Cater to Califano, 10 August 1966; Cohen to Cater, 27 June 1966, EX FA 2, WHCF, LBJ Library.

17. The Hunt task force grew like Topsy, with anthropologist Oscar Lewis being subsequently invited to add sociological weight on the culture of poverty; Susan Gray of George Peabody College on educating the parents of the poor; Joseph Reid as a child welfare specialist; and Marie Costello of Philadelphia's Health and Welfare Council—at Hunt's suggestion, to "help with the Catholics in getting any program [that is, family planning and contraception] passed," (Memorandum, Califano to President Johnson, 15 October 1966, EX FA 2, WHCF, LBJ Library). Other members of the task force were Robert Cook of Johns Hopkins University, John Goodlad of the University of California at Los Angeles, Edmond Gordon of Yeshiva University, Halbert Robinson of the University of North Carolina, George Tarjan of Los Angeles' Neuropsychiatric Institute, and Lois Murphy of the Menninger Clinic, with both Cater and Gaither as White House representatives. Hunt had written widely on the Montessori method and preschool enrichment as antidotes to cultural deprivation, and his book *Intelligence and Experience* (New York: Ronald, 1961) was the most frequently cited source in the report, although Oscar Lewis's *The Children of Sanchez* was frequently cited as an authoritative source on the debilitating effects of the culture of poverty. Bronfenbrenner had published quite recently (in 1966 and 1967) on the effects of early deprivation in mammals and man and the psychological dimensions of quality and equality in education. The 157-page report was a collective effort, but it especially bears the distinctive imprint of Hunt and Bronfenbrenner.

18. Transcript, "Gaither Oral History Interview," LBJ Library, tape no. 1, 20.

19. "Report of the President's Task Force on Early Childhood Development," 14 January 1967, Task Forces file, container 4, LBJ Library. The Hunt report echoed the Moynihan report's alarm over the disintegration of the inner city Negro family—and, like the Moynihan report, it wrongly blamed it on slavery. This error was not their fault, because the pre- and postemancipation strength of the southern rural Negro family was not discovered by historians until the next decade. The cause was less southern slavery than twentieth-century northern migration; ghetto decay; and, as ever, nationwide racism. But the disaster that Moynihan and Hunt decried was real, escalating, and chilling. It centered on black families that were headed by females and were characterized by poverty, uncontrolled procreation, despair, distrust, alienation, self-contempt, violence and ephemeral escape, and functional illiteracy, with no father role model, a failed and defeated mother role model, and no contact with a working adult. The children of such shattered families were too often both doomed and dangerous.

20. Joseph Califano, interview with author, Washington, D.C., 15 June 1981. Gaither called the Hunt report "really a first rate report," and indeed it was.

21. "A Bill of Rights for Children," 16.

22. Ibid., 24.

23. Memorandum, Estes to Emerson Elliott, 7 December 1966, EX FG 165–64, WHCF, LBJ Library.

24. Memorandum, Cannon to Gaither, n.d., Cater file, LBJ Library, container 39, 2.

25. *Public Papers of the President: Lyndon B. Johnson, 1967* (Washington, D.C.: Government Printing Office, 1968), 55.

26. The tuition tax credit had narrowly failed by a forty-five-to-forty-eight roll-call vote in 1964, and eleven Democrats who voted against it then switched to support in 1967, with seven of them facing reelection races in 1968. Senate Republicans had always heavily favored the tax credit, and southern Democrats opposed it.

27. The complicated maneuvering of 1967 is best followed in Norman C. Thomas, *Education in National Politics* (New York: McKay, 1975), especially ch. 4. The first session of the Ninetieth Congress did pass the Education Professions Development Act, which narrowly saved the Teacher Corps, but the main battles over financing higher education were to be waged in 1968.

28. The quotation is from Ralph Huitt's paraphrase of Lee, in a memorandum to Cater, Wilson, and Manatos, 26 January 1967, Cater file, container 15, LBJ Library.

29. Excluded is Johnson's major request for the creation of a corporation for public television, primarily because it was destined for the Department of Commerce and therefore followed a quite separate procedural and political path from the hearings and voting route of the ESEA and HEA amendments.

30. Memorandum, Huitt to Cater, 30 January 1967, EX LE/ED, WHCF, LBJ Library.

31. *New York Times*, 23 April 1967.

32. Thomas correctly explains that the Quie controversy was not over the amount of aid (Quie's $3 billion for fiscal year 1969 was only $281 million less than the committee bill), nor was it an attempt at no-strings general aid, because Quie had incorporated required expenditures for the educationally deprived, including private-school children.

33. Perkins's elevation to the chair of the House Committee on Education and Labor opened a scramble for subcommittee chairs and jurisdiction in a confused situation. Perkins had chaired the *general* subcommittee, which Edith Green would inherit by dint of seniority, but she passed it along to Roman Pucinski and retained her *special* subcommittee (which was later helpfully renamed the subcommittee on post-secondary education), leaving Congressman Dominick Daniels to chair the *select* subcommittee, whose jurisdiction Ralph Huitt charitably described as "exceedingly vague (for example, 'libraries, and other special education programs')." Unlike Powell, Perkins was a steady, loyal, and weak chairman, and so the stronger personality of Edith Green ultimately dominated several major legislative policy decisions on education in 1967, to the disgust of the White House.

34. Transcript, "Albert Quie Oral History Interview," 30 April 1969, LBJ Library, 24–25.

35. Ibid.

36. Memorandum, Cater to President Johnson, 19 April 1967, Cater file, container 16, LBJ Library.

37. Charles Radcliffe, interview with author, Washington, D.C., 15 June 1982. On 26 April Cater wrote the president that "Quie and Jerry Ford have been engaged in daily negotiations with various lobby groups and have offered one concession after another to get their support. The lobbyists now realize that this is strictly a partisan matter so far as Quie and Ford are concerned. Our best judgment is that we should handle this as a partisan fight."

38. Memorandum, Wilson to President Johnson, 25 May 1967, EX LE/FA 2, WHCF, LBJ Library.

39. Transcript, "Harold Howe Oral History Interview," 29 October 1968, LBJ Library, tape no. 2, 6.

40. William Cannon, interview with author, Washington, D.C., 15 September 1981.

41. As quoted in Eugene Eidenberg and Roy D. Morey, *An Act of Congress* (New York: W. W. Norton, 1969), 212. Hayes was no ideological fan of Edith Green. During the May debates, Hayes chastized his own state of Ohio for being the sixth or seventh richest state and yet being thirty-ninth in what it does for education, and he complained that "when we pass these amendments to give the job of administering the Federal money back to those state administrators . . . it is like taking a drunkard who is convicted of neglecting his children and giving him an extra $100 a month to spend on whiskey, so he can neglect them some more."

42. A prime example is "The Strange Roll of Oregon's Edith Green and her 'Mini-Quie' Amendments," *I. F. Stone's Weekly*, 5 June 1967.

43. Bailey to Howe, 9 June 1967, EX LE/FA 2, WHCF, LBJ Library.

44. Memorandum, Cater to President Johnson, 25 May 1967, Cater file, container 38, LBJ Library.

45. Memorandum, Wilson to President Johnson, 25 May 1967, EX LE/FA 2, WHCF, LBJ Library.

46. Memorandum, Gaither to Califano, 26 May 1967, EX LE/FA 2, WHCF, LBJ Library.

47. Eidenberg and Morey, *Act of Congress*, 212.

48. See generally Numan V. Bartley and Hugh D. Graham, *Southern Politics and the Second Reconstruction* (Baltimore: Johns Hopkins University Press, 1975).

49. *Hearings before the Special Subcommittee on Bilingual Education of the Committee on Labor and Public Welfare*, U.S. Senate, 90th Congress, 1st Session (Washington: Government Printing Office, 1968).

50. *New York Times*, 22 July 1967.

51. *Hearings before the General Subcommittee on Education of the Committee on Education and Labor*, U.S. House of Representatives, 90th Congress, 1st Session (Washington: Government Printing Office, 1968).

52. Harold Howe II, interview with author, New York City, 11 May 1981.

53. Memorandum, Cannon to Cater, 3 July 1967, EX LE/FA 2, WHCF, LBJ Library.

54. Memorandum, Gaither to Califano, 15 August 1967, EX LE/FA 2, WHCF, LBJ Library.

55. Gardner to Hill, n.d., EX LE/FA 2, WHCF, LBJ Library.

56. Memorandum, Huitt to Cater and Sanders, 7 August 1967, EX LE/FA 2, WHCF, LBJ Library.

57. S.428 ultimately became Title VII of Public Law 90–247, the ESEA amendments for 1967, which called for its citation as the "Bilingual Education Act," referred only to "children of limited English-speaking ability" and nowhere specified ethnic entitlements.

58. *Public Papers: Johnson, 1965*, 636.

59. Transcript, "Charles Zwick Oral History Interview II," 1 August 1969, LBJ Library.

CHAPTER 7

1. Memorandum, Cater to President Johnson, 10 February 1967, Cater file, container 16, LBJ Library.

2. "Talking Points," n.d., Bohen file, container 17, LBJ Library. The document does not identify its author or who attended the meeting.

3. The Heller Plan was first proposed to President Johnson when Heller was CEA chairman in 1964 (although Heller had raised it within the Kennedy campaign and administration as early as 1960) and Joseph Pechman's outside task force on intergovernmental fiscal cooperation of 1964 explored how it might be put into effect. Johnson toyed with the notion of tax sharing with the states with few strings attached, but it was opposed by the Bureau of the Budget, which preferred project grants with strings attached; by organized labor, which preferred federal to state leverage; and by big-city mayors, who questioned the priorities and competence of rural and suburban-dominated state legislators. In 1966 Johnson formally rejected such tax sharing, but the Republican block-grant proposal amounted to a partisan and relatively no-strings version of the Heller concept.

4. *Congress and the Nation, 1965–1968* (Washington, D.C.: Congressional Quarterly, 1969), 2:84–88. The administration took a severe battering on foreign aid in 1967, with Congress both authorizing and appropriating the lowest budget levels in the twenty-year history of the program and then attaching to the foreign-aid bill restrictive amendments that curbed the president's authority to conduct foreign policy.

5. The identical wording for the three lead issues appeared in all six of Gaither's discussion summaries (Gaither, the official academic dinner amanuensis, prepared the first six summaries, with Ervin Duggan on Chicago and Fred Bohen on New York preparing summaries in a different format [emphasis added]). Califano's issue that treated blue-collar alienation prompted some lively and sympathetic discussion at Harvard University, where growing Boston racial and class tensions highlighted the danger of whites perceiving Great Society programs as essentially welfare for blacks. But elsewhere the question of alienation quickly shifted to the anti–Vietnam War feeling on the campus and rioting in the ghettos.

6. Levi to Califano, 31 July 1967, Bowen file, container 17, LBJ Library.

7. Memorandum, Califano to President Johnson, 7 June 1967, Bowen file, container 17, LBJ Library.

8. All summaries of the 1967 academic dinners are located in the Bowen file, container 17, and all contain lists of the participants. Gaither did not attend the last two dinner discussions. The Los Angeles meeting was surprising, however, in that there was *no* representation from the University of California at Berkeley, but *six* attended from the California State College System (Stanford University sent seven; University of California at Los Angeles, three; California Institute of Technology, two; and there were two lawyers and one businessman).

9. Ehrlich to Califano, 7 July 1967, Bowen file, container 17, LBJ Library.

10. North Carolina Summary, Bowen file, container 17, LBJ Library.

11. The New York dinner was the least campus-oriented meeting, with the majority of its impressive assemblage having no primary campus affiliation: McGeorge Bundy, Burke Marshall, Pendleton Herring, Alan Westin, Allen Cartter, Paul Ylvisaker, Mitchell Svirdoff, Wallace Sayre, David Truman, and Gerard Piel.

12. Bowen to Califano, 28 August 1962, Bowen file, container 17, LBJ Library.

13. Ehrlich to Califano, 7 July 1967, Bowen file, container 17, LBJ Library.

14. Memorandum, John E. Robson to Califano, 15 August 1967, Bowen file, container 17, LBJ Library.

15. Memorandum, Califano to President Johnson, 2 August 1967, EX WE, WHCF, LBJ Library.

16. Memorandum, Califano to President Johnson, 4 October 1967, EX FG-600/Task Forces, WHCF, LBJ Library.

17. Memorandum, Califano to President Johnson, 11 September 1967, EX FG-600/Task Forces, WHCF, LBJ Library. Johnson approved, "If it does not cost a lot of extra money."

18. Harry McPherson, *A Political Education* (Boston: Little, Brown, 1975), 293.

19. Memorandum, Califano to President Johnson, 30 September 1966, FG 600/Task Forces, WHCF, LBJ Library.

20. Gaither's best recollection was that Johnson insisted on switching Friday and Marland in the interest of regional spread. Gaither, conversation by telephone with author, 7 July 1982.

21. Most documents on the Friday task force are in the Cater file, container 37, LBJ Library.

22. William Friday, interview with author, Chapel Hill, North Carolina, 15 May 1981; William Cannon, interview with author, Washington, D.C., 15 September 1981.

23. Memorandum, Hugh F. Loweth (for William B. Cannon) to Task Force, 2 March 1967, Cater file, container 37, LBJ Library.

24. "Notes on the Task Force Meeting, March 17 and 18, 1967," Cannon to Task Force Members, 29 March 1967, Cater file, container 37, LBJ Library. According Cannon's summary, Calkins challenged Pettigrew, arguing that "educational parks may not be the answer because (a) ability grouping demands may undercut them and (b) they will intensify an already major problem in ghetto areas—the lack of community institutions—and may work against [the] need to make ghettos decent areas with good living [conditions] and good schools" (ibid.).

25. Ibid.

26. Cannon, interview with author, Washington, D.C., 15 September 1981.

27. Memorandum, Cannon to Task Force, 27 April 1967, Cater file, container 37, LBJ Library.

28. "Status of Education Task Force Deliberations," 17 May 1967, container 414, OMB Records Division, National Archives.

29. *Report of the 1966 Task Force on Education*, 30 June 1967, Task Force File, container 4, LBJ Library. The internal debate over the unrestricted general aid formula for higher education pitted Harrington against DuBridge, with the University of Wisconsin president calling for equal flat amounts per student, and the president of California Institute of Technology for equal proportions of instructional costs. The final report compromised on a combination of both, arguing that an instructional cost formula would be theoretically ideal, but that adding a flat per capita amount would help boost instructional costs at junior colleges and four-year nonresearch colleges, where instructional costs had been unrealistically depressed.

30. Friday, interview with author, 15 May 1981. Also painful is the irony of President Friday's subsequent decade-long battle with the federal courts and the

Office of Education, especially under the Carter administration, over integrating North Carolina's predominately white and black campuses, for he had been the task force's strongest proponent of the recommendations for black-white campus pairing as a prelude to "joint program development, sharing of faculty, and academic facilities which can be jointly used [because] increasing contact and cooperation between Negro and white institutions . . . can speed later racial integration" (Friday report, 86).

31. Memorandum, Cater to President Johnson, 12 July 1967; Cannon to Cater, 13 July 1967, EX FG/600, WHCF, LBJ Library.

32. This quotation is from page 46 of the Friday report, which refers to general aid as "a deferred goal."

33. *New York Times*, 21 August 1967. On 25 August the *Times* editorially endorsed the Johnson/Friday position but observed that the federal government's major precedent for categorical aid in education derived less from the ESEA of 1965 than from the NDEA of 1958, and it urged the prompt extension of "categorical emergency funds" to such riot-torn cities as Newark.

34. "A Political Analysis of the Background for New Legislation in the Field of Education," Tab 1, *Report of the Interagency Task Force on Education*, October 1967, Cater file, container 39, LBJ Library.

35. Ibid.

36. Memorandum, Howe to Califano, 23 October 1967, Cater file, container 39, LBJ Library. In his report to Director of the Budget Schultze, task force member Emerson Elliott agreed that the ambitious Friday recommendations were too expensive to contemplate at that time, but he could not resist adding, full in the Cannon tradition, that the Friday report's "moon shot" educational education recommendations "will be successful only if we can construct some functioning interagency mechanisms so that the contacts which NSF and NFAH have with the academic and artistic communities can be brought in to ventilate the stodgy educationists" (Memorandum, Elliott to the director, 30 October 1967, container 413, OMB Records Division, National Archives.

37. Memorandum, Gorham to the secretary, 13 November 1967, EX ED, container 4, WHCF, LBJ Library.

38. Memorandum, Gorham to the secretary, 13 November 1967, EX ED, container 4, WHCF, LBJ Library.

39. More often than not, the notes or memorandums of senior BOB personnel reflected an unusually ironic, antibureaucratic, and even mischievous tone. Emerson Elliott soberly noted of the 12 December meeting that "Gaither, ever the sphinx, busily took notes but made no comment." The following day, Carey reported with delicious irony that Gardner and Howe had denounced any program of general aid (as ever) "at this time," but then Howe had introduced a nine-point package that in effect called for general aid for higher education by another name. The meeting was interrupted when Califano, Gardner, and Schultze were called away to deal with more pressing matters. Carey wrly recorded, "Absent Califano, Schultze and Gardner, the survivors addressed attention to Howe's nine point program. It appeared that the Gardner-Howe distaste for general aid did not extend to the nine points." The BOB note-takers were especially and characteristically acerbic. Carey opposed an adult educational program as "recreational education for the middle class," called a telecommunications proposal "old-fashioned hogwash," and complained that excessively detailed federal earmarks actually

discouraged state and local governments from comprehensive planning; but he conceded that the current DHEW proposals could be worse: "We couldn't lose anything—the programs are already lousy and we have failed in cut-backs" (Memorandum, R. C. Carlson to Carey, 5 October 1967, container 413, OMB Records Division, National Archives). BOB's Steffen W. Plehn wrote Carey flatly that DHEW's current proposal for undergraduate financial aid was "a nonrecommendation for a non-program (that is, meaningless)" (Memorandum, Plehn to Carey, 6 October 1967, container 413, OMB Records Division, National Archives).

40. "Report of the Task Force on Child Development," 7 November 1967, Task Forces file, container 20, LBJ Library.

41. Transcript, "Charles Zwick Oral History Interview," part 2, LBJ Library, 1 August 1969, 16–17.

CHAPTER 8

1. Transcript, "Gardner Ackley Oral History Interview," 7 March 1974, 2, LBJ Library, 16. See also David C. Mowery and Mark S. Kamlet, "Killing the Messenger: Fiscal and Budgetary Policy Processes in the Johnson Administration" (Paper delivered at the annual meeting of the American Historical Association, Los Angeles, 28 December 1981). Johnson had originally called for a 6 percent tax surcharge in January of 1967, but he sent no specific message or bill to Congress until August. For Johnson's view, see *The Vantage Point* (New York: Holt, Rinehart, and Winston, 1971), ch. 19.

2. Telegram, Califano to President Johnson, 3 January 1968, EX FA 2, WHCF, LBJ Library.

3. *Public Papers of the President: Lyndon B. Johnson, 1968* (Washington, D.C.: Government Printing Office, 1969), 1:83–112.

4. *New York Times*, 11 February 1968. The *Times* unhappily editorialized on 7 February that "education this year has had to bow to the budgetary consequences of the war in Vietnam," but that there was a danger in a loss of momentum, and "the dismal conditions in the nation's slums and the riots and alienation that spring from them are a reminder that this is not the time for reducing or deferring preventive action."

5. John W. Gardner, "Remarks" (delivered at the annual meeting of the American Statistical Association, Washington, D.C., 27 December 1967). The Cater files in the LBJ Library reveal a consistent series of memorandums to the president reminding him that he had not spoken to his loyal and able Republican secretary of health, education, and welfare recently, and that Gardner deserved and could use some presidential jollying.

6. John W. Gardner, interview with author, Washington, D.C., 7 May 1981. Upon leaving the government, Gardner launched Common Cause.

7. Transcript, "Charles Schultze Oral History Interview," 28 March 1969, LBJ Library, 2, 28.

8. Transcript, "Samuel Halperin Oral History Interview," 24 February 1969, LBJ Library, 10–11.

9. Ibid., 12.

10. See Hugh Davis Graham, "Short-circuiting the Bureaucracy in the Great Society: Policy Origins in Education," *Presidential Studies Quarterly* (Summer 1982): 407–20.

11. Harold Seidman, *Politics, Position, and Power*, 3d ed. (New York: Oxford University Press, 1980), 91.

12. *Vantage Point*, chapter 18. Johnson claimed that he told George Christian of his decision in September of 1967.

13. Memorandum, Califano to President Johnson, 10 June 1967, Bowen file, container 14, LBJ Library.

14. Ibid.

15. The group included Califano, Gaither, Bohen, Cater, McPherson, Panzer, Hardesty, John Roche, Matthew Nimetz, Stanley Ross, DeVier Pierson, Charles Maguire, Lawrence Levinson, Edward Hamilton, William Jordan, George Reedy, George Christian, Thomas Johnson, Lloyd Hackler, and John Robson.

16. Memorandum, Hardesty to Califano, 26 March 1968, Bowen file, container 14, LBJ Library. As John Dean was later to exclaim, "They throw big rocks in this town."

17. Memorandum, Robson to Califano, 28 March 1968, Bowen file, container 14, LBJ Library.

18. See Hugh Davis Graham, "On Riots and Riot Commissions: Civil Disorders in the 1960s," *The Public Historian* (Summer 1980): 7–27.

19. Califano, Gaither, and Levinson solicited and reported to the president the advice of public affairs deans Brewster Denny (University of Washington), Stephen Bailey (Maxwell School at Syracuse University), Donald Price (Kennedy School at Harvard University), Marver Bernstein (Woodrow Wilson School at Princeton University), plus Richard Neustadt at Harvard University and Wallace Sterling at Stanford University. Sterling, who had recently retired, recounted Stanford's embarrassing difficulties with the intrusive Herbert Hoover, and Johnson was unanimously advised not to make the dean's job impossible by meddling in academic policy or administrative matters, and not to accept appointment as a member of the faculty, other than perhaps as an occasional lecturer.

20. [President] James K. McCrocklin to President Johnson, 27 May 1968, EX PP 14, WHCF, LBJ Library; President Johnson to [Regent Chairman] Frank C. Erwin, Jr., 18 May 1968, EX PP 14, WHCF, LBJ Library.

21. The standard analysis is Thomas E. Cronin, *The State of the Presidency*, 2d ed. (Boston: Little, Brown, 1980). Cronin was a member of Johnson's premier class of White House Fellows.

22. Harry McPherson, *A Political Education* (Boston: Little, Brown, 1972), 268.

23. President Johnson was so badly burned by the Revenue and Expenditure Control Act of 1968 (H.R. 15414-P.L. 90–364) that he signed the bill into law on 28 June in private, without the customary ceremonies.

24. Memorandum, Manatos to Sanders, 27 April 1968, EX LE/FA 2, container 38, LBJ Library.

25. Quoted in *Congressional Quarterly Almanac, 1968* (Washington, D.C.: Congressional Quarterly, 1968), 493.

26. Ibid., 498.

27. See J. Leiper Freeman, *The Political Process* (New York: Random House, 1965).

28. Douglass Cater, *Power in Washington* (New York: Vintage, 1964).

29. Hugh Heclo, "Issue Networks and the Executive Establishment," in *The New American Political System*, ed. Anthony King (Washington: American En-

terprise Institute, 1978): 87–124. See also Heclo, *A Government of Strangers* (Washington: Brookings, 1977).

30. Transcript, "Charles Zwick Oral History Interview," 1 August 1969, LBJ Library, 2, 17.

31. Cater, "The Political Struggle for Equality of Educational Opportunity," in *Toward New Human Rights*, ed. David C. Warner (Austin: Lyndon B. Johnson School of Public Affairs, 1977), 335.

32. Two able analyses are Lawrence E. Gladieux and Thomas R. Wolanin, *Congress and the Colleges* (Lexington, Mass: D. C. Heath, 1976); and Chester E. Finn, Jr., *Education and the Presidency* (Lexington, Mass: D.C. Heath, 1977).

33. Stephen K. Bailey, *Education Interest Groups in the Nation's Capital* (Washington: American Council on Education, 1975); Charles Lee, interview with author, Washington, D.C., 30 June 1981. In the 1970s, Lee concentrated on lobbying the appropriations committees, much as the education lobbies had won over the authorization committees in the 1960s.

34. Minutes, Cambridge Meeting, 3 June 1968, Academic Dinner files, WHCF, LBJ Library. Attending from the White House staff were Califano, Cater, Gaither, and Nimetz.

35. Ibid.

36. *Talent Development: An Investment in the Nation's Future*, July 1968, Task Forces file, container 9, LBJ Library.

37. Since Miller was assistant secretary for education, he submitted the report to Califano through Secretary Cohen. Memorandum, Miller to the secretary, 5 July 1968; Cohen to Califano, 17 July 1968, Task Forces file, container 9, LBJ Library.

38. The thirteen-member task force contained five college and university presidents plus William Cannon (by then deputy director of the National Endowment for the Arts); Wilson Riles, the prominent black educator from California; and its vice-chairman was Hale Champion.

39. Memorandum, B. H. Martin to the director, 14 November 1968, container 413, OMB Records Division, National Archives.

40. Report of the Task Force on the Administration of Federal Program of Academic Science, October 1968, Task Forces file, container 27, LBJ Library. The report contains the two Califano memos of appointment and also the BOB analysis by Hugh Loweth, dated 25 October.

41. Meeting notes of Emerson Elliott, 17 December 1968, container 413, OMB Records Division, National Archives. Gaither presided, and the attendees included Cohen, Bennett, Rivlin, Howe, Zwick, Hornig, Carey, and Elliott.

42. On the Nixon reorganization, see Otis L. Graham, Jr., *Toward a Planned Society* (New York: Oxford University Press, 1976), ch. 5.

43. "Toward a Long-Range Plan for Federal Financial Support for Higher Education," December 1968, 26, Task Forces file, container 27, LBJ Library.

44. Summary Report, White House Task Force on Education, 11 October 1968, Task Forces file, container 27, LBJ Library.

45. Memorandum, R. C. Carlson to the director, 21 November 1968, container 413, OMB Records Division, National Archives.

46. *Vantage Point*, 328. This is the section where Johnson discusses the task forces and refers to their approximately 300 members as "my Brain Trust."

47. Memorandum, Califano to President Johnson, 7 November 1968, EX LE, WHCF, LBJ Library.

48. Annual Message to the Congress on the State of the Union, 14 January 1969, *Public Papers: Johnson, 1968*, 2:1263–70.

CHAPTER 9

1. A balanced and informed exploration is Henry J. Aaron, *Politics and the Professors: the Great Society in Perspective* (Washington: The Brookings Institution, 1978).
2. See for instance Frederick M. Wirt, "Education Politics and Policies," in *Politics in the American States: A Comparative Analysis*, ed. Herbert Jacob and Kenneth N. Vines, 3d ed. (Boston: Little, Brown, 1976). A useful review of this literature and a restatement of its critique is Allan Rosenbaum, "Federal Programs and State Governments: On Understanding Why 40 Years of Federal Efforts Haven't Fundamentally Altered Economic Inequality in American Society" (Paper delivered at the 1978 meeting of the American Political Science Association, in New York City).
3. Eugene Bardach, *The Implementation Game: What Happens after a Bill Becomes a Law* (Cambridge: MIT Press, 1977). See also George C. Edwards III, *Implementing Public Policy* (Washington: Congressional Quarterly Press, 1980); and Robert T. Nakamura and Frank Smallwood, *The Politics of Policy Implementation* (New York: St. Martin's Press, 1980). Two early studies of implementation failures are Martha Derthick, *New Towns In-Town* (Washington: Urban Institute, 1972); and Jeffrey L. Pressman and Aaron Wildafsky, *Implementation* (Berkeley and Los Angeles: University of California Press, 1973).
4. Howard Ball, Dale Krana, and Thomas P. Larth, *Compromised Compliance: Implementation of the 1965 Voting Rights Act* (Westport, Connecticut: Greenwood Press, 1982).
5. Claude E. Barfield, *Rethinking Federalism* (Washington: American Enterprise Institute, 1981).
6. Robert S. Friedman, "State Politics and Highways," in *Politics in the American States*, ed. Herbert Jacob and Kenneth N. Vines, 2d ed. (Boston: Little, Brown, 1971).
7. Milbrey Wallin McLaughlin, *Evaluation and Reform: The Elementary and Secondary Education Act of 1965, Title I* (Cambridge, Mass.: Ballinger, 1975), 119.
8. Quoted in Jerome T. Murphy, "Title I of ESEA: The Politics of Implementing Federal Education Reform," *Harvard Educational Review* 41 (February 1971): 42.
9. James S. Coleman et al., *Equality of Educational Opportunity* (Washington, D.C.: Government Printing Office, 1966). A reanalysis of the Coleman data conducted at Harvard University corrected many alleged errors but generally sustained Coleman's main conclusion. See Frederick Mosteller and Daniel P. Moynihan, eds., *On Equality of Educational Opportunity: Papers Deriving from the Harvard Faculty Seminar on the Coleman Report* (New York: Random House, 1972); and Gerald Grant's review of the Harvard restudy in *Harvard Educational Review* 42 (February 1972), 109.
10. See Martin T. Katyman and Roland S. Rosen, "The Science and Politics of the National Assessment," *The Record* 71 (1971): 571–86.
11. Stephen K. Bailey and Edith K. Mosher, *ESEA: The Office of Education Administers a Law* (Syracuse: Syracuse University Press, 1968), 222. The evidence

they cite in footnote 16, all from 1967, includes the critical study *Racial Isolation in the Public Schools* (Washington, D.C., U.S. Commission on Civil Rights, 1967).

12. Joel S. Berke and Michael W. Kirst, *Federal Aid to Education* (Lexington, Massachusetts: Heath, 1972).

13. Federal aid averaged 8 percent of per-pupil expenditure in the sample districts, with local taxes accounting for approximately half and state equalization formula aid for the remainder.

14. Berke and Kirst, *Federal Aid*, 45.

15. McLaughlin, *Evaluation and Reform*. See also Aaron Wildafsky, *Speaking Truth to Power: The Art of Policy Analysis* (Boston: Little Brown, 1979), ch. 13, on education.

16. Norman C. Thomas, *Education in National Politics* (New York: David McKay, 1975), 230. The reference to Lowi was to his *The End of Liberalism* (New York: W. W. Norton, 1969).

17. Julie Roy Jeffrey, *Education for the Children of the Poor: A Study of the Origins and Implementation of the Elementary and Secondary Education Act of 1965* (Columbus: Ohio State University Press, 1976).

18. For a sampler of these debates, see Donald M. Levine and Mary Jo Bane, *The "Inequality" Controversy: Schooling and Distributive Justice* (New York: Basic Books, 1975). A superior recent analysis is Diane Ravitch, *The Troubled Crusade* (New York: Basic Books, 1983), ch. 5.

19. For a defense of the goals and achievements of the Great Society (but not of its inflated expectations and naïveté), see Sar Levitan and Robert Taggart, *The Promise of Greatness* (Cambridge, Mass.: Harvard University Press, 1976), ch. 6.

20. Samuel Halperin, "ESEA: The Positive Side," *Phi Delta Kappan* (November 1975), 147-51. See also Ralph W. Tyler, "The Federal Role in Education," *The Public Interest*, 164-87.

21. Halperin, "ESEA," 151.

22. Ibid. Halperin, interview with author, Washington, D.C., 22 April 1981.

23. Halperin celebrated ESEA's bar mitzvah in "ESEA Comes of Age: Some Historical Reflections," *Educational Leadership* 36 (February 1979): 349-53.

24. William W. Wayson, "ESEA: The Negative Side," *Phi Delta Kappan* (November 1975), 151-56.

25. Ibid., 151, 153.

26. See Jackie Kimbrough and Paul T. Hill, *The Aggregate Effects of Federal Education Programs* (Santa Monica: Rand, 1981).

27. The allusion is to Peter Hall's *Great Planning Disasters* (London: Weidenfeld and Nicholson, 1980), which concentrates on such megadisasters (or near disasters) as London's third airport, the Anglo-French Concorde, San Francisco's BART, and Sydney's Opera House.

28. Robert Benjamin, *Making Schools Work* (New York: Continuum, 1981). A former reporter for the *Cincinnati Post* and later with the *Baltimore Sun*, Benjamin's research and writing was supported by a Ford Foundation grant in affiliation with Halperin's Institute for Educational Leadership at George Washington University. See also Sara Lawrence Lightfoot, *The Good High School* (New York: Basic Books, 1983).

29. Lorraine M. McDonnell and Milbrey W. McLaughlin, *Education Policy and the Role of the States* (Santa Monica: Rand, 1982). See also Paul T. Hill, *Enforcement and Informal Pressure in the Management of Federal Categorical Pro-*

grams in Education (Santa Monica: Rand, 1979); Paul T. Hill, *Do Federal Education Programs Interfere With One Another?* (Santa Monica: Rand, 1979); and Paul Hill, Joanne Wuchitech, and Richard Williams, *The Effects of Federal Education Programs on School Principles* (Santa Monica: Rand, 1980).

30. McDonnell and McLaughlin, *Education Policy*, ix.

31. Kimbrough and Hill, *The Aggregate Effects of Federal Education Programs*.

32. See, for example, *Compensatory Education Study* (Washington: National Institute of Education, 1978); Edward Zigler and Jeanette Valentine, eds., *Project Head Start* (New York: Free Press, 1979). On evaluating education programs, see Robert F. Boruch and David S. Cordnay, eds., *An Appraisal of Education Program Evaluations: Federal, State, and Local Agencies* (Washington: U.S. Department of Education, 1980); and Senta Raizen and Peter Rossi, eds., *Program Evaluation in Education. When? How? To What Ends?* (Washington: National Academy of Sciences, 1980).

33. Carl F. Kaestle and Marshall S. Smith, "The Federal Role in Elementary and Secondary Education, 1940–1980," *Harvard Educational Review* (November 1982), 384–408.

34. Ibid., 400.

35. Ibid., 405.

36. McDonnell and McLaughlin, *Education Policy*, xii.

37. But in this connection see Hugh Davis Graham, "Liberty, Equality, and the New Civil Rights," *South Atlantic Quarterly* (Winter 1980), 82–92.

38. *Washington Post*, 27 November 1981.

39. Ibid.

40. Somewhat surprisingly, the Reagan administration promised to increase federal aid to black colleges while generally reducing aid to all the other colleges. The political compromise was a relatively wide access to Title III funding, but with set-asides for predominantly black and Hispanic colleges.

41. Noel Epstein, *Language, Ethnicity, and the Schools: Policy Alternatives for Bilingual-Bicultural Education* (Washington: Institute for Educational Leadership, 1977).

42. Ibid., 7. Epstein cited a USOE-sponsored study of thirty-eight bilingual projects for Hispanic children that found that 70 percent of the pupils were dominant in English, not Spanish, for test-taking purposes.

43. Joseph A. Califano, Jr., *Governing America* (New York: Simon & Schuster, 1981), 313.

44. Harold Howe II, interview with author, New York City, 11 May 1981.

45. Abigail M. Thernstrom, "Language: Issues and Legislation," *Harvard Encyclopedia of American Ethnic Groups* (Cambridge, Mass.: Harvard University Press, 1980), 619–29.

46. Ibid., 624. See Malcolm N. Danoff, *Evaluation of the Impact of ESEA Title VII Spanish/English Bilingual Education Program* (Palo Alto: American Institutes of Research, 1978).

47. Thernstrom, 625. In 1981 the Department of Education published a thorough review of the literature on bilingual education by two of its staff members, Keith A. Baker and Adriana A. de Kanter. Their assessment of twenty-eight studies of transitional bilingual education programs concluded that the evidence did *not* justify the federal government's exclusive reliance on the bilingual method, nor did it support the necessity of teaching nonlanguage subjects in the child's

native tongue. But immersion (TESOL) programs showed promising results that merited more program attention (consult Keith A. Baker and Adriana A. de Kanter, "*The Effectiveness of Bilingual Education* [Washington, D.C.: Office of Planning, Budget, and Evaluation, U.S. Department of Education, 1981]). A parallel study in 1981 by Alan L. Ginsberg and Beatrice F. Birman for the Department of Education concluded that only one million children needed language help, not 3.6 million as the Carter administration had claimed, and that the evidence indicated that TESOL was more effective than the bilingual approach (see the *Washington Post*, 29 September 1981).

In 1983 a Twentieth Century Fund Task Force on Federal Elementary and Secondary Education Policy chaired by Robert Wood, Lyndon Johnson's former under secretary of HUD, concluded that American elementary students must learn to "read, write, speak, and listen in English" and so recommended that "federal funds now going to bilingual programs be used to teach non-English-speaking children how to speak, read, and write English" (see the *New York Times*, 6 May 1983, and the *Chronicle of Higher Education*, 11 May 1983).

48. Richard Rodriguez, *Hunger of Memory* (Boston: Godine, 1981). Rodriguez was so tortured by the unfairness of affirmative action policies, which rained Ivy League professorial offers on him while virtually ignoring his white doctoral colleagues at Berkeley, that he declined them all and left academe.

49. *Washington Post*, 13 March 1982.

50. An excellent recent analysis of American higher education is George Keller, *Academic Strategy* (Baltimore: Johns Hopkins University Press, 1983).

51. During the period from 1976 to 1982, the city of Philadelphia was able to dismiss only 24 of its 13,000 teachers; a typical dismissal took two years and involved extensive legal fees.

52. Perceptive recent discussions of the causes of the decline in education include *The New Republic*'s education issue of 18 April 1981 and Phil Keisling's three-part series in the *Baltimore Sun*, 20, 21, and 22 October 1982. Keisling reports that when the Lemon Grove School District in southern California gave to all of its properly degreed and certified teachers a literacy test scaled to eighth-grade levels, 35 percent flunked one or more parts.

53. Diane Ravitch, *The Troubled Crusade: American Education, 1945–1980* (New York: Basic Books, 1983), 316.

54. Ibid.

55. Diane Ravitch, "Scapegoating the Teachers," *The New Republic* (7 November 1983): 27.

Method and Sources

Normally an essay on method would not be necessary for a study based on archival sources, because historical research in archival evidence has been a staple over the centuries, and I certainly claim no major innovation here. In the United States since the administration of Franklin D. Roosevelt, the development of the presidential library system has somewhat regionalized archival access to documentary evidence from the executive branch, and the presidential libraries in Boston and Austin contain rich lodes of material from the 1960s that are only beginning to be tapped. (Unfortunately, the important Nixon archives have remained closed because of litigation.) My research is basically grounded in the Kennedy and Johnson archives, especially the massive holdings in the Lyndon Baines Johnson Library and Museum in Austin, Texas. But the key to my sense of *perspective* on those millions of White House documents lies elsewhere—primarily in three sources.

The most important, and the one that I had least anticipated at the beginning, was the archival repository of the Bureau of the Budget in the National Archives in Washington, D.C. And thereby hangs a tale. Wilbur Cohen loves to describe Lyndon Johnson's decision-making process as essentially an exercise in *triangulation*. Joe Califano would typically send the president a file of memorandums full of policy recommendations for his night reading, each with a space, or "box," to be marked "approve" or "disapprove." On the major items, Johnson would neither typically approve nor disapprove. Instead, he would scribble something like "Check this with Clifford and Fortas"—or with Mansfield and Russell and Long, or whomever, always seeking policy consensus before he committed himself. Similarly, my research hinged on a triangulation that I had not initially foreseen. One party was obviously the president and his

White House staff. The second was the world of the mission agency involved in education, be it DHEW, most often USOE, but also NSF, NIH, OST, and others. The third would normally have involved Congress. But the literature on Congress is abundant, and congressional hearings and votes are almost instantly available. What I sought was another third leg of the policy stool for primary research—not Congress, which was important and was attracting scores of fine congressional scholars, upon whom I heavily relied—but instead the Bureau of the Budget. The BOB files in the National Archives are a gold mine, especially because they can provide that crucial dimension of internal executive branch triangulation that Wilbur Cohen talked about, and they tend to do so with refreshingly nonbureaucratic candor. Typically during the midsixties, LBJ's semisecret task forces would propose a brace of new program proposals, the line agencies would respond nervously and sometimes resentfully, and the policy and program analysts in BOB would reply with the confidence and sometimes the cockiness that signaled the élan of a bureaucratic elite, viewed from the perspective of their jealously guarded role as keepers of the institutional memory and the integrity of the executive branch. So, like LBJ, I have enjoyed my triangulation, but with a slightly different clientele. Indeed, because one cannot ignore Congress, my triangle in effect became a quadrangle, with White House task forces proposing new program ideas, and with responses flowing in from the line agencies, from the relevant congressional committees, and always from the Bureau of the Budget. So my book flows from this quadrangular vortex, which makes the analysis very complicated—but complicated it *was*. Nevertheless, the evidence necessary to clarify this complex process of policy evolution is abundant.

The oral history interviews in the presidential libraries are an excellent and easily accessible source of contemporary perspective and candid opinion, especially because the interviewers were usually well informed and asked hard, probing questions. The transcripts are usually available on interlibrary loan, although several require permission. I greatly profited from reading the interviews of the following persons:

Hugh Gardner Ackley	Anthony Celebrezze
Lucile Anderson	Wilbur Cohen
David Bell	Nolan Estes
Joseph Califano	Myer Feldman
Douglass Cater	James Gaither

Kermit Gordon
Samuel Halperin
Ben Heineman
Donald Hornig
Harold Howe II
Phillip S. Hughes
Dwight Ink
Francis Keppel
Henry Loomis
Harry McPherson
John Macy

Mike Manatos
Peter Muirhead
Walter Mylecraine
Richard Neustadt
Albert Quie
Wayne Reed
Charles Schultze
David Seeley
James Sundquist
Charles Zwick

Actually, the Califano interview is not a standard oral history transcript, but rather a taped interview with Robert Hawkinson. It is both puzzling and regrettable that Califano, Moyers, and Sorensen did not leave proper oral histories. Also lacking, given my research interests, are oral history transcripts for William Cannon, Edith Green, Wayne Morse, Carl Perkins, and Adam Clayton Powell. The best of the Kennedy oral history collection is Myer Feldman's unusual seven-volume interview; at the LBJ Library it is a close race for honors between the interviews of Wilbur Cohen and Harry McPherson.

Unlike typical social science researchers, I did not use personal interviews as a primary substantive source of evidence. Nevertheless, I requested twenty interviews and conducted eighteen of them. All were on record, but none was formally structured or taped. They varied widely in length and informational value (three were by telephone, including one of the best and longest, with James Gaither in San Francisco), but all were helpful and are warmly appreciated:

Henry Aaron
Joseph Califano
William Cannon
William Daniel Carey
Douglass Cater
Wilbur Cohen
Myer Feldman
William Friday
James Gaither

John Gardner
Samuel Halperin
Catharine Heath
Paul Hill
Harold Howe II
Francis Keppel
Joseph Laitin
Charles Lee
Charles Radcliffe

No one refused to talk to me on the record, although I was unfortunately unable to connect logistically with Sorensen and Moyers in New York.

The heart of the presidential libraries is the White House Central Files (WHCF), and also the crucial aide files. The chief repository for education legislation in the John F. Kennedy Library in Boston is in the Myer Feldman file, but the Sorensen file is important also. In the Johnson Library, the best source is in the rather massive file of James Gaither (138 linear feet), but other good sources include the files of Bill Moyers (91 linear feet), Joseph Califano (77 linear feet), Douglass Cater (37 linear feet), Lawrence O'Brien (35 linear feet), Harry McPherson (26 linear feet), Fred Bohen and Matthew Nimetz (5 linear feet each). There is also an education subject file of 11 linear feet, and an important series of task force files from the Gaither collection.

During his tenure as president, Lyndon Johnson directed federal departments and agencies to prepare narrative histories with supporting documents for inclusion in the presidential archives. These sixty-four administrative histories vary widely in volume and quality, ranging from the eighteen volumes and twelve archive containers on the Department of Health, Education, and Welfare, to a slim report on the Committee on Purchases of Blind-Made Products. Fortunately, the thousand-page history of the United States Office of Education is one of the most objective and richest in detail. The Bureau of the Budget administrative history is also excellent.

Finally, in Washington, two important archives were convenient to my home and university location in Maryland. Most important was the OMB Records Division of the National Archives. But also important was the Office of Education Historical Policy Files, which at its core is essentially the remarkable collection compiled carefully over the years by Dr. Catherine Heath and deposited in the NIE Library. The collection contains 131 volumes of policy files (thirty-four linear feet) alphabetically arranged by subject, approximately 600 volumes (forty-three linear feet) of publications on educational topics, and approximately 90 volumes (six linear feet) of congressional hearings and committee reports. The ERIC system of information retrieval was of only modest assistance in my research, but ERIC was understandably not constructed with a research project like mine in mind, which connects broad policy questions to specific archival documents. The secondary sources I needed were easily identified and available, and the rest was a matter of archival digging. ERIC, on the other hand, operates mostly in the broad middle, connecting researchers with highly specific and often highly technical questions and interests across the extraordinarily broad spectrum of education research.

Bibliographically, one should begin with Fred Greenstein, Larry Berman, and Alvin Felzenberg, *Evolution of the Modern Presidency* (Washington: American Enterprise Institute, 1977). Thomas E. Cronin deservedly owns the turf on *The State of the Presidency* (Boston: Little, Brown, 1980). The best primary guide to the Kennedy presidency remains Theodore Sorensen's *Kennedy* (New York: Harper & Row, 1965). There is no equivalent comprehensive memoir for the Johnson years, but Johnson's memoirs, *The Vantage Point* (New York: Holt, Rinehart, and Winston, 1971), was co-written by a host of aides, and the Johnson presidency is ably assessed in Robert A. Divine, ed., *Exploring the Johnson Years* (Austin: University of Texas Press, 1981), especially Divine's chapter 1 on LBJ, and my chapter 5 on education. By far the best memoir by a Johnson aide is Harry McPherson's *A Political Education* (Boston: Little, Brown, 1972). Califano's *A Presidential Nation* (New York: W. W. Norton, 1975) is disappointing. Eric Goldman's *The Tragedy of Lyndon Johnson* (New York: Knopf, 1969) is perceptive, but it is also obviously self-serving.

Students of the recent history and policy evolution of American education are fortunate to have available Diane Ravitch, *The Troubled Crusade: American Education, 1945–1980* (New York: Basic Books, 1983); her citations and bibliographic essay constitute an excellent reference source for the postwar period. The standard contemporary studies on federal education policy during the 1960s are Stephen K. Bailey and Edith K. Mosher, *ESEA: The Office of Education Administers a Law* (Syracuse: Syracuse University Press, 1968); Eugene Eidenberg and Roy D. Morey, *An Act of Congress* (New York: W. W. Norton, 1969); and Julie Roy Jeffrey, *Education for the Children of the Poor: A Study of the Origins and Implementation of the Elementary and Secondary Education Act of 1965* (Columbus: Ohio State University Press, 1976). Add to that Norman C. Thomas, *Education in National Politics* (New York: McKay, 1975); and the able dissertation of Robert E. Hawkinson, "Presidential Program Formulation in Education: Lyndon Johnson and the 89th Congress" (Ph.D. diss., University of Chicago, 1977). Also recommended is the doctoral dissertation of José Chavez, "Presidential Influence on the Politics of Higher Education: The Higher Education Act of 1965" (University of Texas at Austin, 1975). Philip Reed Rulon has written an unconvincing defense of LBJ as *The Compassionate Samaritan* (Chicago: Nelson-Hall, 1981). Chester E. Finn, Jr., *Education and the Presidency* (Lexington, Mass.: Heath, 1977), is the best book on the Nixon administration, and is essential to understanding the presidential politics of education generally.

Superior books on aspects of the presidency and the federal government that range beyond education and that analyze the domestic policy processes of government include the following: Henry Aaron, *Politics and the Professors* (Washington: The Brookings Institution, 1976); Patrick Anderson, *The Presidents' Men* (Garden City: Doubleday, 1968); Thomas E. Cronin and Sanford D. Greenberg, eds., *The Presidential Advisory System* (New York: Harper & Row, 1969); Richard F. Fenno, Jr., *Congressmen in Committees* (Boston: Little, Brown, 1973); Otis L. Graham, Jr., *Toward a Planned Society* (New York: Oxford University Press, 1976); Hugh Heclo, *A Government of Strangers* (Washington: The Brookings Institution, 1977); Stephen Hess, *Organizing the Presidency* (Washington: The Brookings Institution, 1976); Richard Tanner Johnson, *Managing the White House* (New York: Harper & Row, 1974); Louis W. Koening, *The Chief Executive* (New York: Harcourt, Brace, Jovanovich, 1975); Sar A. Levitan and Robert Taggert, *A Promise of Greatness* (Cambridge, Mass.: Harvard University Press, 1976); James T. Patterson, *America's Struggle Against Poverty, 1900–1980* (Cambridge: Harvard University Press, 1981), especially parts 3 and 4; Emmette S. Redford and Marlan Blissett, *Organizing the Executive Branch* (Chicago: University of Chicago Press, 1981); Francis E. Rourke, *Bureaucracy, Politics, and Public Policy* (Boston: Little, Brown, 1969); Harold Seidman, *Politics, Position, and Power* (New York: Oxford University Press, 1970); and James L. Sundquist, *Politics and Policy: The Eisenhower, Kennedy, and Johnson Years* (Washington: The Brookings Institution, 1968).

Superior journal articles in the same category are: Carl M. Brauer, "Kennedy, Johnson, and the War on Poverty," *The Journal of American History* 69 (June 1982): 98–119; William D. Carey, "Presidential Staffing in the Sixties and Seventies," *Public Administration Review* 29 (September/October 1969): 450–58; Thomas E. Cronin and Norman C. Thomas, "Educational Policy Advisors and the Great Society," *Public Pol-*

icy (Fall 1970); Nathan Glazer, "On Task Forcing," *The Public Interest* (Spring 1968): 40–45; Hugh Heclo, "Issue Networks and the Executive Establishment," in *The New American Political System*, ed. Anthony King (Washington: American Enterprise Institute, 1978); Hugh Heclo, "The OMB and the Presidency," *The Public Interest* (Winter 1975): 80–98; William Leuchtenburg, "The Genesis of the Great Society," *The Reporter*, 21 April 1966, 36–39; Richard E. Neustadt, "The Presidency and Legislation: The Growth of Central Clearance," *American Political Science Review* 48 (1954): 641–71; [Hugh Sidey] "The White House Staff vs. the Cabinet: Hugh Sidey Interviews Bill Moyers," *Washington Monthly* (February 1969): 2–8, 78–80; Nancy Kegan Smith, "Presidential Task Force Operation During the Johnson Administration," mimeographed guide, LBJ Library, 26 June 1978; Norman C. Thomas, "Presidential Advice and Information: Policy and Program Formulation," *Law and Contemporary Problems* 35 (Summer 1970): 540–72; Norman Thomas and Harold Wolman, "The Presidency and Policy Formation: The Task Force Device," *Public Administration Review* 29 (September/October 1969): 459–70; James Tobin, "The Political Economy of the 1960s" in *Toward New Human Rights*, ed. David C. Warner (Austin: Lyndon B. Johnson School of Public Affairs, 1977), 33–50; James Q. Wilson, "The Rise of the Bureaucratic State," *The Public Interest* 41 (Fall 1975): 77–103; and Adam Yarmolinsky, "Ideas Into Programs," *The Public Interest* 2 (Winter 1966): 70–79.

Index